Fragmented Identities

Additional praise for *Fragmented Identities: Popular Culture, Sex, and Everyday Life in Postcommunist Romania*

"Denise Roman's fine book should be read as a kind of '*flânerie*,' expressing the feel of everyday personal life in post-1989 Romania, but it also displays solid methodological reflection and scholarly culture. The way in which it moves between these two dimensions, between theory and lived experience, is what gives the study its special charm—even for a nonspecialist reader.

Denise Roman places post-1989 Romania on view for us, a society taken apart, a society resisting without any object of resistance, attached to a golden age without a golden age that can be located anywhere, clinging to a dream of the West while at the same time rejecting that West. Romania experiences itself as ringed with shadows: there is the figure of the Jew who embodies Evil, the Other as Evil. Women are lost between the imagined calm of a return to the home and a militant feminism of the Anglo-American kind. These women speak a great deal through the author's pen: they speak humor, self-hatred, a need to leave—to leave for somewhere else. They are real women, and the author has been able to hear what they say from within their private lives.

Denise Roman's extreme talent is what is needed to infuse knowledge with feeling, as she puts her heart into studying the course of a country with seemingly no clearly defined plans for the future, carried along by a hybrid identity.

This book is an indispensable means of illuminating the complex tensions of a Romanian identity driven both to banalize and to reject integration. The author has been able to set before us the East European combination of dynamism and conservatism: she is the guide who walks with serious mien and poses questions, at the bends in the road."
—**Catherine Durandin**, National Institute of Oriental Languages and Civilizations, Paris

"Ms. Roman is anything but a detached traveler, although she does bring to her writing a most insightful and often amusing account of the state of politics and identity in Bucharest. But this is politics and identity in no common understanding of those terms. Skillfully teasing her own innovative interpretations from the insights of historians, sociologists, political, feminist, and cultural theorists, Ms. Roman . . . dismantle[s] old conceptions and convincingly reconstruct[s] new ones about the 'politics of life' in Eastern Europe today. By brilliantly bringing together disparate strands of thought in truly innovative, provocative, and sometimes even sly ways, she has written not only an outstanding piece of academic scholarship, but a real 'page turner.'"
—**Debra Renee Kaufman**, Northeastern University; author of *Rachel's Daughters*

Fragmented Identities

Popular Culture, Sex, and Everyday Life in Postcommunist Romania

Denise Roman

For the inspiration and warm support offered, please accept my gratitude and, not in the last instance, my book.

Sincerely,

Denise Roman

08/03

LEXINGTON BOOKS
Lanham • Boulder • New York • Oxford

LEXINGTON BOOKS

Published in the United States of America
by Lexington Books
A Member of the Rowman & Littlefield Publishing Group
4501 Forbes Boulevard, Suite 200, Lanham, Maryland 20706

PO Box 317
Oxford
OX2 9RU, UK

All photographs (including cover) are courtesy of the author.

British Library Cataloguing in Publication Information Available

Library of Congress Cataloging-in-Publication Data

Roman, Denise, 1965–
    Fragmented identities : popular culture, sex, and everyday life in postcommunist
Romania / Denise Roman.
       p. cm.
    Includes bibliographical references and index.
    ISBN 0-7391-0574-4 (cloth : alk. paper)
    1. Popular culture—Romania. 2. Arts—Romania. 3. Romania—Social
conditions—1989– I. Title.

HN647 .R66 2003
306'.09498—dc21   2002152538

Printed in the United States of America

♾™ The paper used in this publication meets the minimum requirements of American
National Standard for Information Sciences—Permanence of Paper for Printed Library
Materials, ANSI/NISO Z39.48–1992.

To my parents and to Vlad,
And to those Romanian adolescents of the 1980s
who believed in freedom and rock 'n' roll.

Contents

Photographs

Acknowledgments

My special thanks go to Dr. Ananya Mukherjee-Reed from York University, Canada, who provided me with constant support, encouragement, stimulating intellectual exchange, and, last but not least, priceless friendship in voicing my Eastern European positionality. For her warm help and smart insights into my work I wish to bring thanks to Dr. Sandra Whitworth from York University, Canada. I also wish to express my gratitude to Dr. Joan W. Scott from the Princeton Institute for Advanced Study and to Dr. Warren Magnusson from University of Victoria, British Columbia, for helping me bring out some valuable nodal points in my book. To Shurli Makmillen go my heartfelt thanks for her camaraderie and invaluable editorial assistance. Finally, I wish to thank my editors at Lexington Books and Rowman & Littlefield, Jason Hallman, Rebekka Brooks, and Brian Richards, for their warm and inspired support of my book.

Various grants and scholarships, and one fellowship, have helped me write this book: the Dean of Faculty of Graduate Studies Fellowship for academic excellence, York University, Canada; the Canadian Federal Government Special Opportunity Grants for Female Doctoral Students; the Canadian International Development Agency grant; and the Hadassah International Research Institute on Jewish Women junior scholar fellowship, Brandeis University.

Some academic centers and summer schools that have helped me formulate the project for this book are: the European Union Network of Interdisciplinary Women Studies in Europe (NOISE) Summer School under the directorship of Dr. Rosi Braidotti, held in Pisa, Italy, in 2000; the Women's Studies Program from Northeastern University, in Boston; York University Center for International and Security Studies, Toronto, Canada; and the University of California at Los Angeles Center for the Study of Women.

For their longtime friendship and support while I researched and wrote this book, I also wish to give thanks to Magdalena Popa and Amato Checiulescu from Toronto, and, for their warm nurturing and deep sense of humanity, to Ursula Hannah from Victoria, British Columbia, and to Jeanne and Bill Maloney from Sudbury, Massachusetts. For offering some important comments regarding queer identity and politics in Romania, I wish to thank Adrian Coman from ACCEPT-Romania.

Finally, as moments of inspiration and support of this book, I thank my parents in Romania: my father, a writer, violinist, and a child Holocaust survivor; my mother, whose literary scholarship has gracefully interwoven Eastern and Western intellectual legacies, thus inspiring my curiosity for and understanding of diverse cultures; and the subtle yet enduring memory of my beloved grandmother who lived throughout most of Eastern Europe's twentieth century tormented history. I also thank my husband, who helped me produce the pictures for this book, thus enabling me to show the reader that version of Bucharest most familiar to me as a one-time Bucharestian. The 1980s "Blue Jeans Generation" of youth mentioned in this book, a generation of freedom and rock 'n' roll to which I ineluctably belonged, has inspired me to bring the past, present, and future together in this book, and to continue with what I once idealistically perceived was that generation's drive: the absence of limits.

Faithful to my destiny as a "global citizen," I had to relocate several times while writing this book: East-to-West and West-to-more-West, and back again. In fact, I wrote this book in several cities: Victoria, Vancouver, Toronto, Boston, Los Angeles, and Bucharest. All these "nomadic" *rites de passage* have opened up my understanding of so many liminal subjectivities, themselves fascinating microcosms of diversity. I am thankful for the sense of human tragedy and victory, of our very palpable existence, that these experiences have given me.

Although some issues addressed in the following pages have been previously presented in earlier publications, my evolving interests and understandings have stirred new ideas, conclusions, and occasionally the use of new theoretical frameworks, all of which have meant what I hope is a richer apprehension of such topics as gender and anti-Semitism. This said, I still gratefully acknowledge copyright permission granted for the following previously published material, which is diversely adapted throughout this book: "The Mythical Jew: Anti-Semitism, Intellectuals, and Democracy in Post-Communist Romania," *Nationalities Papers* 29 no. 3, 2001, 419-439, permission granted from Taylor and Francis, www.tandf.co.uk; and "Gendering Eastern Europe: Pre-Feminism, Prejudice, and East-West Dialogues in Post-Communist Romania," *Women's Studies International Forum* 24 no. 1, 2001, 53-65, permission granted from Elsevier Science. Unless otherwise stated, all the translations from the Romanian belong to this author, as does the copyright on photos and photomontages.

PART ONE
EVERYDAY LIFE

Chapter One

A Flâneur[1] *through Bucharest at the End of the Twentieth Century*

The billboards that shine big and high on both sides of the Bucharest-Otopeni road, a road linking the Otopeni airport with downtown Bucharest, are perhaps the best indicators of what postcommunist Romanian everyday life has become. The smiles and seminaked bodies of colorfully photographed young local or foreign girls pictured on these billboards are indicative of the degree of consumer culture that has finally reached the Romanian citizen after 1989. Advertising a wide range of products—tobacco, oil, shopping malls, tires, paints, and appliances—the billboards are crowded one after another in numeric aggressiveness and cramped display. It's now or never, the billboards seem to say. Downtown Bucharest is jammed with cigarette advertisements covering half a block, while the celebrated character from the American TV serial "Dallas," "J.R."—a character played by the actor Larry Hagman—displays an urgent smile on a wide billboard advertising Russian LUKOIL.

A type of "Dallas"-mania has twice hit Romania. First, in the late 1970s, when the national television station presented it as an ideologically crucified symbol of "decadent capitalism." The second time was in the early 1990s, its signification displaced with one of progressive consumerism, as if trying to give lessons in capitalism. No wonder that many Romanians have imitated the representations conveyed by "Dallas" and, according to public knowledge, there is at

3

least one Southfork ranch replica built by a *nouveau riche*[2] somewhere in the midst of rural Romania, near the city of Slobozia.

Today Bucharest combines a variety of urban styles stretching back from medieval times. Feudal inns (*han* or *caravanserai*),[3] such as the famous *Hanul lui Manuc*, are juxtaposed with Ceaușescu's megalomaniac architectural plans— including his Palace, second in size only to the Pentagon, and the newly built civic center surrounding it, the latter aptly labeled "the communist Disneyland."[4] No wonder that one Romanian author thinks of this postcommunist eclectic architecture, which coalesces signs of medievalism, modernism, French-inspired nineteenth- and early twentieth-century urbanism, a traditional Romanian *Brâncovenean* style, "socialist realist" artistry, and postcommunist villas of the *nouveaux riches*—themselves challenging proofs of aesthetic eclecticism—a hodgepodge, or willy-nilly "postmodernism."[5] This stylistic combination of communist kitsch and interesting, occasionally chic, European and Oriental influences can ultimately become striking for the new visitors in town, who are thus constantly reminded that they find themselves at the threshold of cultures and aesthetics.

For the last decade of postcommunism, stray dogs have become one of the most annoying aspects a stroller through the city could encounter, worse perhaps than the roads and their abysmal chuckholes—deadly menaces to any solid car—or the unmanaged garbage. Although other countries have experienced a booming industry in pet ownership and culture in recent years,[6] such a practice is occluded in Romania by the existence of a burgeoning population of stray dogs. These unfortunate creatures are a sad testimony to a time when Ceaușescu leveled down entire portions of the city where many people had lived in old, semirural residences, with a house, a small garden, some poultry, and a watch dog. Left by their owners in the street, over the past twenty years these dogs went through an uncontrolled reproduction and now cause dozens of bites as well as political debates over their suggested euthanasia or deportation to the countryside. Nonetheless, there exists a small but growing pet culture—seen mainly through the existence of urban pet clinics—which can be best understood as a sign of prestige and a marker of the economic status of the *nouveaux riches*.[7]

These signs of affluence lie in sharp contrast to the city's population of street children, who spend their time living underground in the sewage system, or gathering in the railway station neighborhood of *Gara de Nord*. They live under the effect of hallucinatory substances, mainly a local chemical originally designed to clean the parquetry. Called *Aurolac*, this substance lends its name to its young consumers; Bucharestians call street children *Aurolaci*.

Elsewhere the *flâneur* can easily access the Internet in a variety of Internet cafés that have started to populate the urban environment of Bucharest and other major cities.[8] The Internet cafés from *Piața Rosetti* or *Calea Victoriei* offer Internet access, e-mail, network chat and games, and bar services for some modest prices. Public *cyber-postcommunism*—as I call this new techno-global condition of postcommunism—is one of the major powers of globalization, one that connects urban youth, unifying and diversifying their tastes, aspirations, and political ideas on a daily basis. Cyber-postcommunism can at once offer a broad range of local and foreign messages, from cinema and fashion, Romanian humor or sci-fi clubs, to neo-Nazi, feminist, and queer activism websites. The average consumer of public Internet is young, urban, with some knowledge of English language, and a fan of Western popular culture.

Beautiful hotels display their new or restored façades everywhere in Bucharest—*Lido*, *Athénée Palace Hilton*, *InterContinental*, *Crown Plaza Flora*, or *Sofitel*—and the *flâneur* can now enjoy a variety of international cuisines: Chinese, French, German, Greek, Indian, Italian, Lebanese, Korean, or Hungarian. "McDonald's," "KFC," and "Pizza Hut" have opened their doors for some years now, and their prices classify them as rather expensive yet desirable places for gatherings, mainly for youth.

Today Bucharest has developed one of the most striking casino cultures, attracting gamblers from all over the region, and also from countries where gambling is religiously prohibited, such as Turkey or Israel. Among the most famous ones gathering an eclectic community of *nouveaux riches*, artists, political personalities, foreigners, and prostitutes are *Palace Casino*, *Princess Casino*, *Victoria Casino*, or *Plaza Casino*. Jazz clubs and discos such as *Blues Café*, *Swing House*, *Studio Martin*, or *Lăptăria Enache* (Enache's Dairy) are youth's most preferred places of gathering, while adult entertainment has brought postcommunist Romania in line with international cabaret, striptease, and erotic show culture. Some of these are *Blue Moon*, *Flamingo Club*, or *Crazy Bull*—the last one featuring male striptease. A former French burlesque-style cabaret culture existed in urban Romania prior to 1989, creating isolated small communities of love affairs, intrigue, and transfers of information, connecting the nomenklatura and their sons and daughters with bar singers, ballerinas, prostitutes, foreigners, and *Securitate* personnel.[9] During communism, the atmosphere at the notorious *Bar Melody*, *Athénée Palace*, or *Salonul Spaniol* (the Spanish Salon) seems to have preserved the glorious years of a Bucharest described as the "little Paris" by Countess Waldeck in her acclaimed novel *Athene Palace*.[10]

Shopping malls such as *Bucureşti Mall* are comparable to their Western counterparts, serving mainly the *nouveaux riches*. In a country where the monthly average salary is around US $100, ranging up to US $400 for some trained professional categories, the price for a refrigerator is about US $120, a washing machine costs around US $140, while a Sony TV set ranges anywhere from US $120 to US $300. Youth generally wander passively through this mall, rarely consuming its products, except perhaps for an ice-cream or an expensive ticket to *Hollywood Multiplex*, the mall's cinema, where the advertising invites the passerby to its "10 super-halls with air conditioning," "clear image on gigantic screens," and "spatial acoustic effects." Along with the shopping mall there are other Western-imported concepts and services, such as fitness clubs, aerobics, and body-building (such as *Salon Monalisa, Api Estetic,* or *Henriette Body Line Center*), although the entire symbolism conveyed by this new subculture directly addresses the upper middle classes. Apparently, the rest of the population is entirely a *flâneur,* less of a consumer of Western services and products.

Today Bucharest's walls expose an increasing number of graffiti in competition with tobacco billboards. Postcommunist graffiti conveys an entire political mythology, from nationalist, anticommunist, anti-Western, anti-Semite, and anti-Roma messages, to sexist, derogatory, and obscene rhetoric.[11] As an artifact, postcommunist graffiti is a reminder of the great theatrical space of the 1989 Revolution and its subsequent street demonstrations and camps that have animated Bucharest afterwards, in 1990 and 1991, a time when the city had literally become a political and dramaturgic space, a spectacle of power devolution.

Downtown, the famous "gypsy" flower sellers have survived the 1989 Romanian Revolution and, with their lively colored, flowered, long, thick, and overlayered skirts, they give Bucharest a romantic flavor; apparently immortal, they seem to unite the dawns with the twilight of the twentieth century. Today and in competition with them, new flower shops sell bulbs and seeds from the Netherlands, orchids from Singapore, and artificially bred roses, thus ending the monopoly that the seemingly eternal red and white carnations had attained during the last communist years of floral penury.

Western fashion is pervasive all over Bucharest, attracting its potential upper-middle-class consumers through shining and beautifully decorated shop windows of small but pretentious boutiques lined up along cosmopolitan boulevards such as *Calea Victoriei, Brătianu, Bălcescu,* or *Magheru.* With their high prices, Italian "Stefanel," American "Levi's," "Lee," and "Wrangler," and British "Mark's & Spencer" are only a few famous names that can be seen on Bucharest's major boulevards. In their midst one cannot forget the cheap mirage of faded glory of stores like *Eva, Unirea, Cocorul,* or *Magazinul Tineretului* (Youth's Store), that brought consumer goods to the average Romanian living in communism.

A growing population of cell phone users can be spotted at each step: people talk on their cell phones in the street, while driving, taking the bus, the tram, or a cab, while yelling, running, or smoking. Cell phones are everywhere and they seem to defy class boundaries. *Connex, Cosmoron, Dialog, SunTel, Telemobil,* or *Xpress* are the main cell phone companies responding to the time-space compression and new dynamism of life practices wrought by postcommunist changes. Thus ends the sad and archaic communist telephone system symbolized by a gloomy, semigothic institution, *Palatul Telefoanelor* (The Telephone Palace), a testimony of times when people literally had to wait for many years for others to move or die in order to obtain a telephone number.[12]

Postcommunist Bucharest seems to be defined by its noises, its sounds, and cries, which constitute as they do the city's tumultuous and unique *buzz*: cars honking, street dogs barking, church bells praying, rap and *manele* music irruptions, people's talk, youth's commotion, and, here and there, lingering in the disarticulated peace of a late evening or early morning, the occasional cry of Bucharest's more rare than ever turtledoves. However, cars dominate the sound system of this urban landscape. Everywhere the *flâneur* will encounter—and would eventually be stopped, honked, startled, almost hit by—cars galore. Today *Dacia*, the famous Romanian brand of cars produced during communism in association with the French Renault, does not reign anymore. Some of the most expensive Western cars can be spotted on Bucharest's major routes. Visible to everybody, cars represent a sign of economic status and, to the average citizen, they seem to be valued more than real estate ownership.

To the *flâneur*'s eye, Bucharest offers a new generation of dry cleaners, privatized public toilets, ATMs, an imposing World Trade Plaza, beauty centers, sex shops, photocopiers, private clinics and pharmacies, private banks, and, for the daring, investment brokers. Streets have changed their names, monuments go up and down, public parks can still accommodate passersby on a hot summer day, and football games still reign and bring the public chanting in the street. Finally, in the summer's twilight, few narrow, cobbled streets still offer the smell of Bucharest's ageless linden trees.

The *flâneur*'s voyage through Bucharest has captured some important elements of the new economic, social, cultural, and political order that is under construction in Romania, such as: advertising, consumption, graffiti, street children, poverty, youth, popular culture, gender, queer, *nouveaux riches*, hate speech, and public cyber-postcommunism. On this descriptive background, one can then ask: What will the *flâneur* encounter when entering the time and space of postcommunist Romania, as exemplified by the city of Bucharest? Indeed, what are the discourses, identities, and practices of everyday life most striking to the stroller in town?

1.1 Larry Hagman, alias "J.R.," from the celebrated American TV serial "Dallas," advertises Russian *LUKOIL* on the façade of *Dalles* Hall, located on *Nicolae Bălcescu* Boulevard, in Bucharest.

1.2 In the Civic Center: Ceauşescu's Palace, *Casa Poporului* (People's Palace), today the residence of the Parliament and other constitutional bodies (seen from *Piaţa Constituţiei,* up, and from *Piaţa Unirii,* down).

1.3 The famous revolutionary, anticommunist, and monarchist graffiti on the wall of the Bucharest University as viewed from *Piața Universității*. Recalling the 1989 Revolution, its victims, and protests, this place is also locally referred to as "Tiananmen Square II." In the summer of 2001, the new mayor of Bucharest, Traian Băsescu, covered the graffiti with white paint.

1.4 Downtown Bucharest, at *Piața Universității*. Built in a European cosmopolitan architectural style, the buildings represent: the Romanian Commercial Bank, Bucharest City Museum, and the University. The crosses are a remembrance of the revolutionary massacre from December 1989.

1.5 The concert hall *Ateneul Român* (up), the famous hotel *Athénée Palace* (middle), and *Piaţa Revoluţiei* (named after the 1989 Revolution) (down) as viewed from *Piaţa George Enescu* on *Calea Victoriei*.

1.6 Bucharest's old financial center: *Stavropoleos* Street (upper left) and the old Romanian bank and trust *Casa de Economii şi Consemnaţiuni, CEC* (bottom right), on *Calea Victoriei*.

1.7 Kilometer zero in old Bucharest, on *I. C. Brătianu* Boulevard at *Sfântul Gheorghe Nou.*

Notes

1. *Flâneur* is a poetic figure symbolizing the disinterested walker, the stroller. It was used by the French Romantic poet Charles Beaudelaire and was then symbolically transferred in the more political works of Walter Benjamin and Michel de Certeau. Today the *flâneur* has become a common marker for the detached, insightful, and amused traveler.

2. Here the notion of postcommunist *nouveau(x) riche(s)* takes the less sophisticated sense of "new money" (as opposed to "old money"), a simplified sense that is partly motivated by the *nouveaux riches'* highly volatile character in postcommunism, and partly by this book's concentration on certain practices of everyday life—aesthetical, with regards to the *nouveau(x) riche(s)*—and on micropolitics (as opposed to macropolitics). Used in this way, the notion of *nouveau(x) riche(s)* is not automatically made equivalent with the notion of "bourgeoisie," which this book also uses to designate the precommunist bourgeoisie as class, and its aesthetical, "bourgeois," "legitimate" taste formation, as this will be explained in chapter 3, "Aesthetics and Politics," following

Pierre Bourdieu's class-based system of taste classification. In postcommunist Romania, unlike the more recently used term *nouveau(x) riche(s)*, which conveys a symbolism of the present and future, the notions of "bourgeoisie" and "bourgeois" generally encapsulate a past-oriented mythology, occasionally filled with a sense of social criticism for some or nostalgia for others. (Also, with regards to the gendered nature of Romanian language, I note that the general Romanian parlance uses only the masculine form—*nouveau/x riche/s*—discarding the feminine form—*nouvelle/s riche/s*.) Pierre Bourdieu, *Distinction: A Social Critique of the Judgement of Taste*, trans. Richard Nice (Cambridge: Harvard University Press, 1984).

3. On the Romanian inns, see Şerban Cantacuzino, "Inns, Churches, Parks and Avenues," in *Bucharest: A Sentimental Guide*, ed. Aurora Fabritius, Erwin Kessler, and Adrian Solomon, trans. Florin Bican, Alina Cârâc, Michi Constantinescu Fărcaş, Daniela Neacşu, Adrian Solomon, Monica Voiculescu, and Ioana Zirra (Bucharest: The Romanian Cultural Foundation, 2001), 33.

4. Augustin Ioan, "Bucharest—Memory Walled-In," in *Bucharest: A Sentimental Guide*, ed. Aurora Fabritius, Erwin Kessler, and Adrian Solomon, trans. Florin Bican, Alina Cârâc, Michi Constantinescu Fărcaş, Daniela Neacşu, Adrian Solomon, Monica Voiculescu, and Ioana Zirra (Bucharest: The Romanian Cultural Foundation, 2001), 167.

5. Ioan, "Bucharest," 173.

6. See Adele Marie Barker, "Going to the Dogs: Pet Life in the New Russia," in *Consuming Russia: Popular Culture, Sex, and Society Since Gorbachev*, ed. Adele M. Barker (Durham: Duke University Press, 1999), 266-77.

7. Since 2001, the newly elected mayor of Bucharest, Traian Băsescu, has started a radical operation of neutering or plainly eliminating the stray dog population of Bucharest. His measures were often encountered by local protests.

8. In 2000, Romania had 800,000 Internet users and 32 personal computers per 1,000 people. World Bank, *2000 World Development Indicators*, <www.worldbank.org> (24 June 2002).

9. In the early 1980s, Bucharest was widely animated by the famous love affair between Ceauşescu's son, the late Nicu Ceauşescu, and the "Melody" bar singer Jeanina Matei.

10. R. G. Waldeck, *Athene Palace* (New York: Robert M. McBride & Company, 1942).

11. See also Mircea Cărtărescu, "Nuova guardia: Ura şi galeriile de fotbal" [Nuova Guardia: Hatred and Football Galleries], *Dilema* no. 357 (December 1999), <http://www.algoritma.ro/dilema/357/MirceaCA.htm> (10 January 2000).

12. Today, the former national telephone company is in a joint venture with the Hellenic Organization of Telecommunications (OTE).

Chapter Two

Discourses, Identities, and Practices of Everyday Life

Located in Southeastern Europe, Romania borders Ukraine in the North and East, the Republic of Moldavia and the Black Sea in the East, Bulgaria in the South, Yugoslavia in the Southwest, and Hungary in the West. It has an area of around 238,391 square kilometers[1] and a population of 21.7 million, of which 53 percent is urban.[2] With a legal system based on French civil law and a language belonging to the family of Romance languages, Romania was home to precommunist elites who were predominantly educated in French high culture, while the country at large remained peasant. In 1947 the country became a republic under communist rule, and in 1989 emerged from this regime with an impoverished economy and an outdated industrial base, a residue of forced industrialization and modernization.[3] Finally, with a new 1991 Constitution, Romania enjoys political pluralism and is engaged in a difficult economic restructuring with a view toward European Union and NATO integration.

According to the preliminary results of the 2002 census, the country's ethnic population numbers some 89.5 percent Romanians, 6.6 percent Hungarians,[4] 2.5 percent Roma,[5] while other national minorities include Germans, Jews, Ukrainians, Croatians, Czechs, Greeks, Poles, Armenians, Serbs, Tartars, Turks, Slovaks, Italians, Bulgarians, Lipovenean Russians, and, more recently and in connection to the postcommunist flourishing of international small commerce,

Chinese. The main religion is Christian-Orthodox and a variety of Roman-Catholic, Greco-Catholic, Reform, Pentecostal, Baptist, Unitarian, Judaic, and Muslim faiths are also professed.[6]

After more than a decade of postcommunist transformation, Romania experiences today some of the most significant challenges to traditional and communist forms of identity construction and production of subjectivities. Romania's citizens have emerged from communism tired and angry after decades of economic, social, cultural, and political deprivations, which culminated with the various infringements of basic rights under the rule of their last communist leader, Nicolae Ceauşescu. It can realistically be said that, perhaps with the exception of Albania under Enver Hoxa, Romania experienced one of the cruelest forms of communism under Ceauşescu, who initiated his own brand of communism, "Ceauşescuism,"[7] or national-communism, a mixture of Marxism-Leninism, autocracy, and nationalism. Cruelty toward his dispirited subjects led to the only bloody revolution—among the otherwise "velvet" transitions—when, in December 1989, Ceauşescu became the prey of citizens' movements and was shot on Christmas Day. Politically, postcommunist Romania has alternated leftist or center-leftist governments, in various degrees of an ex-communist heritage and allied in the early 1990s with the (ultra)nationalists, with center-right governments. Faced with trans-European integration Romanian civil and political societies are traversed by whirlpools of nationalist versus globalist ideologies. Overall, human, ethno-religious, gender, and sexual rights, as well as environmental issues are largely perceived as external importations. These new ideas of democratic acceptance of otherness have not been absorbed into current political and public culture and discourses, although—as will be presented throughout this book at least with regards to feminism and queer—several non-governmental organizations (NGOs) do exist within civil society and, although funded mainly by international organizations, they promote various forms of democratic activism, pushing toward either liberal, egalitarian, antidiscrimination policies or difference politics and affirmative action.

Drawing mainly from the tumult of everyday life experiences, this book discusses some of the discourses, subjectivities, political identities, experiences, and practices in postcommunist Romania. It will focus on issues of popular culture—and the way aesthetics, youth identity, and hate speech (anti-Semitism) emerge from it—as well as on gender and sexuality—in the form of women, queer, and politics. More specifically, the section on popular culture first starts by engaging in a comparison of communist and postcommunist aesthetics explained as a change from "socialist realism" into what will be called here, drawing from Mikhail Bakhtin,[8] *postcommunist carnivalesque.* This analysis is destined to frame the aesthetic condition and subject-formative experiences of postcommunist urban popular culture, as these will be discussed in the subsequent chapter on youth. Thus, chapter 4 will present the identity construction of the Romanian urban youth in communism and postcommunism—introduced here as the "Blue Jeans Generation" and "Generation PRO"—a form of resistance-identity that remains to this day indissolubly intertwined with various discourses and practices of popular culture. Postcommunist popular culture is also analyzed in terms of hate speech, an often unacknowledged yet widespread discourse that constructs derogatory identifications and representations, here exemplified by the discourse of anti-Semitism as "the mythical Jew." The third part, on gender and sexuality as identity construction and identity politics, makes an analysis of the way women are constructed as discursive and political subjects in postcommunism. This discussion about gender and sexuality becomes more intricate in the book's final analysis of the queer subject in present-day Romania.

At a more fundamental level and through the empirical material explored, this book also problematizes the cultural and political notions of *identity construction* and *identity politics* or, as expressed by Michel Foucault, "technologies of the self" that structure subjectivities and "technologies of power" that structure political identities.[9] In other words, issues of identity construction are here broken down into their constituent elements: *the practices* or *experiences* that *discursively construct subjectivities.* In this case of an analysis of Romanian communism and postcommunism, such practices of *identification,* indeed such *experiences,* will be understood through an interrogation of processes of oppression and resistance, and processes that construct "the other." These processes are expressed in and by "discourse," here understood, following Foucault, not only as "technologies of sign systems,"[10] but as "a set of rules which at a given period and for a given society define . . . [t]he limits and forms of the *sayable* . . . [its] conservation . . . memory . . . reactivation . . . [and] appropriation" by individuals, groups, or classes.[11] "[D]iscoursing subjects form a part of the discoursing field. . . . Discourse is not a place into which subjectivity irrupts; it is a space of differentiated subject-positions and subject-functions."[12] In other words, according to Rosi Braidotti, a feminist philosopher and a student of Foucault: "Discourse is the network of circulation of texts, meant both as material, institutional events and as symbolic or 'invisible' effects. A text is a term in a network that creates meaning, values, and norms and distributes them in a social context."[13]

With respect to the many constructions of *identity* and *subjectivity* available in the literature, those most important here draw from the reflections of Braidotti. She discusses *identity* as a matter of "the unconscious," thus suggesting a psychological/psychoanalytical basis to identity, while, at the same time, relationally juxtaposing it to the consciously engaged "political subjectivity": "identity bears a privileged bond to unconscious processes, whereas political subjectivity is a conscious and willful position. Unconscious desire and willful choice do not always coincide."[14] Braidotti proposes such definitions based on the tradition of poststructuralism;[15] for her "the politics of subjectivity":

refers both to the constitution of identities and to the acquisition of subjectivity, meant as forms of empowerment or entitlements to certain practices. The French term *assujettissement* renders both levels of this process of subjectification: it is both a material and a semiotic process that defines the subject through a number of regulative variables: sex, race, age, and so forth.[16]

Terminologically, this book starts from Braidotti's conceptualization of subjectification, while also recognizing the parlance of "political identities." Indeed, in the North American political (as opposed to psychological/psychoanalytical) discursive practices—at least feminist and queer—*subjectivities* are discussed mainly as cultural yet political practices of identity construction, as everyday life experiences, and as subject-positionings. *Political identities* on the other hand are here referred to as those subjectivities that are politicized through the voice of social movements and *identity politics*. Thus, to Braidotti's definition of *subjectification* I also add the notion of *experience* formulated by the feminist historian Joan W. Scott. Scott has cogently articulated *experience* as the basis for constructing political identities; she develops a critical, nonessentialist understanding of identities, and deconstructs them into dynamic, historicized, and discursively situated subjectivities, practices of subjectification, or subject-creating experiences. Following Scott, "the sense of political possibility" is "not the discovery of an identity, but a sense of participation in a movement," its practices, historicized experiences, and discursively created subjectivities: "To think about experience in this way is to historicize it as well as to historicize the identities it produces . . . focusing on processes of identity production, insisting on the discursive nature of 'experience' and on the politics of its construction."[17]

In this sense, and for the purposes of this book focused on the Eastern European/Romanian multifaceted, yet fragmented, subject, I will use the notion of *subjectivity* as a cultural and political practice, and as a subject-creating experience that stems out from the intersection of the unconscious with semiopen/semiaccepted everyday life existential routines. However, the notion of *identity*—here understood as *political identity*—refers to the power play and negotiation that politicizes forms of subjectivity through the voice of social movements and subsequent inclusive politics and public policies. Thus, while subjectivities overwhelmingly inhabit the private/public realm of civil society, political identities are those subjectivities that have managed to come out from the amorphous texture of everyday life practices—practices that create subjects through experiences of oppression and resistance—and have thus permeated political society, which they wish to make more inclusive, more tolerant, and more democratic. In other words, for this author, subjectivity refers to that poststructuralist conceptualization that considers individuals in a process of self-identification and fluid, dynamic, positioning as subjects within various crisscrossing experiences, practices, and discourses. Identity on the other hand is gained through identity politics of social movements, which are socially dynamic forces that politicize subjectivities through claims of inclusion, thus transforming them into articulated political identities. Finally, the nexus between subjectivity and identity in this understanding is also highly influenced by civil society's fluidity—as is the post-totalitarian Eastern European case—or its more argumentative articulation—as is the case of differently dynamic Western civil societies. As I will argue in this book with regards to Eastern European/ Romanian identity politics, during the first decade of postcommunist transformation, political state apparatuses were in various degrees at pains to recognize all subjectivities'—the ones that are considered democratic at least by Western standards, such as feminism and queer—claims to inclusion. Therefore, to follow on this example, feminist or queer claims in Romania are—and, in the case of a recently legalized queer subjectivity, socially and morally speaking, continue to be—forcefully relegated to the realm of ethico-religious subjectivities, without being recognized as political identities. And this is possible even if, as is the case of queer today, frameworks of legality that can enable a more vocal political identity, do exist. This is also why, in the queer case, due to the absence of clear-cut queer identities and queer social movements—and, as will be explained throughout this book, in line with most recent research of the post-Soviet queer subject or the nonpathologization of same-sex relations in non-Western contexts—this book's narrative refers to queer in terms of queer subjectivity, not queer identity—*political identity*—per se.

In keeping with this line of thought—centered as it is on the notions of *experience-based subjectivities* and *subjectivity-based political identities*, and focused on aesthetical, youth, hate speech, gender, and queer discourses and identifications located in various everyday life practices—this book shows that, in light of both precommunist and communist subject-formative patterns, present Romanian society proves to be inhabited more by *subjectivities*, as *practices* and *experiences* generated through oppression and resistance, and less by *political identities*, which, furthermore, as they are understood in Western democratic politics, are built up on notions of cohesive solidarity, social movements, and vocal identity politics of inclusion/exclusion. In other words, due to the political texture of its empirical background, I suggest here that present Romanian society proves to accommodate an uneven balance between *subjectivities* or practices and experiences of identity construction—that are in focus here—and *political identities* or the politics of social movements that have prominence in other such discussions addressing more articulated public expressions of civil society.

Accordingly, various gender and women subject-formative experiences and (anti)feminist practices are discussed here *in the absence* of a significant feminist movement or political identity. Similarly, queer subjectivity and queer experiences of oppression and resistance are discussed *in the absence* of clear-cut queer identity and politics, and some urban youth subject-formative experiences through popular culture are discussed *in the absence* of (politically inclusive) youth politics. The research also makes a discursive analysis of hate speech, here exemplified by anti-Semitism, which inhabits as an anachronism—and particularly in the near absence of the Jewish minority itself—various Romanian discursive spaces, of which popular culture is one. Similar to the absence of feminist, queer, or youth political identities mentioned above, anti-Semitism as a discourse can function *in the absence* of a significant Jewish entity, organized minority, and subsequent Jewish politics.

Finally, the connection between *subjectivities* as *practices and experiences of identity construction* and *identity politics* of *social movements* is acknowledged here as an important equation of identity politicization. In the context of Romania's difficult postcommunist transformation and gradual democratization of civil society, this connection is presently characterized by fluidity and transnational politics, and less by local, vocal mundane politics. Hence, the focus of the book is primarily on *identity construction* (and its constituent practices, discourses, subjectivities, and everyday life experiences) and only secondarily on *identity politics*, which, as a politics of social movements, represents a developing possibility today. This apprehension of identity politics seems to constitute a somewhat more pragmatic image of democratic identity and politics in present Romania.[18]

At the empirical level, my use of the concept of identity starts from the notion of "duplicity," a duplicitous identity explained as a form of *dedublare*, and a term employed by the sociologist Gail Kligman in her seminal work on reproductive politics in Ceauşescu's Romania.[19] Yet, as with Braidotti's notion of subjectification, here too I displace the main paradigm, "duplicity," by bridging it with Susan Gal and Kligman's later notion of "fractals"[20] and with Michel de Certeau's concept of "everyday life."[21] According to Kligman:

> Romania's socialist edifice was constructed on false reports, false statistics, deliberate disinformation, and false selves as well. . . . Duplicity became a mode of communicative behavior; conscientious lying was customary practice. Each was a characteristic form of *dedublare*, which all together spun the threads of complicity.
> *Dedublare* . . . roughly means division in two, or dual or split personalities. In the context of Ceausescu's Romania, it generally referred to distinctive representations of the self: a public self that engaged in public displays of conformity in speech and behavior, and a private self that may have retreated to the innermost depths of the mind to preserve a kernel of individual thought.[22]

What permits the construction of the concept of "duplicity" here is the author's recognition of a sharp division between the public and private spheres under Romanian communism, which, as a consequence of totalitarianism, engendered the split of spheres and selves. This allows, as Kligman says, "the resulting psycho-social problem and drama of the double-self or the split between the 'true' and 'false' self."[23] Kligman also constructs the notion of "duplicity" as a cultural practice used as a "communicative mode" under communism and an "internalized" "second nature."[24] Other notions are explained in order to highlight in juxtaposition the central concept of "*dedublare*" such as "*smecherie*," or individual cunning behavior.[25] Nevertheless, in the later work of Kligman with Susan Gal, the authors do not confer this public/private division—of spaces and selves—the same sharpness of boundaries. Instead they generate a concept, as expressed above, of "fractals," a fractality dynamic through history, and having blurred borders in fact. According to Gal and Kligman, dichotomies (public and private) nest intrinsic divisions creating endless "fractals":

> Activities, identities, and interactions can be split into private and public parts, and each of these parts can be split again, by the same public/private distinction. The result is that within any public one can always create a private; within any private one can create a public. . . . Another way to say this is that everyday public and private distinctions—whether of activities, spaces, or social groups—are subject to reframings and subdivisions in which some part of the public is redefined as private, and vice versa.[26]

This new concept of "fractal" seems to represent a more comprehensive operational term since its explanatory area can account for the diverse subject-formative experiences and discourses existing in the embedded private/public fractalities of communism and postcommunism, avoiding sharp segregations that feminist, postcolonial, and Cultural Studies have criticized for some decades now as "essentialism."[27] At a more profound level, as used in *The Politics of Duplicity*, the concept of "duplicity"/"*dedublare*" appears to predominantly reflect one nuance of subject-formation, a subject-creative experience generated in the shift, in the performativity between public and private spheres/selves. The use of this nuance inescapably conveys ideas of disempowerment, while ethically reducing experiences of subjectification to "conscientious lying," "complicity," "true" and "false" selves, "schizophrenic duality," and "kissing the hand one cannot bite."[28] Yet, as proved by the rich empirical material of *The Politics of Duplicity*, the concept "duplicity"/"*dedublare*" also engenders empowering connotations, which are conveyed by an everyday life practice and politics of survival, whereby the citizens did manage to subvert and displace the system on an individual basis; and Kligman also says in one instance, "People were manipulated by, but also manipulated, 'the system.'"[29] On a similar note, Slavenka Drakulić says, people "survived" the system and "even laughed."[30] It is on this empowering notion of duplicity, a *resistance-duplicity*, that some topics of this book (such as youth and, selectively, queer and women) will rest upon. This *everyday, life-based resistance-duplicity* emanated from the grassroots, from the quotidian existence of the average citizen faced with the imperative of constantly negotiating with the strictures of a totalitarian regime, and should empower with a politics of resistance the bodies, voices, and agency of various subjects located in diverse, counter-hegemonic experiences. I also hope to show that in specific discursive spaces the strictures of the regime were not so rigorously enforced, suggesting niches of subversiveness and alternative subject-formations, as in the discussion of youth and, occasionally, women and queer subjectivities.

In light of these considerations, my concept of identity is fundamentally based on the empowering practice and politics of everyday life, as this notion has been conceived by Michel de Certeau in his *The Practice of Everyday Life*. For de Certeau, everyday life is a political site of conflict and negotiation between the weak and the powerful, between dominant and dominated. Writing in a French existentialist, semiotic, and poetic spirit, de Certeau considers the practice of everyday life as a war of "tactics"—which John Fiske calls "guerilla tactics"[31] and Umberto Eco discusses as "semiotic guerilla warfare"[32]—fought by the weak against the great and well-organized military strategy of the powerful. Guerilla tactics refers to a daily harassing of the forces of the powerful, never challenging them in open fight, but constantly maintaining an opposition and resistance to the dominant social order, besieging the dominant and obtaining quotidian small victories. Everyday life is a continuous process of conflict, resistance, challenge and negotiation, whereby "the powerful construct 'places' where they can exercise their power"—"cities," "workplaces," and "houses"—while "the weak make their own 'spaces' within those places": "A place is where strategy operates; the guerrillas who move into it turn it into their space; *space is practiced place*."[33] The tactics of everyday life are ways of subverting dominant orders by the use of "trickery," "ruse," "deception," "manipulation," and adaptation:

> Innumerable ways of playing and foiling the other's game (*jouer/déjouer le jeu de l'autre*), that is, the space instituted by others, characterize the subtle, stubborn, resistant activity of groups which, since they lack their own space, have to get along in a network of already established forces and representations. People have to make do with what they have. In these combatants' stratagems, there is a certain art of placing one's blows, a pleasure of getting around the rules of a constraining space . . . there is a skill that has its connoisseurs and its esthetics exercised in any labyrinth of powers, a skill ceaselessly re-creating opacities and ambiguities—spaces of darkness and trickery. . . . Even the field of misfortune is refashioned by this combination of manipulation and enjoyment.[34]

To conclude, John Fiske argues that everyday life "is characterized by the creativity of the weak in using the resources provided by a disempowering system while refusing finally to submit to that power."[35]

No doubt, such a perspective has importance for a study of everyday life under authoritarian political conditions, such as those from Eastern Europe under communism. Under such circumstances, everyday life becomes a matter of daily small victories, or "guerilla tactics," fought against the dominant discourse of the "disempowering system," a practice of petty and duplicitous physical and psychical negotiations and adaptation of "places into spaces" through "trickery," and, ultimately, a practice of bodily and intellectual survival.

From a methodological perspective, it is important to recognize that, as a form of lived experience with its specific material and semiotic associations, Eastern European everyday life in general has remained, until the fall of communism, outside Western direct experience and subsequent theorization.[36]

However, Eastern European everyday experience owes its present conceptualization to the importance conferred in contemporary Western Cultural Studies—as this will be explained below—to the notion of everyday life and its Foucauldian politics of microstructures. Accordingly, *micropolitics* as *the politics of everyday life* and as a bottom-up politics arising from an empirical model of *lived experience* can now be theorized as a plurality of sites of struggle, resistance, and contestation to dominant, totalitarian power—a micropolitics empowering marginal, subaltern groups to find an identitary voice in the *polis*. As expressed earlier, such a micropolitics of everyday life makes possible for the first time an analysis of the communist *microreality*, as the daily life of the average citizen, with its small, hour-by-hour and minute-by-minute "guerilla tactics" and petite victories over dogmatism, scarce economic resources, and physical and psychical fear. Such an everyday life represents a Foucauldian understanding of power functioning at the level of surfaces and nodal points, capillary and ubiquitous, power circulating through individuals and their quotidian practices.[37] Finally, everyday life under communism can thus be understood as a life of meager survival strategies largely expressed in the creation of the second economy; in unofficial philosophic, literary, artistic, and youth private associations; in rock 'n' roll subculture and political jokes spread on the politically subversive corridors of workplaces and educational institutions, while taking a walk in the park, or in the kitchen while sipping from an ersatz-coffee: "in the sphere of daily life, the struggle was waged, often on an unconscious level, by the people themselves as they sought to live within the strictures imposed by the regime."[38]

Throughout this book the narrative of popular culture uses more semiotic and poststructuralist definitions such as those suggested, among others, by Raymond Williams in his *Keywords*.[39] Williams defines culture in three ways, all of which can enlighten the practices, discourses, identities, and experiences of everyday life in communist and postcommunist Romania. First, culture as an "abstract noun" can be comprehended as "intellectual, spiritual and aesthetic development" in general.[40] This definition is correlative with a second one, whereby culture refers to "a particular way of life, whether of a people, a period, a group, or humanity in general,"[41] which can be located in various cultural formations spanning the history of Europe, Buddhist or Muslim Asia, Africa, or, as is the case here, Eastern Europe. In the words of John Storey, these are "lived cultures or cultural practices," including the more novel study of sports, holidays, and even "youth subcultures."[42] It is here that I locate the bulk of this book's analyses of subject-formations and discourses through popular culture, such as youth subjectivity, hate speech as a discourse that intersects popular culture with politics, and—as will be presented in subsequent chapters—some instances of teenager girls', women's, and queer experiences of subjectification through popular culture. Williams refers to culture in a third way, as "works and practices of intellectual and especially artistic activity . . . music, literature, painting and sculpture, theater and film,"[43] or, as Storey again expresses from a poststructuralist perspective, "signifying practices," "producers of meanings," or "cultural texts," from "poetry, the novel, ballet, opera and fine art . . . [to] soap opera, pop music and comics."[44] This last sense of "culture" will serve to apprehend the experience of constructing youth subjectivity through popular culture as a form of political, yet artistic, resistance-identity, and underlies the aesthetic passage from "socialist realism" to what I am calling here *the postcommunist carnivalesque.*

Popular culture also works at the level of everyday life and practices, at a Foucauldian *micropolitical* level.[45] Since Foucault, power has been revealed as discursive and located in specific, micropolitical contexts, of which popular culture is one. Accordingly, the "politics of popular culture *is* micropolitics" and its tactic is one of everyday life.[46] Popular culture relates to daily power negotiations in what I call *biostructures* such as the family, the workplace, the school, in various formal and informal, smaller or larger associations, and the city. Then, it follows that *popular culture is a biopolitical culture* created in the private/public spheres of civil society, from where it stems out as a form of reactive energy and a counter-hegemonic cultural moment challenging a dominant, authoritarian political society and its hegemonic, official cultures. Such a perspective is useful to understand everyday life as *lived life* under communism, and popular culture as a site of an ongoing *micropolitical* struggle endowed with erosive, counter-hegemonic, and delegitimating discursive powers. Importantly, my use of the notion *biopolitics* is different from the one employed by Michel Foucault, for whom "biopolitics" is "the endeavor, begun in the eighteenth century, to rationalize the problems presented to governmental practice by the phenomena characteristic of a group of living human beings constituted as a population: health, sanitation, birthrate, longevity, race."[47] Unlike Foucault's use of this concept as a policy, here I use the notion of biopolitics as a terminological alternative to what would otherwise be called *life (micro)politics,* or *the politics of lived life,* understood as micropolitics fundamentally created by active human beings. When applied to popular culture, my notion of *biopolitics* is also designed to emphasize that such a popular culture is human, it is alive, it is *bio(s),*[48] and it is also *political* in nature and scope; it is *biopolitical.* Finally, this biopolitical sense of micropolitics highlights the idea that popular culture is actually created by individuals rather than being imposed on them—as some previous theories of popular culture as "mass culture" or alienated "one-dimensional" human beings had suggested, such as those of Theodor Adorno, Max Horkheimer,[49] and Herbert Marcuse[50] from the Frankfurt School.[51] In this sense, I also use the notion *biostructures* to emphasize the humanly alive character of these political structures—the family, the workplace, the school, various formal and informal, smaller or larger associations, and the city—in which, from an everyday life standpoint human beings have agency at all times, thus engendering micropolitics. This symbiotic human-structure perspective inspires a notion of political structures that are alive due to their dynamic connection to agency-creative human beings.[52]

Following Walter Benjamin's *Illuminations*, where he celebrates "the work of art in the age of mechanical reproduction,"[53] my notion of popular culture also makes reference to that highly democratic nuance of it, which is engendered by the passage from "auratic,"[54] high, classical cultures, and political histories, to democratic, popular, even pop culture or *street theory*, social histories, and Cultural Studies. In this sense, *popular culture is* in my understanding *a minimalist form of Cultural Studies.*[55]

Finally, my notion of popular culture also follows Lawrence Grossberg, for whom, as indicated by complex and often contradictory terms such as "mass, elite, legitimate, dominant, folk, high, low, midcult . . . civilized versus vulgar, dominant versus subordinate, authentic versus inauthentic, self versus other, same versus difference," popular culture is also a terrain of cultural diversity, the site of identity construction and lived popular experience.[56] Popular culture is revealed as an intersecting point of hybrid cultural practices, of pluralism. In this sense, by expressing cultural diversity, popular cultural becomes a politically important moment in the struggle to democratize the politics of identity recognition within the public sphere, which will also be presented in the case of communist and postcommunist Romania, particularly in what regards youth, gender, and queer politics.

On a different, terminological plane, in regards to the much debated notion of postcommunist "transition"—without excluding other conceptualizations, yet following the literature on "Postcommunist" and "Development" Studies regarding "transition" or "transformation"—this book finds that the notion "transformation" better expresses the complex socioeconomic and political processes that are taking place in Eastern Europe since 1989, compared, for example, with the governmental political "transitions" that took place in Latin America, and which do not involve comparable grand socioeconomic changes, in spite of local effects under "structural adjustment policies." Also, my witnessing and understanding of postcommunism conceptualizes it not only as a nondeterministic transformational process, but also as a *syncretic condition* where local and global, synchronic and diachronic discourses meet—of interest here being those that engender subjectivities and political identities.

With regards to *diachronic discourses*, or the recirculation of previous symbolic, discursive systems in postcommunism, the present discussion may come down to understanding the fact that "transformations," "transitions," and revolutions usher in new political regimes. These regimes must then try to construct a new ideology, a new symbolic order, a new culture, and a new vocabulary, which can enable discoursing subjects to locate themselves within newly emerging discourses. In other words, social changes are accompanied by discursive, symbolic changes. But in the immediate aftermath of such a transformation, there might be a period of discursive crisis, when the new political, economic, and cultural order has yet to build a new discursive order, a new vocabulary, which is bounded by what Michel Foucault calls "the limits and forms of the *sayable*," and which Richard Rorty discusses as the "final vocabulary":

> All human beings carry about a set of words which they employ to justify their actions, their beliefs, and their lives. These are the words in which we formulate praise of our friends and contempt for our enemies, our long-term projects, our deepest self-doubts and our highest hopes. They are the words in which we tell, sometimes prospectively and sometimes retrospectively, the story of our lives. I shall call these words a person's "final vocabulary."[57]

In other words, as Serguei Alex Oushakine explains through his notion of "post-Soviet aphasia,"[58] when grand transformations occur, subjects cannot engage in a new discursive production of subjectivity because they are locked into previous symbolic systems, which I call diachronic discourses; hence, an overwhelming nostalgic *psyche* pervades the postcommunist societies. In this sense, the new subjects remain prisoners of their settled "final vocabularies," a concept by which, as introduced above, Rorty means a set of primary value-words—such as "good," "right," "beautiful," "true"—that stand beyond definition, functioning as the inner experiential "text/test."[59] Finally, the relevance of such diachronic discourses for this book is not only that it stresses the eclectic, syncretic nature of postcommunism, but also that it emphasizes *lines of continuity with precommunism*. Furthermore, from a standpoint of everyday life, this situation of continuity and discursive syncretism should bring evidence to the fact that communism did not manage to entirely dismantle Romanian precommunist society, particularly outside the range where power was exacted directly (as is the case of the long-lasting influence of the Christian-Orthodox Church, Romanian nationalism, peasant culture, or select, urban, precommunist, "bourgeois" lifestyles, for example). Moreover, and in connection with the concept of *resistance-duplicity*, communism did not succeed in completely crushing people's resistance to totalitarianism, nor—as presented in this book—their myriad expressions of difference, such as is evident in youth counter-culture, alternative femininities, and even everyday resistance. As a consequence, *postcommunism must be understood not only as a blunt reaction to communism, but as a profound transformation and a discursive hybrid stemming out from an ample past that transcends totalitarianism into precommunism, while also continuously coalescing Western influences.*

In the end, my occasional use of "Eastern Europe" and "Romania" together or loosely interchangeably does not wish to convey notions of corporate, uniform entities, or amorphous, identical experiences of subjectification, identity politics, or everyday life textures. My infrequent shifting use of these comparative terms is explained through broad, nonessentialist, pluralistically common historical trends of at least communism and early postcommunism, both with their situated, local, intersecting, synchronic and diachronic discourses counterposed to a correlated scholarly notion of "West," yet symbiotically intertwined in an "East-West" relationship.

Methodology

This book uses the epistemology of Cultural Studies and Feminist Theory. Cultural Studies is understood as an interdisciplinary field gathering paradigms and theories concerned with culture, identity, discourses, and practices, together with concepts that are derived from anthropology, sociology, psychology, linguistics, literary criticism, art theory, media and communication studies, political science, history, and philosophy. Relevant for the purpose of this book, Cultural Studies generally—but not exclusively—focuses on identity construction and representations of "the other" within various postmodern,[60] cultural, feminist, poststructuralist, psychoanalytical, postcolonial, and environmental critiques of canons, and—given the special attention paid to signs, codes, and texts—on discourse analysis.

With paradigms created by a gallery of respected names such as Raymond Williams, Stuart Hall, Michel Foucault, Roland Barthes, Michel de Certeau, Pierre Bourdieu, Jean Baudrillard, and Edward Said—to name only a few—Cultural Studies has increasingly become a transnational discipline that coalesces, as explained, various critiques of canons in politics and academic fields.[61] Changing its focus from early analyses centered on "codes" and "meanings" to "difference" and "otherness," as Simon During explains, since the 1980s Cultural Studies has become a fulcrum of pan-subjectivity politics, of "cross-identification," "micropolitics," "rainbow alliances," and "dialogical" differences."[62] The phenomenon of globalization has also brought forth the importance of the transnational in the interconnection of such levels as economic processes, the "global popular," new technologies, and information flows and communication systems. The emphasis on globalization also revalorized the relevance of a global politics of location and positionality, while this new global cultural economy was revealed as "disjunctive," functioning throughout many levels of "global cultural flows" and "imagined worlds," and transcending classic nation-state politics.[63] As Arjun Appadurai metaphorically expresses, contemporary "global culture" is the politics of the "mutual cannibalization" of "sameness and difference," of the "triumphantly universal and the resiliently particular."[64]

A transnational academic discipline today, Cultural Studies focuses on an increasing repertoire of newly politicized issues: from Michel de Certeau's "everyday life" (*le quotidien*), science, nature and the body, difference feminism, and sex and queer theory, to the public sphere and the media, and, last but not least, to a global popular culture. Relevant for this book, Cultural Studies analyzes today the ways in which identities are culturally and globally produced, reproduced, hybridized, consumed, and renegotiated in a double-movement of economic and cultural flows.[65]

However, the idea that Cultural Studies could be applied to analyses of Eastern Europe is quite novel. As Catriona Kelly, Hilary Pilkington, David Shepherd, and Vadim Volkov explain in their luminary introduction to *Russian*

Cultural Studies,[66] the Soviet Union has been Western politics' "most significant 'other'" for more than half a century of communism and Cold War. Accordingly, these authors suggest that when it comes to Russia and the Soviet Union, such arguments as those used in the "binary oppositions of East and West, high and low, major and minor, perennial and ephemeral, old and new, political and apolitical" appear to be welcome and legitimate, yet they "would command little respect if applied to French, German, British, or American history"[67]:

> But it is perhaps time to recognize that Russian history is neither more nor less complex and illogical than the histories of other European countries; that causative processes have been diverse and unpredictable here as elsewhere; and that these processes may not be subsumed into easy conflicts between "intelligentsia" and "people," "Westernizers" and "Slavophiles" or into generalizations about "autocratic" and "totalitarian" societies. The indisputable fact that Russia has never (yet) had an Anglo-American style democracy should not be elevated into proof of the country's eternal capacity for repression. Some at least of the mechanisms of government under both tsars and Soviets, such as bribery and patron-client networks, are found in other European countries too (from Ireland to Italy).[68]

From a comparative perspective, these authors' descriptions of the symbolic appropriation of Russia and the Soviet Union by the West can be usefully applied to the rest of (communist) Eastern Europe. In this sense, the seminal studies developed by Larry Wolff[69] and Maria Todorova[70] represent a comprehensive introduction to the topic of historical construction of Eastern Europe and the Balkans as "the other," as imagined and displaced myths. As Kelly, Pilkington, Shepherd, and Volkov convey, the bulk of literature on communism has concentrated on the realm of *high politics*. The repressive character of the state and its bureaucracies, the dictatorial impulses of its leaders, the totalitarian nature of the regimes, and arms competition have, until recently, constituted traditional topics, as have the official economy of shortages versus the unofficial second economy, the lack of freedoms and dissent, and the neutralization of civil society. However, the significant mutations that were taking place in the realm of everyday life, indeed the way life was lived at the grassroots by the denizens of the region day-by-day, hour-by-hour, and minute-by-minute, were neglected. As these authors cogently suggest, the lasting hegemony of "political history" (versus social or cultural history) in communist and postcommunist studies lay in the strongly ideological texture of the postwar political climate, which had in fact determined the "binary models" of the Cold War whereby communism (Soviet Union/Eastern Europe) was imagined as "the 'other'" (or "totalitarianism") versus "the West" (or democracy).[71] These authors also explain that social scientists used either the totalitarian model (democracy versus totalitarianism), or modernization theory, which stressed communism's unique route to development;[72] but both theories were operating at the level of "economic determinism" and "cultural insensitivity."[73] Another Western approach focused on political culture, employing the problematic category of the *homo sovieticus*, or the New Socialist Being—a stereotype characterized by alleged internalized ethical, ideological, or "cultural impediments to democratization."[74] These "grand theories" and the difficulty of gathering primary data, of field research, are the main factors credited by Kelly, Pilkington, Shepherd, and Volkov to have impeded the creation of a discipline that I would call Eastern European Cultural Studies. Lacking the political chances for sustained travel and research in Eastern Europe, Western social scientists were left with the bias-prone alternative of applying ideologically cosmeticized "media texts and governmental statements,"[75] as well as the declarations of dissident-intellectuals, themselves of various persuasions.[76] This represented at best a "top-down" approach to the study of society, culture, and politics, leaving aside forms of cultural production and the sensitive *daily lived life* and interaction of individuals with the *negotiated construction of their identities*. As Kelly, Pilkington, Shepherd, and Volkov conclude, these theories fail to penetrate the complex nature of "identity formation" and "cultural practices" during communism. In this sense, the Eastern European sociocultural universe was reduced to a "fictitious generalized average, based on public opinion-polling methods."[77]

In spite of this, present Western studies of Eastern European societies and politics have started to show a growing interest in culture beyond studies of nationalism, mainly through an increasingly gender-sensitive approach to the region. In other words, today there is a growth in culturally oriented studies of Eastern Europe, due to further processes of democratization in the West, such as the civil rights movement, feminism, and queer politics.[78]

At present, the application of Cultural Studies to the study of Eastern Europe is taking on some of the issues that are animating contemporary Cultural Studies in the West, among which are "globalization and localization; domination and subordination; identity formation; and . . . diversity, difference, and fragmentation,"[79] gender politics, queer, environment, class, ethnicity, religion, age, ableness, literature, TV and media, the university, popular culture, and folklore. These issues are brought to bear on *the daily lived life* and interaction of individuals with the *construction of their identities* (in this case, during communism and postcommunism).

Finally, it is this focus that Cultural Studies bears on fragmentation, on difference and diversity on the one hand, and the notion of dispersed subjectivities struggling for recognition as political identities in Romania on the other hand, that have ineluctably suggested the title of this book, *Fragmented Identities*.

The other important set of epistemologies that grounds this book is Feminist Theory.[80] And I am not referring here to any one in particular from the varied feminist theories that constitute the corpus of this knowledge—liberal, socialist, radical, African-American, existentialist, postcolonial, postmodern, performative, queer, or *écriture feminine*—to name some of them. What is of interest here is the specific contribution that this body of knowledge has brought as a critique of canons in politics and academic disciplines. Thus, it is not the focus on sex, gender, or sexuality that makes feminist theories a valuable epistemology here—although the discussion in the book will undeniably make gender and queer analyses—but certain particularities of this body of literature that transcend the immediate focus on women and gender. First, I would like to mention that, like Cultural Studies, Feminist Theory stresses interdisciplinarity, employing paradigms and methods from many fields in the social sciences and humanities. Second, Feminist Theory valorizes the entire move toward a nonessentialist difference, which, following Third Wave/postmodern feminism, has displaced essentialist, segregationist notions of difference from Second Wave radical feminist persuasions toward unbound, differed diversity—what Jacques Derrida calls *Différance*.[81] In this sense, the critical standpoint in Feminist Theory today goes well beyond a focus on gender or women. As this book will express along its narratives, as a critical theory of identity construction, Feminist Theory valorizes and problematizes the intersection of many axes of subjectification. Gender, sexuality, ethnicity, race, religion, age, or ableness are subject-positionings which, as African-American feminists like bell hooks, Deborah King, and Audre Lorde have expressed it for some years now, are indissolubly interlocked at the level of everyday life and its materiality.[82] This Third Wave feminism of pluralism is ultimately a feminism that transcends its own name of *feminism*—i.e., focused on women and gender—into *postfeminism*. Thus, *postfeminism* represents a wider critical epistemology that has become contiguous today with other theorizations that challenge notions of essentialism or ethnocentric universalism, such as postcolonial, postmodern, and environmental theories, and poststructuralism, psychoanalysis, and Cultural Studies.

To sum up, while Cultural Studies' relevance here is its focus on epistemologies of everyday life, on micropolitics, and on experiences of subjectification, Feminist Theory as postfeminism provides foundation for a critical, oppositional rhetoric that is indissolubly embedded in a discourse of identity construction and democratic identity politics in communist and postcommunist Romania.

Lastly, from a methodological standpoint grounded in feminist and postcolonial understandings of *an author's positionality*, or *the author's voice*, it is also important to recall here my pluralistic location as an author within a *hybrid Diasporic sensitivity*: Eastern and Western.[83] Thus, the standpoint here is liminal yet multiple: it is a location that, valorizing an interface with various theoretical and empirical experiences, is at the same time gendered, Eastern European (Romanian),[84] and North American. These experiences are in turn traversed and translated into Western discourses by using both Western and Romanian scholarship. In this sense, my knowledge is "situated"[85] in various empirical and theoretical positionalities, understood as multiple, intersecting "epistemological communities"[86]; it is "perspectival."[87] This shift, this continuous and dynamic performativity of one's authorial voice between epistemological universes, makes for a case of what Rosi Braidotti calls "nomadic writing."[88] Thus, employing the hybrid standpoint as the location of the author's voice (Walter D. Mignolo calls this "border gnoseology,"[89] Alberto Moreiras discusses it as a "counterpolitics of location,"[90] and Geeta Kapur considers it a "local-global" point "from where I speak"[91]), I will engage throughout this book in explaining certain ways in which subjectivities are discursively created, political identities are constructed in a counter-hegemonic exercise, and some segments of life are lived in communist and postcommunist Romania as a micropolitics of the quotidian.

This book is selective in its Romania-focused topics of study, although some inferences can be extrapolated in the context of other Eastern European societies, politics, and identities. Thus, this is not a book about an elusive corporate concept of "postcommunist Romania"—theoretically and empirically speaking *there are many Romania-s*, not only one in particular, even within Diasporic Romania(s). Nor is this a book on Romanian popular culture, gender, sexuality, anti-Semitism, youth, aesthetics, communism, postcommunism, and politics in general. Accordingly, I will discuss only some *discourses, subjectivities, political identities,* and *practices of everyday life* in postcommunist Romania—and their connection with communism and its heritage. My discussion will not only valorize the vantage point of Cultural Studies and Feminist Theory, as explained above, but, selectively, will also answer to a lack of previous analytical introspection into such specific "technologies of the self" and "technologies of power." Such experiences and expressions, united by their everydayness and their construction as forms of resistance, are also connected by their situatedness in sub-civil society *biostructures* such as the family and close, informal networks of friends, or in small, youth or other cultural associations, groups, or events within the private/public structures of everyday life. As expressed before, the discourses and experiences analyzed here are politically united by a condition of presence/absence, that is by the fact that, on the background of a postcommunist fluid civil society, they can exist as practices of identification and discursive constructions of subjects *in the absence* of correlated, organized, cohesive identity politics or social movements. Finally, looking into such practices of identification also serves as a means to understand processes of democratization of the Romanian postcommunist civil society, of the way "the other"—women, Jews, queer, youth—is constructed on a background of Romanian conservative, national-communist, and more recent Western discourses.

Empirically, the focus here falls on urban Romania of the late 1980s and the first decade of postcommunist transformation, and takes a gravitational standpoint in the city of Bucharest. This passage in time from the 1980s to the 1990s captures an important symbolism characterizing both political regimes— communism and postcommunism—as their underlying popular culture and select processes of identity construction were significantly overlapping in the late 1980s. Thus, the empirical foundation of this book resides in field research conducted mainly in Bucharest in 1996 and 1998-2001. I analyzed Romanian scholarly, literary, and journalistic texts, TV and Radio talk- and artistic shows, news and advertisements, statistics, and Internet resources; I had discussions with various youth and adults who were adolescents during the 1980s, with select performers and composers of Romanian pop music, *muzica uşoară*, and with various feminist scholars and queer politics activists; and, occasionally, as was explained above regarding my *voice* as an author, I inescapably situated myself as a tourist in my own skin while strolling as a *flâneur* in my native Bucharest. From a theoretical perspective, I have employed both Western and Eastern European/Romanian scholarly literature, particularly those narratives or theories of feminism, queer, youth, popular culture, aesthetics, nation, and identity that proved relevant for a study of Romania, communism, and postcommunism, while also drawing occasional East-West comparisons.

Notes

1. Romania.org, "Facts and Figures," <http://www.romania.org> (24 June 2002).
2. This data follows the preliminary results of the 2002 census. *Recensământ 2002* [Census 2002], <http://www.recensamant.ro/> (17 July 2002). According to the 1992 census, the total population of Romania was about 23 million. See Irina Moroianu-Zlătescu and Ioan Oancea, *The Legislative and Institutional Framework for National Minorities from Romania* (Bucharest: The Institute on Human Rights, 1992).
3. See also Romania.org, "Facts and Figures."
4. From 8.9 percent according to the 1992 census. Moroianu-Zlătescu and Oancea, *The Legislative and Institutional Framework*, 7-8.
5. From 1.6 percent according to the 1992 census. Moroianu-Zlătescu and Oancea, *The Legislative and Institutional Framework*, 7-8.
6. *Recensământ 2002*.
7. See Trond Gilberg, *Nationalism and Communism in Romania: The Rise and Fall of Ceausescu's Personal Dictatorship* (Boulder: Westview Press, 1990), 49-57.
8. See Mikhail Bakhtin, *Rabelais and His World*, trans. Helene Iswolsky (Bloomington: Indiana University Press, 1988).
9. Michel Foucault, "Technologies of the Self," in *Ethics: Subjectivity and Truth. Essential Works of Foucault 1954-1984*, vol. I, ed. Paul Rabinow, trans. Robert Hurley and others (New York: The New Press, 1998), 225.
10. Foucault, "Technologies of the Self," 225.
11. Michel Foucault, "Politics and the Study of Discourse," in *The Foucault Effect: Studies in Governmentality*, ed. Graham Burchell, Colin Gordon, and Peter Miller (Chicago: The University of Chicago Press, 1991), 59-60.
12. Foucault, "Politics and the Study of Discourse," 58.
13. Rosi Braidotti, *Nomadic Subjects: Embodiment and Sexual Difference in Contemporary Feminist Theory*. (New York: Columbia University Press, 1994), 260.
14. Braidotti, *Nomadic Subjects*, 166.

15. On poststructuralism, see also Denise Roman, "Poststructuralism," in *Encyclopedia of Postmodernism,* ed. Victor E. Taylor and Charles E. Windquist (New York: Routledge, 2001), 308-10.

16. Braidotti, *Nomadic Subjects,* 99.

17. Joan W. Scott, "Experience," in *Feminists Theorize the Political,* ed. Judith Butler and Joan W. Scott (New York: Routledge, 1992), 23, 26, 37.

18. This book concentrates only on those subject-formative experiences and democratic political identities that regard women, queer, and youth. Thus, my book does not address other identity politics, vocal indeed, that exist in present Romania, such as working-class politics or the ethnic politics of various minority or majority groups, and which, unlike the Jewish minority today, have a substantial empirical grounding as entities in Romanian society and politics. Nevertheless, some of their subject-formative experiences will often touch upon more generic topics, such as ethno-gender politics in postcommunist Romania.

19. Gail Kligman, *The Politics of Duplicity: Controlling Reproduction in Ceausescu's Romania* (Berkeley: University of California Press, 1998).

20. Susan Gal and Gail Kligman, *The Politics of Gender after Socialism: A Comparative-Historical Essay* (Princeton: Princeton University Press, 2000), 13, 41.

21. See Michel de Certeau, *The Practice of Everyday Life,* trans. Steven F. Rendall (Berkeley: University of California Press, 1984).

22. Kligman, *The Politics of Duplicity,*15.

23. Kligman, *The Politics of Duplicity,* 15.

24. Kligman, *The Politics of Duplicity,* 265 ens. 70, 73.

25. Kligman, *The Politics of Duplicity,* 265 en. 70.

26. Gal and Kligman, *The Politics of Gender after Socialism,* 41.

27. On critiques of "essentialism," see Elizabeth Grosz, "A Note on Essentialism and Difference," in *Feminist Knowledge: Critique and Construct,* ed. Sneja Gunew (New York: Routledge, 1992), 332-44; Chandra T. Mohanty, "Under Western Eyes: Feminist Scholarship and Colonial Discourses," in *Dangerous Liaisons: Gender, Nation, & Postcolonial Perspectives,* ed. Anne McClintock, Aamir Mufti, and Ella Shohat (Minneapolis: University of Minnesota Press, 1997), 255-77; and Trinh T. Minh-ha, "Not You/Like You: Postcolonial Women and the Interlocking Questions of Identity and Difference," in *Dangerous Liaisons: Gender, Nation, & Postcolonial Perspectives,* ed. Anne McClintock, Aamir Mufti, and Ella Shohat (Minneapolis: University of Minnesota Press, 1997), 415-9.

28. Kligman, *The Politics of Duplicity,* 15; 265 ens. 70-2.

29. Kligman, *The Politics of Duplicity,* 15.

30. Slavenka Drakulić, *How We Survived Communism and Even Laughed* (New York: HarperPerennial, 1993).

31. John Fiske, *Understanding Popular Culture* (New York: Routledge, 1991), 19.

32. Umberto Eco, *A Theory of Semiotics* (Bloomington: Indiana University Press, 1976), 150 and *Travels in Hyperreality* (London: Picador, 1986).

33. Fiske, *Understanding Popular Culture,* 32-3. My emphasis.

34. de Certeau, *The Practice of Everyday Life,* 18.

35. Fiske, *Understanding Popular Culture,* 47.

36. A notable exception in the Romanian case is the path-breaking work of Katherine Verdery and Gail Kligman. See for example Katherine Verdery, *Transylvanian Villagers: Three Centuries of Political, Economic, and Ethnic Change* (Berkeley: University of

California Press, 1983) and *National Ideology under Socialism: Identity and Cultural Politics in Ceauşescu's Romania* (Berkeley: University of California Press, 1991); and Gail Kligman, *The Wedding of the Dead: Ritual, Poetics, and Popular Culture in Transylvania* (Berkeley: University of California Press, 1988).

37. Michel Foucault, "Two Lectures," in *Power/Knowledge: Selected Interviews and Other Writings, 1972-1977*, ed. Colin Gordon (New York: Pantheon Books, 1981), 98-9.

38. Adele Marie Barker, "The Culture Factory: Theorizing the Popular in the Old and New Russia," in *Consuming Russia: Popular Culture, Sex, and Society Since Gorbachev*, ed. Adele M. Barker (Durham: Duke University Press, 1999), 21.

39. Raymond Williams, *Keywords: A Vocabulary of Culture and Society* (London: Fontana, 1983).

40. Williams, *Keywords*, 90.

41. Williams, *Keywords*, 90.

42. John Storey, *An Introduction to Cultural Theory and Popular Culture*, 2nd ed. (London: Prentice Hall/Harvester Wheatsheaf, 1993), 2.

43. Williams, *Keywords*, 90.

44. Storey, *An Introduction to Cultural Theory*, 2.

45. Michel Foucault, "Two Lectures," 78-108.

46. Fiske, *Understanding Popular Culture*, 56. My emphasis.

47. Michel Foucault, "The Birth of Biopolitics," in *Ethics: Subjectivity and Truth. Essential Works of Foucault 1954-1984*, vol. I, ed. Paul Rabinow, trans. Robert Hurley and others (New York: The New Press, 1998), 73.

48. *Bios* means "life" in Ancient Greek.

49. Max Horkheimer and Theodor Adorno, "The Culture Industry: Enlightenment as Mass Deception," in *The Cultural Studies Reader*, ed. Simon During, 2nd ed. (New York: Routledge, 1999), 32-41.

50. Herbert Marcuse, *One-Dimensional Man: Studies in Ideology of Advanced Industrial Society* (Boston: Beacon Press, 1992).

51. On popular culture as "made by the people, not produced by the culture industry," see also Fiske, *Understanding Popular Culture*, 24.

52. This idea would ultimately be contiguous with the feminist notion of "cyborg" developed by Donna Haraway as a physical, intellectual, and political intersection of the human being with nature and machine. Donna Haraway, "A Manifesto for Cyborgs: Science, Technology, and Socialist Feminism in the 1980s," in *Feminist Social Thought: A Reader*, ed. Diana T. Meyers. (New York: Routledge, 1997), 501-31.

53. Walter Benjamin, *Illuminations*, ed. and Introduction by Hannah Arendt, trans. Harry Zohn (New York: Shocken Books, 1968), 217-51.

54. Benjamin, *Illuminations*, 222-3.

55. On a link between popular culture and Cultural Studies, see also Braidotti, *Nomadic Subjects*, 38, 260.

56. Lawrence Grossberg, *We Gotta Get out of This Place: Popular Conservatism and Postmodern Culture* (New York: Routledge, 1992), 75.

57. Richard Rorty, *Contingency, Irony, and Solidarity* (Cambridge: Cambridge University Press, 1989), 73.

58. Serguei Alex Oushakine, "In the State of Post-Soviet Aphasia: Symbolic Development in Contemporary Russia," *Europe-Asia Studies* 52, no. 6 (Sept. 2000): 991-1016.

59. For a similar use of the Rortian paradigm in the Russian case, see Theresa Sabonis-Chafee, "Communism as Kitsch: Soviet Symbols in Post-Soviet Society," in *Consuming Russia: Popular Culture, Sex, and Society Since Gorbachev*, ed. Adele M. Barker (Durham: Duke University Press, 1999), 363.

60. According to Chantal Mouffe, understood as a "critique of universalism, humanism, and rationalism," of "the idea of a universal human nature, of a universal canon of rationality through which that human nature could be known, as well as the traditional conception of truth," the "postmodern" refers to "the main currents of twentieth-century philosophy"—not solely to "poststructuralism" or a generic "postmodernism." Among these philosophical currents stand "Heidegger and the post-Heideggerian philosophical hermeneutics of Gadamer, the later Wittgenstein and the philosophy of language inspired by his works, psychoanalysis and the reading of Freud proposed by Lacan, [and] American pragmatism." Chantal Mouffe, "Feminism, Citizenship, and Radical Democratic Politics," in her *The Return of the Political* (London: Verso, 1993), 74.

61. On a history of Cultural Studies, see Storey, *An Introduction to Cultural Theory*; Andrew Milner, *Contemporary Cultural Theory: An Introduction* (London: UCL Press, 1994); and Simon During, "Introduction," in *The Cultural Studies Reader*, ed. Simon During, 2nd ed. (New York: Routledge, 1999), 1-28.

62. During, "Introduction," 13.

63. Arjun Appadurai, "Disjuncture and Difference in the Global Cultural Economy," in *The Cultural Studies Reader*, ed. Simon During, 2nd ed. (New York: Routledge, 1999), 221-2.

64. Appadurai, "Disjuncture and Difference," 229-30.

65. Some notable country-based collections of essays in Cultural Studies are William Kidd and Siân Reynolds, eds., *Contemporary French Cultural Studies* (London: Arnold/ New York: Oxford University Press, 2000); Vinay Lal, *South Asian Cultural Studies* (Manohar: Delhi, 1996); David Forgacs and Robert Lumley, eds., *Italian Cultural Studies: An Introduction* (New York: Oxford University Press, 1996); Catriona Kelly and David Shepherd, eds., *Russian Cultural Studies: An Introduction* (Oxford: Oxford University Press, 1998); and Neil Campbell and Alasdair Kean, *American Cultural Studies: An Introduction to American Culture* (New York: Routledge, 1997).

66. Catriona Kelly, Hilary Pilkington, David Shepherd, and Vadim Volkov, "Introduction: Why Cultural Studies?," in *Russian Cultural Studies: An Introduction*, ed. Catriona Kelly and David Shepherd (Oxford: Oxford University Press, 1998), 1-17.

67. Kelly, Pilkington, Shepherd, and Volkov, "Introduction," 1-2.

68. Kelly, Pilkington, Shepherd, and Volkov, "Introduction," 3.

69. Larry Wolff, *Inventing Eastern Europe: The Map of Civilization on the Mind of the Enlightenment* (Stanford: Stanford University Press, 1994).

70. Maria Todorova, *Imagining the Balkans* (New York: Oxford University Press, 1997).

71. Kelly, Pilkington, Shepherd, and Volkov, "Introduction," 4.

72. On modernization theory as "Russian mismodernization," see the line of thought started by Barrington Moore Jr.'s classic *Social Origins of Dictatorship and Democracy: Lord and Peasant in the Making of the Modern World* (Boston: Beacon Press, 1966) and continued by his student, Theda Skocpol, in her *States and Social Revolutions: A Comparative Analysis of France, Russia, & China* (Cambridge: Cambridge University Press, 1979).

73. Kelly, Pilkington, Shepherd, and Volkov, "Introduction," 4.

74. Kelly, Pilkington, Shepherd, and Volkov, "Introduction," 5.

75. Kelly, Pilkington, Shepherd, and Volkov, "Introduction," 4.

76. On dissident-intellectuals, see Vladimir Tismaneanu, *Fantasies of Salvation: Democracy, Nationalism, and Myth in Post-Communist Europe* (Princeton: Princeton University Press, 1998).

77. Kelly, Pilkington, Shepherd, and Volkov, "Introduction," 5.

78. Kelly, Pilkington, Shepherd, and Volkov, "Introduction," 4.

79. Kelly, Pilkington, Shepherd, and Volkov, "Introduction," 6.

80. Different from my use of the notion "Feminist Theory" here, my general application of the concept "feminism" throughout this book conveys both meanings of "feminist theorizations" and "women's and gender politics."

81. Jacques Derrida, *Positions*, trans. and annot. Alan Bass (Chicago: The University of Chicago Press, 1981), 39-96.

82. bell hooks, *Yearning: Race, Gender, and Cultural Politics* (London: Turnaround, 1991); Deborah K. King, "Multiple Jeopardy, Multiple Consciousness: The Context of a Black Feminist Ideology," in *Feminist Social Thought: A Reader*, ed. Diana T. Meyers (New York: Routledge, 1997), 220-42; and Audre Lorde, "Age, Race, Class, and Sex: Women Redefining Difference," in *Dangerous Liaisons: Gender, Nation, & Postcolonial Perspectives*, ed. Anne McClintock, Aamir Mufti, and Ella Shohat (Minneapolis: University of Minnesota Press, 1997), 374-80.

83. On the dual, liminal, or "insider-without" position of the Eastern scholar in the Western context, see also Minh-ha, "Not You/Like You."

84. Ultimately, I must acknowledge that even my originating experiential point—Romanian—is to be understood here within a comprehensive civic-based definition of the political subject and as a form of (temporary yet significant) socialization, not as an ethnic situatedness.

85. On the notion that "knowledge is situated," see Donna Haraway, "Situated Knowledges," in her *Simians, Cyborgs, and Women* (London: Free Association Books, 1990), 183-202.

86. On the notion of "epistemological communities," see Lynn Hankinson Nelson, "Epistemological Communities," in *Feminist Epistemologies*, ed. Linda Alcoff and Elizabeth Potter (New York: Routledge, 1993), 121-59.

87. On the notion that knowledge is "perspectival," see Sandra Harding, "Rethinking Standpoint Epistemology: What Is 'Strong Objectivity'?," in *Feminist Epistemologies*, ed. Linda Alcoff and Elizabeth Potter (New York: Routledge, 1993), 49-82; and Elizabeth Grosz, "Bodies and Knowledges: Feminism and the Crisis of Reason," in *Feminist Epistemologies*, ed. Linda Alcoff and Elizabeth Potter (New York: Routledge, 1993), 187-215.

88. Braidotti, *Nomadic Subjects*, 15-28.

89. Walter D. Mignolo, "Globalization, Civilization Processes, and the Relocation of Languages and Cultures," in *The Cultures of Globalization*, ed. Fredric Jameson and Masao Miyoshi (Durham: Duke University Press, 1998), 51.

90. Alberto Moreiras, "Global Fragments: A Second Latinamericanism," in *The Cultures of Globalization*, eds. Fredric Jameson and Masao Miyoshi (Durham: Duke University Press, 1998), 84.

91. Geeta Kapur, "Globalization and Culture: Navigating the Void," in *The Cultures of Globalization*, ed. Fredric Jameson and Masao Miyoshi (Durham: Duke University Press, 1998), 192, 204.

PART TWO
POPULAR CULTURE

Chapter Three

Aesthetics and Politics: From "Socialist Realism" to "Postcommunist Carnivalesque"

- What is the difference between a fairy tale in the West and a fairy tale in the East?
- A fairy tale in the West starts with words "Once upon a time there was . . ."
A fairy tale in the East starts with the words "Once upon a time there will be . . ."

— East European political joke[1]

Today, more than ten years after the fall of the official communist, ascetic, anticonsumerist ideology and the emergence of the underground second market consumer society into the public sphere's broad daylight, a new aesthetic sensibility seems to dominate in the rationality of postcommunism. With no clearly dividing line between highbrow and lowbrow, such a cultural logic exposes as main features an unprecedented carnivalesque flamboyance attuned to a relative kitsch culture, a consumption language and symbolic system reduced to a converted communist set of market and aesthetic discourses, and more recent transnational influences that are locally hybridized.

As explained in the previous chapter, due to impressive postcommunist economic, political, and cultural changes, life in Eastern Europe is a matter of syncretism. As such, its new culture, popular culture—the focus here being urban popular culture—combines original elements with imitative postures, traditionalism and nationalism with Westernism, and can include nostalgia for or rejection of either precommunist or communist pasts. In postcommunism, popular culture is at its apogee, making postcommunism a social and cultural formation that resignifies and hybridizes communist popular culture by displacing signifier from signified, reordering its symbols under a new logic, and mixing it with precommunist pasts and more recent imported markers. Overall, it can be seen as a synchronic/diachronic collusion of lowbrow and working-class taste with precommunist "bourgeois," elitist, and conservative aesthetics and Western influences. This new urban aesthetics opposes high to popular culture, highlighting an elusive, "fractal,"[2] and shifting private/public, dividing line. Finally, after 1989, Eastern European popular culture began to function under the preeminent logic of what the West generally calls "consumption logic."[3] Under this logic, Eastern European urban popular culture favorably signifies Western popular culture, which thus becomes the object of local imitations, particularly in the absence of a dominant public cultural discourse after the fall of communism.

In order to link this context of postcommunist transformation with the discursive construction of subjectivities, I turn to the system of taste classification and aesthetics developed by the French sociologist Pierre Bourdieu in his *Distinction: A Social Critique of the Judgement of Taste.* Bourdieu finds in social classes, with their upbringing and educational formative experiences, the foundation for the structuring of aesthetic taste and cultural practices.[4] His investigation reflects a fundamental aesthetic condition: culture is used in correspondence with the way it has been acquired, and taste functions "as a marker of 'class,'" creating "cultural pedigrees."[5] Education thus mediates the entrance into cultural "high" and "low" orders. Claiming that "the 'eye' is a product of history reproduced by education,"[6] Bourdieu concludes that:

> Taste classifies . . . the classifier. Social subjects, classified by their classifications, distinguish themselves by the distinctions they make, between the beautiful and the ugly, the distinguished and the vulgar, in which their position in the objective classifications is expressed or betrayed.[7]

Bourdieu's "popular aesthetic," or "popular taste," represents the "working-class aesthetic," and it is of a particular analytical interest insofar as it has entered postcommunism—here understood as a post-"proletarian" cultural system— through symbolic displacements. "Popular aesthetics"—as the working class's aesthetics—previously belonged to the proletarian, communist state: it was official and enforced, it was "socialist realism," and it was a form of public culture. This "popular," "proletarian" aesthetics should not to be confused here with one of the central terms of this book, (urban) popular culture, understood as a set of semiopen, semiprivate/public (sub)cultures or counter-narratives produced as anticultures from a micropolitics of the urban quotidian that in turn invades public culture. Thus, it can be said that the communist system functioned under the cultural hegemony of "popular aesthetic," a "socialist realist" aesthetic of the proletarian state *par excellence.* Some of this aesthetic also is discussed in the next chapter focusing on youth and musical subcultures.

Apprehending the cultural logic of postcommunism as functioning through a recombination and recycling of precommunist and communist symbolic systems leads me to call the resultant postcommunist aesthetics, drawing from Mikhail Bakhtin,[8] *the logic of carnivalesque.* In this view, one can think of the aesthetical limits of the previously mentioned postcommunist "final vocabulary," or "limits of the *sayable,*" as ones that combine recirculated "socialist realist" aesthetics—displaced, as will be shown, from propaganda, communist artifacts, and paraphernalia to postcommunist carnivalesque and kitsch—with more modern and postmodern, Western symbols brought about by postcommunist participation in a wider circulation of information, politics, and semiotic orders.

"Socialist Realism"

Communist, urban, public culture inherited precommunist "bourgeois" elitist and conservative cultural systems together with a large, rural, folkloric, peasantist symbolic universe, which, through communist urbanization and industrialization, spread into cities creating a hybrid *urban-peasant* culture. Reordering these two symbolic systems, aesthetically the "proletarian," "socialist realist" taste automatically expected every image to unequivocally perform a certain function, while this art-reality relationship was valued on the background of ideology, communist moral virtues, and aesthetic ideas of "agreeableness."[9]

Indeed, Bourdieu reminds us that the distance between art and life is what separates high culture from popular aesthetic and, while the former makes culture a sort of a "sacred" enclave detached from life and politics, the latter commends the spectators' so-called "profane"—personal, artistic, and political—participation.[10]

A "legitimate taste" belongs to the dominant class—the precommunist bourgeoisie, in this case—which is the richest in educational capital and thus shows an interest for "legitimate" works of art. In Romania, the bourgeoisie followed Western lifestyle models, especially Parisian. In the nineteenth and early twentieth centuries, Bucharest—the urban focus of this book—was a modern city, having electric light since 1899.[11] Bucharest's interwar architecture gathered French imperial, neoclassic, neogothic, neo-Romanian/Brâncovenean, and cubist styles.[12] The French architect Albert Galleron had erected *Ateneul Român,* a dearly enjoyed concert hall neighboring such famous European grand hotels as the *Athénée Palace,* located at the corner of *Piața Atheneului* (today *Piața George Enescu)* and elegant avenue *Calea Victoriei,* the Romanian *Champs-Elysée.* Bucharest had a New York-style skyscraper and two famous parks: *Cișmigiu,* designed after New York's Central Park, and *Parcul Libertății* designed by the French architect Eduard Redont.[13] Bucharest also enjoyed a debonair culture of literary cafés that had become "real social institutions" during those times—"Kübler," "Terasa Oteteleşanu," "Café de la Paix," and "Capşa"—gathering some of the most famous Romanian authors and artists influenced by the aesthetics of Symbolism.[14]

In his study of the "Bucharest Chic," Dan C. Mihăilescu enumerates the Bucharestian bourgeoisie's lifestyles and tastes at the intersection of nineteenth and twentieth centuries:

> assiduous frequentation of dancing parties, fencing and gentlemen's clubs, horse races and theaters; membership with committees and commissions, and philanthropic organizations; yearly voyages abroad, summer retirement to the "estate," or nearby the royal castle of Peleş in wintertime; fashion, gossip, flirting, five-o'clock teas, *au jour* readings, skating in Cişmigiu Gardens, the art and customs of dueling, pigeon shooting, charity balls, whist, patronage of the arts, weddings-baptisms-funerals, varnishing days and opening nights, dinner parties, horseback riding, court trials, flower fights in public parks, spiritualism séances, palmistry, Masonic lodges, oneiromancy, physiognomy, the almanack of the nobility, the rules of *cotillon*, the philosophy of gastronomy, gilded visiting cards, season tickets (and first-tier seats) at the National Theater, heraldry, and so on and so forth.[15]

Interwar Bucharest and its bourgeoisie is described in the same spirit by Countess Waldeck in her memorable *Athene Palace*, recalling Calea Victoriei, "the Korso," which "was dear to the hearts of Bucharestians. It was the bourgeoisie of Bucharest which made the Korso"[16] and *Piaţa Atheneului*:

> The Athene Palace lined the width of the Piazza Atheneului, Bucharest's magic square that opens on the most glamorous artery of the Near East, the Calea Victoriei. Imagine the White House, the Waldorf Astoria, Carnegie Hall, Colony Restaurant, and the Lincoln Memorial, all standing together around a smallish square blossoming out on an avenue which is a cross between Broadway and Pennsylvania and Fifth Avenues, and you understand what Piazza Atheneului means to Rumania. Here was the heart of Bucharest topographically, artistically, intellectually, politically—and, if you like, morally.[17]

Also, Dumitru Hîncu recollects the traveling habits of the 1930s, from means of transportation such as "the Orient Express, the Arlberg Orient Express, and the Simplon Orient Express," which brought the Bucharestian to Paris in some three to four days; the Băneasa airport; the tramways, buses, coaches, and taxicabs; and the few Rolls Royce, Hispano-Suiza, and Packard brands that could be spotted in the streets of the one-time Bucharestian *belle époque*.[18] Finally, there are the impressions brought by Mihail Sebastian who enjoyed an increasing fame in Bucharest's interwar years, when, populated by demimondaines, love affairs, cafés and restaurants, small talk politics, royalty, and a buoyant literary scene, the city was called, as expressed before, "the little Paris."[19]

In counter-distinction, there is—what Bourdieu calls—a "popular taste" of the working class, the social category with the least educational/cultural capital.[20] In the latter case, popular aesthetics bases its preferences on the "continuity between art and life," "the subordination of form to function," the "demand for participation" and involvement in the work of art, the need for "illusion," and "happy-end" conducive plots, the naïveté of emotional "investment"—of "entering the game"—and the organic need for the abstract signifier to match the signified reality.[21] As the "proletarian taste":

> Popular taste applies the schemes of the ethos, which pertain in the ordinary circumstances of life, to legitimate works of art, and so performs a systematic reduction of the things of art to the things of life. . . . The pure aesthetic is rooted in an ethic, or rather, an ethos of elective distance from the necessities of the natural and social world . . . [whereas] the popular disposition . . . annexes aesthetics to ethics.[22]

In the proletarian state, this was the main law of the "socialist realist" aesthetics: continuity between art—life—and revolutionary politics. This is why, during communism, the working class's aesthetics would refuse to engage in experimental artistic forms detached from reality and immediate signification. As will be discussed later, in postcommunism it is the *nouveaux riches,* least rich in educational capital, who prefer soap operas and, in Romania, the *risqué* musical genre of *manele.*

In fact, it can be argued that there were three types of (sub)cultures and counter-discursive aesthetical subject-formative experiences that constituted and consumed urban public culture under Romanian communism.[23] First, there was an official communist culture—"socialist realism"—which was public, ideologically dogmatic, and aesthetically lowbrow or "proletarian," at the same time as it conveyed conservative, patriarchal, and nationalist mythologies. At its core, such a culture resorted to a mixture of peasantist, workerist, and traditionalist aesthetics as limits of its *sayable,* as subject-formative boundaries; these aesthetic codes had survived in the newly formed, postwar, semiurban, incipiently industrial working classes.

Second, there was the culture of the disengaged intelligentsia, who generally claimed a theoretical descent either from Western thought and its democratic Enlightenment, or from more romantic nationalism. In general, the category of intellectuals was a broad one, stretching from the state bureaucracy and nomenklatura to artists and basically anybody with a college or undergraduate degree. In Romania, the rule of thumb was that a person was considered an intellectual if he or she possessed an undergraduate degree, usually obtained in three or four years. Under communist gerontocracy, doctoral degrees were perceived as a matter of successfully accomplishing the *end* of one's carrier. According to public knowledge, in the last decade of communist rule, only individuals coming from the nomenklatura or party members could pursue doctoral studies, and then only under ideological surveillance. Nevertheless, the *dissident* intellectuals were a select species who, although at the margins of the communist official culture, enjoyed a particular Western attention. This in turn automatically located them as alternative liberal and democratic sources of power, as high culture, in opposition to the official communist culture, which the Westerners perceived as lowbrow and of peasantist-workerist aesthetics. Expressing opposition to the official ideology, these intellectuals were cast out at the margins of the official communist discourse, where they had a liminal position between public and private, official and unofficial; they were located in the dissidence, and ideologically splintered into a broad spectrum that can retrospectively be identified as varying from nationalists, liberals, conservatives, socialists of Western social-democratic persuasions, or plain communists. It can realistically be said that, until today, the dissident-intellectuals have been the most researched political actors in Eastern Europe, occluding other forms of subversive political agency, practices, subject-formative experiences, and discourses, such as the ones that can be found in popular culture. Discussing the Soviet Union—although, comparatively speaking, her inferences can be applied to other communist countries—Adele M. Barker criticizes this Western intellectuals-focused view:

> The tendency in the West to champion those writers who ran afoul of the Soviet system was linked to a much broader tendency to view the Soviet Union as a monolithic totalitarian entity in which the relationship between rulers and ruled was one of domination and subordination—rulership and resistance. The totalitarian model led many westerners to see a country of indoctrinated Communists, on the one hand, and dissidents, on the other . . . [a] society as two monologic nonintersecting narratives.[24]

Although Romania did not have an expressly organized dissidence, such as the Polish Solidarity for example, individual acts of dissidence did exist—as is the case of poet Mircea Dinescu—but such acts were ineffectual both at a political and personal level, aggravating the condition of their initiator.[25] Nevertheless, other less visible intellectual, subversive spaces did exist; some of them have only recently started to be apprehended or publicized as counter-hegemonic, alternative intellectual practices under Romanian national-communism. From within the interstices of society, I can mention here the movement that had captivated many Romanian intellectuals in the 1980s, *Meditaţia Transcendentală* (Transcendental Meditation), a movement that ultimately led to the closing down of the Institute for Psychology. Then, there is the "Noica School," where members gathered such intellectuals as Gabriel Liiceanu and Andrei Pleşu.[26] This school of thought reworked conservative interwar views about modernity, in one instance openly rejecting through the voice of its master, Constantin Noica, and in the name of high, classical, and "elitist" culture,[27] the ideas prompted by the 1960s and 1970s social movements that had traversed Europe—and Foucault's work from *Surveiller et pounir* and *Histoire de la sexualité* vol. I: *La volonté du savoir*—as a matter of "Aesopic" politics of *ressentiment*, obsession with "marginality" versus "classicality," and with "denouncement of oppression."[28] This school, which would often gather at *Păltiniş*, discussed the place of Romanian culture in the European culture as a matter of the relationship between the "idiomatic" (particular) and the "universal."[29] Its thinkers looked for "resistance through culture"[30] to a totalitarian regime and discarded engagement from politics (political action/dissidence)—the latter seen as a matter of contextual and contingent, "impurity of the spectacle," unethical attitude toward culture, "false culture," and "seduction" by "public life"[31]—ultimately seeing dissidents as "victims of an illusion."[32]

Another level of alternative intellectual space to totalitarianism and national-communism came out from the bureaucracy. For example, in the 1970s and 1980s, *Editura Politică*—the ancestor of present *Editura Humanitas*—at that time under the directorship of Valter Roman, a former communist antifascist fighter in the Spanish Civil War and father to present politician Petre Roman, published the collection *Idei contemporane* (Contemporary Ideas). This collection introduced Romanian audiences to those ideas that were then animating Western intelligentsias, ideas of such thinkers as, for example, Louis Althusser, Alvin Toffler, Georg Lukács, Marshall McLuhan, C. Wright Mills, Herbert Marcuse, Claude Lévi-Strauss, Bertrand de Jouvenel, Albert Einstein, Jürgen Habermas, Erich Fromm, Jean-Paul Sartre, Ernst Bloch, Karl Jaspers, Martin Heidegger, and Edmund Husserl. Finally, in the early 1970s, famous Nobel laureates and international personalities were also introduced to Romanian audiences, as they answered questions about celebrity: Ulf von Euler, D. H. R. Barton, Norman E. Borlaug, Frank Macfarlane Burnet, Melvin Calvin, René Cassin, Max Delbrück, Ragnar Frisch, Ragnar A. Granit, Odd Hassel, Werner Heisenberg, W. R. Hess, Dorothy C. Hodgkin, Charles B. Huggins, Alfred Kastler, André Lwoff, Lord Boyd Orr, Lester B. Pearson, George Porter, Glenn T. Seaborg, Hugo Theorell, Jan Tinbergen, Arne Tiselius, Karl Ziegler, Emilio Segré, and Henry Coandă.[33]

Other intellectual or associational—more daring or more reserved—subversive spaces also existed in the 1970s and 1980s, such as the ones generated in the milieus of "the Association of Romanian Apiculturists"; the short-lived "Institute of Futurology" led by Mircea Maliţa, whose goal also included the positive resignification of technology and computers, which the communist ideology had declared "enemy of the human mind"; the activities at various urban *Casa de cultură* (Culture House) or *Şcoala populară de artă* (the Popular School of Art), where—at *Sala Dalles* for example—Romanian-invited lecturers recently returned from shorter or longer trips to the West would recall their Western experiences to an eclectic audience; and "the Union of Romanian Journalists," which played behind the closed doors of *Casa*

Scînteii—the headquarters of the Romanian press—the most recent "James Bond" movies of those times.

Finally, the third (sub)culture and subject-formative experience under Romanian communism was popular culture, a largely urban phenomenon, which was at once unofficial and official, a material and discursive hybrid stemming out from the private realm of everyday life but largely pervading the public sphere and its public culture, where it became "omnipresent."[34] Although popular culture under communism can be analyzed from various everyday life experience-standpoints, important here is the fact that popular culture massively engaged urban youth. As will be presented in the next chapter, which is focused particularly on this connection between popular culture and youth, unlike its position in the West as lowbrow and mass culture, Western popular culture under communism was transformed into *Eastern European youth's high culture par excellence*. However, due to the dichotomous model through which the communist system was generally perceived in the West—communists versus dissidents—popular culture as it expressed itself through representations, practices, and discursively positioned subjectivities in the everyday life of the Eastern Europeans was disregarded until the recent Cultural Studies approaches of postcommunism.

Also important for an analysis of politics and aesthetics—communist and postcommunist—is Roland Barthes's poststructuralist analysis of pleasure and the body. Barthes has created a distinction between pleasure (*plaisir)* and ecstasy (*jouissance*) as moments of joy or plainly erotic readings and writings of a text with the body.[35] A text that produces *jouissance* breaks down the boundaries between reader and text, thus allowing personal, counter-discursive rewritings *with the body*—bodily rebellions—and evasions from the social context; this is a writerly (*scriptible*) text. Conversely, *plaisir* is socially not bodily constructed and it is a mere form of indulging in a text offered by the dominant cultural discourse/ideology; it is a pleasure of relating to and identifying with the hegemonic politics of identity recognition; it is a readerly (*lisible*) text. In what regards the communist aesthetics, I can say that *plaisir* represented the cultural-political identification enforced by the official proletarian aesthetics of "socialist realism." For example, in Romania, official "socialist realism" enforced upon its subjects consensual cultural identities and regime-conformist pleasure, *plaisirs*, expressed through various artistic manifestations—novels, movies, paintings, sculptures, theater, mass shows, and the general cultural propaganda rhetoric—spreading counterfeited emotions. Such an ideological aesthetics was centered on the working-class hero, revolutionary optimism, nationalist ethos, "the Leader-Ceauşescu," and a futuristic society with proletarian happy ending. Simultaneously, an undermining, counter-hegemonic anticulture—popular culture—of the sort expressed by youth, for example, conveyed forms of resistance and subversion to the dominant, communist aesthetics through a politics of rock 'n' roll body writing and *jouissance*.[36] Indeed, as the next chapter discusses, rock 'n' roll represented youth's rewriting of the official text with the body, becoming a popular culture antinarrative and a *counter* subject-formative experience produced against the monotony of *plaisir*, which the discourse of "socialist realism" was.

Shifting analytical points of view, it can also be noted that the world of "socialist realism" was highly gendered, which in turn had aesthetic subjectification consequences. Indeed, in terms of identity construction of masculinities and femininities, working-class men were not expected to have any taste refinement, which was thought of as both feminine and "bourgeois." This invited what Bourdieu calls "a dual repudiation of virility, a twofold submission which ordinary language, naturally conceiving all domination in the logic and lexicon of sexual domination, is predisposed to express."[37] Also, as explained in the next chapters, following the Bolshevik model of the proletarian-woman, women were expected to fit the profile of asexual/androgynous partners, although under the cult of motherhood. This was the gender-based *plaisir* aesthetics imposed by "socialist realism." However, in practice there existed many subversive gendered *jouissance* aesthetics and subject-formative experiences—including the counter-hegemonic experiences of urban youth and the diachronic/synchronic discourses of "bourgeois" or Western femininity or masculinity existent in some urban strata, mainly in the artistic and intellectual environment.[38]

Finally, a "proletarian," popular aesthetic as the aesthetic of the working class is a politically "dominated aesthetic,"[39] or, according to John Fiske, a culture of "subordinate allegiances."[40] Ultimately, with regards to the very syncretic aesthetic nature of communism, its "socialist realist" culture was in fact simultaneously seeking legitimation from, and in opposition to, the precommunist, high-culture, "bourgeois"—"legitimate" in Bourdieu's terms—aesthetics. And, although "socialist realism" wished to conquer or reject such a "bourgeois" culture, in fact it managed only to assimilate and hybridize it with a new "popular" twist. "The choice of the necessary," proletarian aesthetics also expressed "a taste for necessity," "adaptation," "resignation," and, ultimately, of "conformity" to inevitable material conditions,[41] which for Romanians was a reflection of their particular socioeconomic reality from the late 1940s through to the late 1980s.

"Postcommunist Carnivalesque"

The *flâneur*'s visit through Bucharest in chapter 1 attempts to capture some elements of the new popular culture, as well as the new economic, social, cultural, and political order that is under construction in Romania today; and many others remain to be further picked. The list includes: rock music, sports, anecdotes and post-*Bulă* jokes,[42] nightlife culture, pet life versus street dogs, pornography and new women's magazines, tattoos, graffiti, street children, renaming streets, parks, new urbanism, cabs and cars, jargon, advertisements, fast food, fashion, Internet cafés and youth cyber-subcultures, new definitions of public/private, nationalism and hate speech in popular culture, communism as kitsch, cell phones, shopping malls, *nouveaux riches*, a new concept of holidays, consumption, and rap and hip-hop—all contributing toward an understanding of popular culture in postcommunism as the realm of the carnivalesque.

The theory of the carnivalesque, as developed by Russian theorist Mikhail Bakhtin, was used to conceptualize opposition to the rigid, normalizing programs of modernization and pure rationalization of the Stalinist era.[43] Considering popular culture as carnival, a world released through the social body, Bakhtin was rediscovered in the Western discourse on popular culture, once popular culture itself became an aesthetically overwhelming phenomenon unveiling the complex relationships between culture and politics, "the logic of late capitalism,"[44] or postmodernity. Throughout the Middle Ages, the carnival was one of the major forms of popular culture. Through "laughter," "excessiveness," "bad taste," flamboyance, "offensiveness," and "degradation," carnivals combined lowbrow with highbrow tastes, "classical" with "vernacular,"[45] and "performers" with "spectators," parodying social hierarchies, ethics, and the body and its "bodily functions."[46]

Although some theorists find that the carnivalesque is "sublimated" in Western, late modern/postmodern culture in the form of the "literary text," "surrealist art," "advertisement hoarding," "pop festivals," and "jazz concerts,"[47] I suggest that the Bakhtinian moment of popular culture as carnivalesque survives in a climactic form of flamboyance, constituting today one of postcommunism's more noticeable aesthetic subject-formative conditions. Lacking any well-defined style, it is a pastiche combining the old with the new under no readily apparent organizing principle. As Serguei Alex Oushakine expresses, popular culture after 1989 is a matter of "quantity versus quality"[48]; it is divided along gender lines; it is highly unequal in terms of social access to consumption; and, besides more novel Western imported signifiers, it fully recirculates the communist discourse and its artifacts and decors of statues, labels, and paraphernalia under a new rationality, no matter how carnivalesque, parodic, or *kitsch*.

When analyzing the condition of postcommunism, it becomes apparent that we are discussing two forms of kitsch. One notion of kitsch has to do with the political-aesthetical heritage of communism. The other, as Matei Călinescu explains it, comes with the development of modernity,[49] and, as further elaborated by Jean Baudrillard, has to do with the disjointed sign-reality relationship under the rule of fake reality, or "simulacra"—"simulations."[50] In other words, kitsch intersects here with politics and with mass consumption (both under communism and postcommunism).

At the intersection of kitsch and politics in communist and postcommunist popular culture, Theresa Sabonis-Chafee gives useful insights into the heritage of the communist elements of *agitprop*: banners calling for revolutionary and patriotic élan and zeal to gloriously build the socialist society, slogans, poems, patriotic odes and hymns, monuments, and gigantesque political shows held in stadiums.[51] To this list one can add the continuous incantations of the names of great revolutionaries and communist leaders; the myth-making refrain *"Partidul —Ceauşescu—Romania"* resonates in one's ears as an Orwellian simulacrum today. Sabonis-Chafee goes on to expose the way in which such artifactual memorabilia becomes sentimental "kitsch debris" in postcommunism, parodically resignifying communism as the "Kitsch Empire."[52] If, under communism, kitsch was part of the regime—it was state policy, state kitsch; it was "socialist realist" aesthetics, and it was propaganda—in postcommunism and its recirculation of previous symbolic systems, kitsch has moved from state policy into the realm of popular culture and its everydayness, relinquishing any ideological parameters and becoming simply a matter of popular culture aesthetics.

The other form of kitsch has to do with the evolution of modernity as a mass empowering/disempowering phenomenon. As a huge effort to modernize and produce mass consumption, communism also produced a quantity of consumption products often identifiable as kitsch. In Romania, many items of household hardware, clothing, furniture, and decoration entered this category which combined old, traditional ideas and techniques about an artisan-based manufacturing process with more industrialized assembly-line concepts, and notions of scarcity and substitution of some materials' original uses with others or with more novel materials such as plastic (hard or fiber).[53] In postcommunism, with its "open-ended indeterminacy,"[54] kitsch has become integral to the entire hedonistic spirit of the transformation. As "one of the most typical products of modernity" that has entered in a stage of presentism in the late twentieth century, kitsch is, as Călinescu expresses, a result of "[t]he phenomenon of compulsive consumption, the fear of boredom, and the need for escape, combined with the widespread view of art as both play and display."[55] Also integral to the logic of the postcommunist carnivalesque aesthetics, kitsch now relies on new notions of consumption and definitions of beauty or legitimate taste; in other words, on a vague combination of previous and simultaneous, local, or Western hybridized aesthetic styles and the kaleidoscopic world of the flea market.

Inherent in the overarching recirculation of different symbolic systems in postcommunism is the discourse of the postcommunist consumption, here understood as a symbolic, novel lifestyle and a subject-formative experience dominated by a new bourgeoisie, the *nouveaux riches.* Such a discourse is expressed through the language of the communist dichotomic consumption terminology, which, at its turn, stood divided between the discourse of the official economy of shortages and the discourse of the unofficial black market or second economy. Serguei Alex Oushakine speaks of the postcommunist consumption as an "imaginary" one, due to its phantasmatic and "mythical" nature.[56] This means that postcommunist consumption behavior resorts to previous, communist market-related practices and discourses, and, by extracting them from their situated past, relocates their symbolism into the present under a new and largely incoherent logic dominated by "the quantity of style."[57]

However, as Barker suggests, one cannot consider post-1989 Eastern Europe a young consumer society, in the sense that it arguably learns only today the practices of consumption. In the last two decades of communist rule, in the 1970s and 1980s, *Eastern Europe already was a consumer society*; the pervasive second economy or the black market stand as testimony to this peculiar situation. Nevertheless, as a consumer society but unlike its Western counterpart, communist Eastern Europe was a prestige-based consumption society, and not a "monied" one.[58] In other words, like elsewhere in Eastern Europe, access to consumption was based on prestige in Romania, such as that acquired through a certain positioning within the nomenklatura or as a cultural personality, and particularly through involvement in the widespread system of personal relations, traffic of influence, and *baksheesh*. Such an access to consumption transcended class association and was not a function of economic capital—as understood in market-based societies—but of political prestige or ideological capital. *Romanian communist society was a prestige-based society founded on status-related access to possession and consumption* in spite of the assertions of equality and classless society in official discourses.

In postcommunist Europe, quantitative consumption, which refers to the economic capital of the *nouveaux riches*, does not necessarily claim Bourdieu's "legitimate taste of luxury," which ultimately belonged to a corresponding precommunist "bourgeois," high-culture capital. Due to their formative experiences as a working class with their lowbrow, proletarian aesthetics "of necessity," such a postcommunist new bourgeoisie is unable to express a taste for "legitimate aesthetics" or high culture—which has never existed in their educational repertoire in the first place. The new postcommunist subject of consumption, owner of economic and, occasionally, political power, does not have high-culture capital and thus resorts to "*excessiveness*," as the working class's *imagined* taste of "luxury"[59]—a taste formed during "socialist realism." By supplanting quality with quantity, the *nouveaux riches* become a consumerist class, using as forms of aesthetic identification excessiveness, flamboyance, kitsch, immediate pleasure, and art-life firsthand artistic connection. In other words, the *nouveaux riches* choose "to express 'the taste of luxury' in terms of 'taste of necessity.'"[60] What they want is to *live* deeply, to feel existence, and their ethics is one of joy. In the same vein, Călinescu refers to the modern subject of kitsch culture as the "kitsch-man," who, seeking for "effortless enjoyment," "tends to experience as kitsch even nonkitsch works or situations . . . involuntarily mak[ing] a parody of aesthetic response."[61]

A quick look into the picture of such a new consumption subject in urban Romania would show both women and men wearing two or three thick gold chains, gold bracelets and rings, and showing off their expensive cars, while their villas and apartments—which belong to a new concept of upper-middle-class suburbia—on the other hand, are advertised in a social environment that makes no effort to cosmeticize its poverty. The *nouveaux riches* rarely go to classical music or even rock 'n' roll concerts. Instead, they hold expensive dinners and parties in costly restaurants and nightclubs where the controversial musical genre of *"manele"* rules,[62] and are the customary clients of a new casino culture of gambling, striptease, and prostitution. They spend their holidays abroad and rarely, if at all, engage in any intellectual activities, such as reading books, which have apparently succumbed under the new vogue of recently broadcasted Latin American tearjerker "telenovela."[63] Against a contemporary shared animal rights sensibility, both men and women wear sophisticated fur coats. Women live under a revived *feminine mystique,* wearing flashy makeup and dressing flamboyantly, which the previous communist ascetic moral code considered either licentious or "bourgeois."

Ultimately, it is not clear if this new kitsch aesthetic does not collide with more "camp" sensibilities. As defined by Călinescu, "[c]amp cultivates bad taste—usually the bad taste of yesterday—as a form of superior refinement. It is as if bad taste, consciously acknowledged and pursued, actually could outdo itself and become its own clear-cut opposite."[64] Be that as it may, "socialist realism" is not dead yet. It is recirculated as kitsch in the cultural logic—practices, discourses, and subject-formative experiences—of contemporary popular culture and its everydayness. Thus, from an aesthetic perspective, postcommunism can be apprehended as a fragmented, flamboyant, and eclectic new artistic sensibility—as carnivalesque.

Finally, blurring high and low taste, and witnessing such extensive identitary and institutional implosions, from an aesthetic, yet political, point of view, postcommunism's popular culture can be understood as *transgressive postmodernism.* One can think of postcommunist popular culture in this way also by virtue of postcommunism's fast collision into Western-based, globalized, postmodern consumption cultures, media, and cyber-information flux.[65] In other words, as a segment of a globalized postmodern culture and in light of postcommunism's functioning through ruptures and discontinuities, one can talk about the postcommunist popular culture as an *information, consumer-oriented, synchronic/diachronic transtemporal, and global-local transgeographic pastiche,* and, by extension, as a *postcommunist-postmodern* popular culture.

Notes

1. C. Banc and Alan Dundes, eds., *You Call This Living? A Collection of East European Political Jokes* (Athens: The University of Georgia Press, 1990), 81.

2. Susan Gal and Gail Kligman, *The Politics of Gender after Socialism: A Comparative-Historical Essay* (Princeton: Princeton University Press, 2000), 13, 41.

3. See also Serguei Alex Oushakine, "The Quantity of Style: Imaginary Consumption in the New Russia," *Theory, Culture, and Society* 17, no. 5 (2000): 97-120.

4. Pierre Bourdieu, *Distinction: A Social Critique of the Judgement of Taste,* trans. Richard Nice (Cambridge: Harvard University Press, 1984), 1.

5. Bourdieu, *Distinction*, 2, 63.

6. Bourdieu, *Distinction*, 3.

7. Bourdieu, *Distinction*, 6.

8. Mikhail Bakhtin, *Rabelais and His World*, trans. Helene Iswolsky (Bloomington: Indiana University Press, 1988).

9. Bourdieu, *Distinction*, 5.

10. Although the notions "sacred" and "profane" have entered the core language of social sciences and humanities, I wish to acknowledge here one of its major sources: Mircea Eliade, *The Sacred & The Profane: The Nature of Religion* (New York: A Harvest Book, 1987).

11. Radu Ioanid, "Introduction," in Mihail Sebastian. *Journal 1935-1944. The Fascist Years*, trans. Patrick Camiller, Introduction and notes Radu Ioanid (Chicago: Ivan R. Dee, 2000. Published in association with the United States Holocaust Memorial Museum), ix.

12. Dinu C. Giurescu, *Distrugerea Trecutului României* [The Destruction of Romania's Past] (Bucharest: Editura Museion, 1994), p. 14.

13. Ioanid, "Introduction," ix-x.

14. Emil Manu, *Cafeneaua literară* [The Literary Café] (Bucharest: Editura Saeculum I.O., 1997), 7-8, 172.

15. Dan C. Mihăilescu, "The Rules of Bucharest Chic," in *Bucharest: A Sentimental Guide*, ed. Aurora Fabritius, Erwin Kessler, and Adrian Solomon, trans. Florin Bican, Alina Cârâc, Michi Constantinescu Fărcaş, Daniela Neacşu, Adrian Solomon, Monica Voiculescu, and Ioana Zirra (Bucharest: The Romanian Cultural Foundation, 2001), 87.

16. R. G. Waldeck, *Athene Palace* (New York: Robert M. McBride & Company, 1942), 17.

17. Waldeck, *Athene Palace*, 11-2.

18. Dumitru Hîncu, "Traveling to Bucharest between the Wars," in *Bucharest: A Sentimental Guide*, ed. Aurora Fabritius, Erwin Kessler, and Adrian Solomon, trans. Florin Bican, Alina Cârâc, Michi Constantinescu Fărcaş, Daniela Neacşu, Adrian Solomon, Monica Voiculescu, and Ioana Zirra (Bucharest: The Romanian Cultural Foundation, 2001), 136-8.

19. See Mihail Sebastian, *Journal 1935-1944. The Fascist Years*, trans. Patrick Camiller, Introduction and notes Radu Ioanid (Chicago: Ivan R. Dee, 2000. Published in association with the United States Holocaust Memorial Museum).

20. Bourdieu, *Distinction*, 16.

21. Bourdieu, *Distinction*, 32-3, 43.

22. Bourdieu, *Distinction*, 5.

23. For a comparative perspective, see also Joseph J. Arpad, "The Question of Hungarian Popular Culture," *Journal of Popular Culture* 29, no.2 (Fall 1995): 9-28.

24. Adele Marie Barker, "The Culture Factory: Theorizing the Popular in the Old and New Russia," in *Consuming Russia: Popular Culture, Sex, and Society Since Gorbachev*, ed. Adele M. Barker (Durham: Duke University Press, 1999), 21.

25. On some reflections of Romanian dissident intellectuals, see Vladimir Tismaneanu, *Fantasies of Salvation: Democracy, Nationalism, and Myth in Post-Communist Europe* (Princeton: Princeton University Press, 1998).

26. On the Noica School and/or the *Păltiniş Diary*, see also Katherine Verdery, "The 'School' of Philosopher Constantin Noica," in her *National Ideology under Socialism: Identity and Cultural Politics in Ceauşescu's Romania* (Berkeley: University of California Press, 1991), 256-301; Vladimir Tismaneanu and Dan Pavel, "Romania's Mystical Revolutionaries: The Generation of Angst and Adventure Revisited," *East European Politics and Societies* 8 (Fall 1994): 402-38; and Denise Roman, "On Survival and Critical Universalism in a Romanian Model in Humanist Culture," in *The European Legacy: Toward New Paradigms* 7, no. 6 (December 2002). Forthcoming.

27. Gabriel Liiceanu, *The Păltiniş Diary: A Paideic Model in Humanist Culture*, trans. James Christian Brown (Budapest: Central European University Press, 2000), 111.

28. Liiceanu, *The Păltiniş Diary*, 24, 62, 65.

29. Liiceanu, *The Păltiniş Diary*, 199.

30. Liiceanu, *The Păltiniş Diary*, 39.

31. Liiceanu, *The Păltiniş Diary*, 176, 178-9.

32. Liiceanu, *The Păltiniş Diary*, xxxi.

33. Interviews with these personalities were conducted by Carol Roman in his *Laureaţi ai premiului Nobel răspund la întrebarea: Există un secret al celebrităţii?* [Nobel Prize Laureates Answer the Question: Is There a Secret to Celebrity?] (Bucharest: Editura Politică, 1971.)

34. Barker, "The Culture Factory," 33.

35. See Roland Barthes, *The Pleasure of the Text*, trans. Richard Miller (New York: The Noonday Press, 1980). Here "text" refers to any type of meaning-creative artifact: books, articles, sculptures, movies, dance, advertisement, or performances.

36. On youth, rock 'n' roll, and *jouissance* in Western culture, see John Fiske, *Understanding Popular Culture* (New York: Routledge, 1991), 51. On Roland Barthes, readerly/writerly texts, and *plaisir* and *jouissance*, see also Denise Roman, "Poststructuralism," in *Encyclopedia of Postmodernism*, ed. Victor E. Taylor and Charles E. Windquist (New York: Routledge, 2001), 309.

37. Bourdieu, *Distinction*, 382.

38. See also chapters 4 on youth and 6 on gender.

39. Bourdieu, *Distinction*, 41.

40. Fiske, *Understanding Popular Culture*, 47.

41. Bourdieu, *Distinction*, 372, 374.

42. *Bulă* was a popular Romanian anecdotal character, a form of everyday life subversive discourse-resistance to communism. Bearing a mix of the wisdom of two other famous folk characters, *Păcală* and *Nastratin Hogea*, Bulă had attained national fame by making a mockery of the Romanian communist regime, its leaders, and its avatars. On a collection of political jokes with *Bulă* until the seventies, see Banc and Dundes, *You Call This Living?*

43. See Bakhtin, *Rabelais and His World*.

44. See Fredric Jameson, *Postmodernism, Or, The Cultural Logic of Late Capitalism* (Durham: Duke University Press, 1991).

45. Fiske, *Understanding Popular Culture*, 81-2.

46. John Storey, *An Introduction to Cultural Theory and Popular Culture*, 2nd ed. (London: Prentice Hall/Harvester Wheatsheaf, 1993), 130-1.

47. Peter Stallybrass and Allon White, "Bourgeois Hysteria and the Carnivalesque," in *The Cultural Studies Reader*, ed. Simon During, 2nd ed. (New York: Routledge, 1999), 388.

48. See Oushakine, "The Quantity of Style."

49. See Matei Călinescu, *Five Faces of Modernity: Modernism, Avant-Garde, Decadence, Kitsch, and Postmodernism* (Durham: Duke University Press, 1987).

50. See Jean Baudrillard, *Simulacra and Simulation (The Body, in Theory: Histories of Cultural Materialism)*, trans. Sheila Faria Glaser (Ann Arbor: University of Michigan Press, 1995).

51. Theresa Sabonis-Chafee, "Communism as Kitsch: Soviet Symbols in Post-Soviet Society," in *Consuming Russia: Popular Culture, Sex, and Society Since Gorbachev*, ed. Adele M. Barker (Durham: Duke University Press, 1999), 362, 366.

52. Sabonis-Chafee, "Communism as Kitsch," 362, 381.

53. However, as a means to pay for Romania's external debt, selected lots of high-quality clothing and furniture were exported to Western Europe during Ceaușescu's regime, particularly in the 1980s. Nevertheless, the discussion here draws attention to the product that reached the average Romanian urban citizen.

54. Călinescu, *Five Faces of Modernity*, 228.

55. Călinescu, *Five Faces of Modernity*, 7.

56. Oushakine, "The Quantity of Style," 104.

57. Oushakine, "The Quantity of Style," 97.

58. Adele Marie Barker, "Rereading Russia" in *Consuming Russia: Popular Culture, Sex, and Society Since Gorbachev*, ed. Adele M. Barker (Durham: Duke University Press, 1999), 7.

59. Oushakine, "The Quantity of Style," 111. Emphasis in the original.

60. Oushakine, "The Quantity of Style," 115.

61. Călinescu, *Five Faces of Modernity*, 259.

62. On "*manele*," see the next chapter on youth and popular culture.

63. My observation of such political actors in Bucharest in 1998-2001—of their discussions and expressed aesthetic preferences—has led me to this last conclusion.

64. Călinescu, *Five Faces of Modernity*, 230.

65. On the relationship between national, or local cultures, and the cultural logic of globalization, see also Mel van Elteren, "Conceptualizing the Impact of U.S. Popular Culture Globally," *Journal of Popular Culture* 30, no. 1 (Summer 1996): 47-89 and John Tomlinson, *Cultural Imperialism* (Baltimore: The Johns Hopkins University Press, 1991).

Chapter Four

"Blue Jeans Generation" and "Generation PRO": Youth, Pop Culture, and Politics

Under a huge slogan on a wall which reads:
"COMMUNISM SHINES LIKE THE SUN"
someone has scribbled with chalk:
"until we all get sunburnt."

— East European political joke[1]

This chapter conceptualizes experiences of subjectification through popular culture from the point of view of one of the most neglected political actors in the current postcommunist transformation: youth. It places youth politics within a popular culture located at the crossroads of the great transformation which postcommunism is, noting where precommunist traditions and histories resurface today, and including communist legacies and the effects of our current, globalized, modern, yet postmodern, world.

Discussing the politics of resistance and subjectification through popular culture and, in particular, through musical subcultures—from classical music and jazz, to pop, rock, disco, punk, rap, and hip-hop—this chapter unveils the de-territorialized character of Western popular culture, one that, as in other

Eastern European contexts, continuously pervaded Romanian forms of public and private culture since early communism. Its analysis of everyday lived life is located at a Foucauldian, sub-civil society level of a politics of quotidian, personalized, and even bodily resistance.

Finally, this chapter discusses Romanian youth as a liminal category situated at the borders of social, economic, and political integration/exclusion, and a bewildered political actor wandering through the great and paradoxical fabric which, in a world of globalization, postcommunism is.

Youth at the Threshold of Communism and Postcommunism

Although youth is a social category that blurs class distinctions, it is youth that has been most associated with popular culture, subculture, counter-culture, and the underground; it is therefore a relevant actor in a study of popular culture in communism and postcommunism. At an analytical level, it can be said that the social category of youth best corresponds to most recent approaches in Cultural Studies, approaches that stress micropolitics, culture, experience, subjectification, and the everyday life. In other words, due to the particularities of its operational field—subversive cultures located mainly in the liminality between private/public spheres—youth becomes a well-designed category for a theory of knowledge based on experience and the structures of the quotidian.

Writing about a France that had already been through the 1968 student movements, Pierre Bourdieu views youth as belonging to a "new spontaneist ideology," perceiving itself to be located outside mainstream institutional frameworks, as the "marginal," the "excluded," a site of "counter-culture," "dream[ing] of social flying," "defy[ing] the gravity of the social field," exulting of an "anti-institutional temperament," "inventing an art of living . . . everyday life . . . the personal sphere . . . and the existential," and obscuring the lines between legitimate, intellectual, and popular taste.[2]

In an American context, Lawrence Grossberg considers youth from a multifaceted perspective: youth has a historical identity as a "generational" personality as well as a "regional" identity structured along various social spaces[3]—such as urban, suburban, and rural—to which, in a world of globalization of cultures, one can also add various geographical locations such as East, West, North, and South. Youth also interacts with various cross-identifications such as race, class, gender, ethnicity, and sexuality. But "the meaning of youth" transcends all these identity axes "and must remain uncertain": "Youth can be a matter of chronology, sociology, ideology, experience, style, attitude."[4] While the politics of youth is "the politics of fun," its social identity is elusive because youth "is a term without its own center," symbolizing that which is not yet existent, the future, while challenging the stabilities incorporated in the past and present.[5] Youth is a cultural, transformational, utopia-searching identity bouncing between extremes and between its potential for rebelliousness and society's ideologically normalizing tendencies to create "docile bodies."[6] Metaphorically, the body of youth is a map, a site of struggle between its antipolitical and antiestablishment impulses and society's ideological powers of subjection, which "attemp[t] to shape the body of youth—to organize its material, ideological and affective life, to monitor its needs, aspirations and behavior."[7] The result of such a political struggle usually makes youth gain an existence outside the social institutional framework, an existence developed through ideological pain. As a consequence, youth is often present through its absence. Such a location is a "unique position . . . formed at the intersection of youth's alienation from the adult world, and . . . the adult realities of everyday life."[8] A form of "performative politics"[9] is then born between social surveillance and the constant exposure of youth's body as a form of protest and struggle, from marching in the street to fashion and rock concert antiestablishment statements. This performative politics is "the politics of youth as spectacle"[10]:

> If society located the body of youth in the spaces of domesticity, consumption, and education (with any transgressions resulting in specific sites of incarceration for the youthful offender), then youth could construct its own places in the space of transition between these institutions: in the street, around the jukebox, at the hop (and later, at the mall). These are all spaces located between the domestic, public and social spaces of the adult world. What the dominant society assumed to be no place at all—merely a transition—became the privileged site of youth's investment . . . offer[ing] the possibility of avoiding social surveillance, a social version of the desperate effort to construct an absolute privacy in one's room, surrounded by the music.[11]

Popular culture has a special relationship with youth. Unlike any other social categories, youth is an active participant, creator, and consumer of popular culture. While the West has alternatively studied youth as a subculture, a lifestyle, or social category, in Romania, like elsewhere in Eastern Europe, the particularity of youth and its pop culture develops along two lines corresponding to communism and present postcommunist transformation.

Under communism and similar to childhood, youth was considered a special sociobiological and ideological category. A youth cultural practice existed and it carved out a distinct space for youth's political identity, an identity conceived in zealously revolutionary terms. The labels *"şoimii patriei"* (the homeland's eagles)—for children under six years old—*"pionier"* (pioneer)—the Romanian version of "boy" and "girl scouts," for children of seven to fourteen years old and in the first eight school elementary grades—and *"utecist"* (from the acronym *U.T.C.* referring to *"Uniunea Tineretului Communist,"* i.e., the communist youth organization)—applied to adolescents of fourteen and older—express these ideological conceptualizations of childhood and youth. All these three practices had their specific rules, associational forms, discourses, and uniforms (orange and navy blue uniform for *"şoimii patriei"*; white, navy blue, and red tie for "*pionieri*"; and light blue and black for "*utecişti*"). Yet, the public discourse addressing the problematic of youth was in fact a strong propaganda toward "building socialism," a propaganda which, by the same token, denied youth its capacity for rebellion, alternative critical thinking, and personal taste—that is, the very possibility of a personalized youth culture.

In the privacy of their rooms, at parties, in schools, and at university gatherings, Romanian youth, particularly those in urban milieus, observed with dedication Western forms of popular culture, as was typical with Eastern European youth in general. However, as explained previously, unlike their Western counterparts, Eastern European/Romanian youth signified these imported Western cultural practices under positive aesthetics, as *high culture*. Particularly toward the demise of communism in the late 1980s, many urban youth semiconsciously refused to enter into the game of a "performative" politics that would have meant interchanging their subjectivity of rebellion with a more consensual, imposed, and conformist youth political identity—previously discussed as *jouissance* versus *plaisir*. This situation was due to their timely capacity for rebellion and detachment from political engagement, the latter being already accepted by such youth as the regime's plain demagogy. To this state of mind were added formative experiences of the late 1970s and early 1980s, experiences strongly permeated by Western signifiers of pop and rock culture, and which have entered Romanian public culture through the second economy or black market. In many cases, it was the sons and daughters of the Romanian nomenklatura who promoted such Western icons. Their position of power through their parents or relatives and their opportunities to travel abroad—from where they would bring back most recent and famous cassettes and videos with Western music and movies—made them successful champions of a subversive politics centered on a de-territorialized Western popular culture. In the mid-1980s, youth from Bucharest and other main cities were well aware of Michael Jackson's, Madonna's, or Prince's music and videoclips, and, their name scribbled on school corridors, in restrooms, on walls, and pavement, "AC/DC" reigned supremely as youth's ultimate idol. This generation of youth also avidly watched American movies—very popular in the late 1980s were Steven Spielberg's and George Lucas's *Indiana Jones*, Jim Abrahams's and David and Jerry Zucker's parody *Top Secret*, and Mel Brooks's comedy *History of the World I*—on a video player or recorder (VCR) that either belonged to their parents, or to their friends, or to their neighbors. The distinction between a video *player* and a VCR was extremely important: in the late 1980s, one paid some 15,000 *lei* for the former and 30,000 for the latter on the black market, while the monthly salary ranged anywhere from 1,000 to 3,000 or 4,000 *lei* and a new *Dacia* car sold for some 70,000 *lei*. A VCR was extremely valuable since it could reproduce movies that could be further distributed on the black market. Apparently, these were the times that initiated the illegal copying of cassettes—movies or music—in Romania, a practice that is undergoing new ramifications in postcommunism as new, international copyright legislation has been recently enforced.

In postcommunism, youth is no longer a social category addressed by official discourses. This however does not mean an empowerment of youth. Caught within the logic of transformation, youth identity has emerged as vulnerable, echoing the feminized traits that can be said to broadly characterize postcommunist societies. Together with gender, queer, and ethnic minorities, youth represents a specifically marginalized category directly exposed to the socioeconomic inequities inflicted by the disarray of post-1989 politics.

Romanian youth undergoes today a multiplicity of experiences of subjectification within globalization and regionalization. Such experiences are: a postcommunist consumer-oriented society, a market economy led by *nouveaux riches* cliques (many times of former communist backgrounds), Western cultural imports perceived as high culture, a highly gendered construction of youth—from dressing and behavioral codes to career aspirations—homelessness and street children, juvenile delinquency, the rise of youth intolerance and exclusionary attitudes vis-à-vis ethnic and queer minorities, prostitution, drugs, and sexualization of youth. However, unlike other social categories, due to this attraction to Western popular culture and the free market with its promised potential of new opportunities, youth proves again to develop the highest sensitivity toward integration into the new age of globalization and dominance of visual culture, partaking in the West-East flux of cultural practices, media and world-scale dissemination of information, from advertising, fashion, and music, to crime and pornography.

Finally, from an axiological point of view, one of the most marked crises of Eastern European/Romanian youth is one of values, with consequences for subjective experience and identity formation. As Luigi Tomasi considers, postcommunist youth undergoes a distancing from ideologies, an increasing stress on individualism although in close competition with nationalism, an emphatic return to religion[12]—even fundamentalism—again in struggle with the values of Western liberal-democratic political signifiers, such as civil society, free market, political pluralism, or gender equity. There is also a general trust in Europe as a historical warrant of successful market transformation and democratization, a Europe nostalgically perceived as a mythical place of return to an original and temporarily lost culture.[13] In the Romanian case, this is translated in an overwhelming discourse of *return to Europe.*

Best reflecting the sensibility of the postcommunist transformation, youth is the most propitious to be affected by the struggle between traditional nationalist versus Westernizing liberal-democratic agendas. Romanian urban youth contin-ues to largely adhere to Western signifiers of a dynamic popular culture, which is imported and hybridized in local contexts. Differently, in rural Romania youth seems to live more distanced from such cultural practices, being caught up in a traditional, peasantist universe of conservative and often nationalist values, in spite of communism's huge effort to urbanize the overwhelmingly rural milieu. The more urban youth is open to Western culture, the more it is prone to support the free market and engage in civil society activities related to human, feminist, and ecological rights.[14]

Overall, with the fall of the communist ideology, the resurrection of the grand, exclusionary theory and practice of nationalism, economic turmoil, and a crisis of subjectivity and cultural disorientation, the historico-temporal conjuncture of the first decade of postcommunist transformation marks a tremendous need for ethical self-redefinition of youth's identity.[15] Correlatively, such a self-signification requires an appropriate political discourse reflecting the governance's inclusive approach to youth's intrinsic needs and difference within the broader social and political spectrum.

"Blue Jeans Generation": The Politics of Pop Culture in Communist Romania

Many Western studies have approached the popular culture of communism under the heading of rock 'n' roll and its political message and capacity to undermine the dogmatism of the Eastern European regimes. Nonetheless, the same studies consider that by the late 1970s and early 1980s the Romanian stage of rock, youth dissent through rock, apparently the entire Romanian musical scene came to an end under the patronage of patriotic songs and "socialist realism."[16] While it may be true that the previously frail freedom of artistic expression, including local rock formations, was crumbling in 1970s Romania, once the regime tightened its national-communist and autarchic tendencies within the Soviet bloc, Romanian pop music by no means came to an end; it was neither transformed solely into vain patriotism, nor transmuted into "light music" (*muzica uşoară*), understood as "euphemism" for pop and rock—as some authors have called it. Romanian pop music, which was locally called *muzica uşoară* or "light music" in counter-distinction to classical or "heavy" music, has a long, precommunist legacy in the Romanian urban stage, a heritage gathering European traditions of operetta and French chansonnette. In other words, there was much more happening in the Romanian popular culture under communism than a reductionist view opposing patriotic-communist "socialist realist" cultures spread through the "panopticon"[17] of the rational media apparatus of the regime on the one hand, to rock as the domain of the subversive on the other. Folk, classic, pop (or "light music," *muzica uşoară*), and jazz (with the acclaimed annual *Sibiu* jazz festival) synchronically and diachronically coexisted on the Romanian stage—besides the more known patriotic and rock genres.

Indeed, there were a number of musical subcultures in communist Romania. First, classic or "heavy" music was a form of music enjoyed by a highly specialized audience gathering the community of musicians from the Romanian conservatories (from Bucharest, *Iaşi*, or *Cluj*) and mainly urban people who had acquired a taste—"bourgeois," or "legitimate" in Pierre Bourdieu's terms—for such a music, which, in many cases, was transmitted through family precommunist musical education. This was a music that belonged to the public domain, to public culture. Second, there was the patriotic music that preached the party, the communist regime, or, in a nationalist way, the glorious Romanian past and its leader, Ceauşescu. As explained in the previous chapter with regards to aesthetics and politics, neither high culture, nor popular, one can bluntly say that this one was a musical form combining march rhythms, sterile lyrics imagining a futuristic society of proletarians, nationalist tonalities, and kitsch. This was one version—the musical one—of "socialist realism."

Finally, in terms of musical subcultures, there were also imported genres, such as a rock style that functioned between public and private, official and unofficial domains. Rock represented urban youth's subculture, an alternative everyday life experience of subjectification pervading popular culture. As was the case with Western youth, rock became Eastern European youth's "very difference from the adult world, a world that, above all else, was regulated, disciplined and boring."[18] What unites youth and rock universally was a potential for rebelliousness and refusal of settled identities: "Rock was about the control one gained by taking the risk of losing control, the identity one had by refusing identities."[19] However, in Eastern Europe the political message was even more bitter since it was directed not only against society but also against the political regime with its enforced autarchic cultural policies and system-conformist identities and *plaisirs*.

Thus, rock subcultures existed and, as alternative, subversive subject-positionings, they functioned at the intersection of public and private spheres. Until the 1970s, *"Cometele," "Cromatic Grup," "Phoenix,"* and *"Sfinx"* functioned as the main Romanian rock groups. As revealed in other Eastern European cases,[20] at first, rock songs were imported directly with their American/English lyrics and music, then they were locally adapted, at first within Romanian lyrics but preserving the Western arpeggios. Finally, genuine Romanian rock music emerged. In the late 1980s, the groups *"Iris"* (and its vocalist Cristi Minculescu), *"Compact," "Compania de sunet,"* the rock singer Dida Drăgan, and *"Holograf"* traveled across Romania performing concerts that combined Romanian with American and English rock music. Never transmitted on radio or television unless under a strict supervision of their lyrics (sung solely in Romanian) and a tempered sound, this music functioned within the mainstream public culture, occasionally as a subversive, other times as an overt musical genre.

Due to its historical traditions, Romanian public culture was deeply influenced by oral traditions even under communism, which is testimony of a country with a recent and overwhelmingly peasantist culture. This level of communication through oral traditions proved to have a deeper accessibility to the average individual than radio or television as the main tools of media and communication in industrialized, rational, Western societies (understood in a Weberian sense). This is why one cannot judge the influence and strength of

Romanian patriotic or rock cultures with the blueprint of Western mass media and communication studies, centered as they are on image, TV, radio, and records distribution. That might be the way in which the industrialized West studies the impact of rationalized, technologically advanced media and communication on the construction of subjectivities, but in this Romanian case the chains of communication responded to—again in a Weberian understanding—a "premodern," less rationalized, peasantist cultural universe. Such a universe functioned under the hegemony of *oral traditions* transmitted from generation to generation, traditions that included folk music (modern ballads, *baladă*), tales, rural festivals, rumor, and (political) jokes[21]—thus, consciously or not, circumventing the media apparatus of the party and the demagogy of the communist regime. The crux of this situation is that public culture should be understood as eclectic, a hybrid that interconnected many subcultures, cultural subgenres, or experiences of subjectification, which, at the level of everyday life practices and systems of beliefs, were by no means psychologically dominated by the party's centralized, top-down media—understood as a framework of subjectification.

Thus, during communism, public culture continued to be overwhelmingly peasantist or urban-peasantist, a culture of oral traditions filled with a quasi-serious everyday life potential for local, peasantist-rural or more cosmopolitan-urban, subversiveness. This is what Michel de Certeau and John Fiske would call the "guerilla tactics" fought from the "spaces within the places,"[22] that is, from a material background of the quotidian—dominated by a condition of syncretism, as explained—that made use of its precommunist traditions, including systems of communication and symbols.

Finally, at a more analytical level, youth was connected and survived communism as a matter of everyday life practices, in small private groups linked by a sense of sharing the same musical or cultural taste, which, in the 1980s, was usually associated with disco, rock, and punk. Before the 1980s, the urban 1970s were widely dominated by the "hippie" culture, which had entered Romania perhaps later than in the West and which had triggered similar—although not as "beatnik" as one could have encountered in Venice Beach, California, for example—youth, individual and group, aesthetic tastes, dress codes, and rebellious attitude. Besides introducing the Romanian youth to the likes of "Yellow Submarine," "Strawberry Fields," and "Imagine," hippie culture also contributed to Romanian youth alternative subjectification by launching the blue jeans fashion. A real *blue jeans mystique* traversed the urban—even some rural—youth generations of the mid-1970s, continuing into the 1980s—here considered as the Romanian *Blue Jeans Generation*.[23] Like Coca-Cola cans and chewing-gum, blue jeans reigned supreme as youth's toughest hard currency. Many Western tourists on the Romanian Black Sea resorts of *Mamaia, Olimp, Neptun, Jupiter*, or *Venus* sold blue jeans on the beach, notoriously reflecting the fact that Romanian citizens could not purchase from the specially created network of hard-currency boutiques designed for foreign tourists, and euphemistically called "shops." On Bucharest's streets of the 1970s, one could spot shier or more overt hippie exposures emerging at a street corner, or dreamingly strolling, or at parties, or during break time at high schools or colleges. Young hippie males would wear long hair gathered in a pony tail and baggy blue jeans, and teenager girls and women in their early twenties would wear mini skirts and clunky sixties footwear, while both genders would expose on their chests wooden or metal crosses or peace symbols. Occasionally, this dressing would combine more rural, peasant shirts, "*ie*" (plural "*ii*"), an item that, with its ethno-folk embroidery, was integral in the hippie costume anyway. Nevertheless, the regime was on their tracks: ultimately, such a dress code was purposely banned in the late 1970s and some groups of "righteous comrades" organized actions with the specific vigilante target—which today might seem as if taken out of a comedy signed by the masters of Soviet humor, Ilya Ilf and Evgeny Petroff—of catching young hippie males in the street and cutting off their pony tails.

Ultimately, according to an everyday life epistemology, youth's existence, subjectification, and potential for subversiveness was located in both private and public structures of the quotidian, in the biostructure of the family extended to the group of close friends and relatives who shared in the same aesthetical tastes of pop culture. Together, such groups created more or less visible strings of subcultures: hippie or rock. However, it remains unclear if, besides their common cultural taste, these groups shared an awareness, a feeling of belonging to a generation—even if subversive—which I call *Blue Jeans*.

Coming back to Romanian public culture under communism, it should be noted that some of the precommunist imported subcultures already hybridized into local styles included classical music and jazz, as well as the tradition of the European chansonnette, which, in the 1970s had evolved into "light music" or *muzica ușoară*. Romanian *muzica ușoară* was drawing on a Latin romantic aesthetics, and it resembled both French and Italian pop music of the 1960s through the 1980s. Although addressing mainly an adult audience, *muzica ușoară* was also a music widely accepted by many generations of youth. Its texts varied from love songs and praises to nature, to songs about Bucharest city that recalled it as precommunist Europe's "little Paris," to those about youth, or holidays. And although promoted by the media, this type of music rarely had patriotic overtones and was the music that the average adult Romanian, Bucharestian, or other would chant or murmur in the street, at work, and in class, *everyday*.

It can realistically be said that, apart from folkloric music, Romanian *muzica ușoară* was by far the most pervasive musical genre in the perimeter of the communist (mainly urban) public culture. Stretching back to early twentieth century, Romanian *muzica ușoară* followed, as explained above, the tradition of the European chansonnette, cabaret, and burlesque. It had produced European hits such as Iosif Ivanovici's "The Danube's Waves" (*Valurile Dunării*) or Richard Stein's "The Bells Sledge" (*Sanie cu zurgălăi*). Some of its early creators had been schooled in Western European conservatories. Among the most famous creators of this genre, gathering both generations educated before and during communism are: Ion Vasilescu, Gherase Dendrino, Ionel Fernic, Mişu Iancu, Nicolae Kirculesu, Elly Roman, Claude Romano, Henri Mălineanu, Edmond Deda, Radu Şerban, Raymond Tavernier, Aurel Mandy, Aurel Giroveanu, Sile Dinicu, Florin Bogardo, Ion Cristinoiu, and Adrian Enescu. In the late 1980s, the most famous Romanian vocalist-stars of *muzica uşoară* were Angela Similea, Corina Chiriac, and Mirabela Dauer, together with the rocker Dida Drăgan and the internationally acclaimed Aura Urziceanu, a professional jazz-singer who, in the 1970s had concerted in North America accompanied by Duke Ellington, Quincy Jones, Dizzie Gillespie, and Ella Fitzgerald.[24] Many Romanian-based national and international festivals celebrated Romanian *muzica uşoară* such as "The Golden Stag" (*Cerbul de aur*) in Braşov, "Nameless Star" (*Steaua fără nume*), the annual "Competition of Melodies" (*Concursul melodiilor*), the annual festival "*Mamaia*," which took place at the Black Sea resort with the same name, the competition "*Bucureşti*," with songs celebrating the city of Bucharest, and many others that would afterwards be broadcasted both on the national television and radio. The essence of this music was highly lyrical, dearly enjoyed by the Romanian public and comparable with the music of Italian Toto Cutugno, Russian Alla Pugaciova, Czechoslovakian Karel Gott, Spanish Julio Iglesias, French Mireille Mathieu, or Hungarian Zsuzsa Koncz—that is, the pop music of the 1970s-1980s, which was also extensively broadcasted in Romania.

Romanian stages also saw some of the most famous foreign performers of those times: in the 1960s and 1970s, the burlesque theater *(teatrul de estradă)* "*Constantin Tănase*" staged Josephine Baker, Neil Armstrong, Mireille Mathieu, Gloria Gaynor, and Connie Francis; in 1970, the rock group "Blood, Sweat and Tears" also performed in Romania;[25] and in the 1980s, Bucharest's famous concert hall "*Sala Polivalentă*" saw the "Boomtown Rats" (1982) and "Smokey" (1983).[26]

Meanwhile, Romanian Television, an institution with a focal political position and capacity for subversiveness under Ceauşescu—which, undoubtedly, deserves a separate study—had developed a genuine show subculture called "*spectacol de varietăţi*" (from the French concept of "*variété* show"). Such shows were usually broadcasted on Saturdays and Sundays and combined a cabaret-style dance with satirical short plays and recitals of *muzica uşoară*. Until the late 1980s, when the TV program was shortened to one channel (from two) and only two hours a day (in the evening), Romanian Television had managed to create the best Hollywoodian escapist imaginary environment, in stark contrast to the average Romanian's daily realities of economic penury.[27] Until the December 1989 revolution, the two channels had already broadcasted, among other British, Italian, and French productions, the main Hollywoodian productions (from musicals such as "An American to Paris" and "Hello Dolly," to "Tarzan" featuring Johnny Weismuller, Shirley Temple movies, and "The Great Gatsby"), the celebrated American TV serials "The Saint," "Time Machine," and "Bewitched," the main American cartoons, from Mickey Mouse to Woody Woodpecker and "the Flintstones"—to mention only a few—and, after 1981, MTV video clips.

Finally, the entire public culture under communism can be seen as a mixture of official and unofficial genres, regulatory ideological "socialist realist" aesthetics and overwhelming spaces of the subversive gathering precommunist oral-peasantist, or high-culture traditions, and Western, imported styles. In other words, Romania was experimenting with many alternative forms of expression, among which, with regards to youth, are recollected the early 1980s Bucharest-based jazz and rock show "*Poezia muzicii tinere*" (The Poetry of Young Music), organized at the theater Lucia Sturdza-Bulandra by the charismatic actor Florian Pittiş;[28] the jazz festival from *Sibiu*; "*Club A*" held by students at the Faculty of Architecture in Bucharest; "*Pop Club*" from the Academy of Economics, which even published a "top ten" of Western pop music;[29] and generally Western and in particular American pop culture obtained from the black market in the form of videos, cassettes, and various disco and rock memorabilia.

From Rock to Rap and "Generation PRO": The Politics of Pop Culture in Postcommunism

As is the case in other Eastern European countries, Romania faces today a boom of artistic expression: new names, styles, fashion, rhetoric, aesthetics, and symbolism embrace the new producer and consumer of Romanian popular culture. As expressed in the previous chapter, postcommunist popular culture is integral in the general ethos of postcommunist aesthetics—*postcommunist carnivalesque*—mixing local with imported signifiers and celebrating the overhead of Western pop culture. Eclecticism is the main feature that defines this new pop subculture, which stands today oriented toward rap and hip-hop styles, although hybridized within local customs, tastes, language, and social realities. This new cultural style is represented in the emergence of a suburban culture. These suburbs were created during the previous communist era, when Ceauşescu sought to develop or extend the urban limits of Bucharest's old and relatively poor, rural peripheries. Today, this music, which is produced and consumed by a generation of postcommunist urban youth, mixes musical elements of American rap and hip-hop with lyrics reflecting the dramatic transformational social realities of Romania. This new generation of urban youth is usually referred to as "*Generaţia PRO*" (Generation PRO), although more traditionalist quarters many times declare "*Generaţia PRO*" a superficial product of the last decade of consumer-oriented ethos, of market transformations, and of Western "copied" symbols. Thus, while in public parlance some might call it "*Generaţia Californizată*" (roughly, "the California-zed Generation"), others would nostalgically contrast it with a perceived perishing of the "Book Generation" (usually referred to by Romanian intellectuals in very French terms as "*la culture du livre*"). This last comparison refers to precommunist and even communist times when, as explained in the previous chapter, aesthetical legitimacy was located in the intellectuals' high culture, not youth popular culture, as is now starting to happen in postcommunism. This present debate over the place of *"Generaţia PRO"* does bring to mind the tremendous need faced by Romania to democratize definitions of culture today, making them more inclusive, and extend the notion of culture beyond its conservative and elitist identification solely with humanist intellectual history, thus including popular culture, civil society's cultural diversity, and the ephemerality of everyday life.

Coming back to rap and hip-hop culture, integral in the postcommunist logic of cultures of despair stands this new style of pop music, one with lyrics that express a highly political form of protest addressed against an increasing poverty and political corruption. With its political message, Romanian rap music takes on the political protest, which in the 1970s and 1980s, had animated rock music and an entire generation of underground, subversive, antipolitical youth subculture. However, unlike its predecessor, rock, contemporary Romanian rap uses a new terminology, which had entered into the core of the language during the last decades of communist, forced urbanization and post-1989 decay of the communist official discourse called *"limba de lemn"* (wooden language). This new idiom has an underlying political message that is a *cri de cœur* against a corrupt politics distanced from the average citizen, whose poverty seems to deepen in line with the national currency's devaluation of the last decade; it is occasionally filled with expletives, sexist, racist, and obscene expressions, which usually accompany—aesthetically and politically—such forms of protest.

In their song titled *"Prostia la putere"* (Idiocy Rules), the group *"Sarmale Reci"* (Cold Rolls) offers such an evocative example of satirical political lyrics:

Nu ştiu cum s-a nimerit (I don't know how it came about)
Nu ştiu cum s-a potrivit (I don't know how it happened)
Că la noi prostia-i la putere (That idiocy rules us now).
Nu ştiu cum s-a întâmplat (I don't know how it happened)
Prin ce fenomen ciudat (Through what strange phenomenon),
Că puterea-i plină de putori (That power is filled with rottenness).
Azi prostia e-n senat (Today idiocy is in the Senate)
Sindicat şi patronat (Trade union and patronage)
Azi prostia e-n foaier (Today idiocy is in the foyer)
Cazinou şi minister (Casino and governmental department)
Prostul n-are nici un chef (The idiot has no wish)
Decât să ne fie şef (But only to be our boss). . . .
Prostul nu e prost destul (The idiot is not idiot enough)
Fără lănţişor şi ghiul (Without [golden] chain and ring)
Daţi-i prostului măcar (Give the idiot at least)
Un celular (A cell phone). . . .
Prostul azi e bătăuş, (The idiot is today a brawler)
Mâine-i mare trepăduş. (Tomorrow he's a hot shot)
Azi e coadă de topor, (Today he is coarse)
Mâine-i mare senator (Tomorrow he is a great senator).[30]

Songs like these, although highly political, are also integral within a wider phenomenon represented, as expressed before, by the rise of a subculture of the semiurban, semirural periphery—the suburb—with its correlative cultural universe. This suburban art genre is called *"muzică de cartier"* (suburb music), a so-called "ghetto" music. Taking its artistic expression from American rap and hip-hop, this new form of politicized pop culture combines a faithfully imported American music with Romanian texts that reflect the impact of postcommunist transformation and politics on the life of the average Romanian suburban youth. It also employs an entire correlated fashion, hair style—pink, blue, yellow, Afro—behavior, and gesticulation, all of which are obviously reminiscent of African-American rappers. Many groups represent the subculture of their own suburb (*"cartier"*). As expressed, they are using a form of unconventional Romanian idiom and a pronunciation that shortens vowels and words, replaces consonants, and, through adding a mixture of jargon, porn, and Roma words, manage to create an entirely new idiom. Among the most celebrated in this category of suburb groups (*"benzi de cartier"*) and vocalists are: *"B.U.G. Mafia"* (representing the suburb *Pantelimon*), *"La Familia," "Il Egal," "Da Hood Justice," "Ganja,"* and the rap singer *"Marijuana."*

On another plane of musical political satire stands the vocalist Ada Milea, who has developed a special musical style that combines an intentional kitsch reiteration of former patriotic songs, modern rhythms, recitative, and theatrical effects and literary formulae. Her celebrated 1999 CD, *"Republica Mioritică România"* (The Mioritic Republic of Romania)—a local euphemism for present Romanian politics of turmoil and corruption—starts with a short but illustrative song titled *"Perspectiva"* (Perspective):

> *Vrei să fii mare in ţara ta?* (Do you want to get important in your country?)
> *Atunci pleacă din ea* (Then leave it)
> *Numai aşa vei progresa* (That's the only way to progress) . . .
> *Numai aşa vei progresa* (That's the only way to progress).[31]

Making a satire of the entire politics and transformation, paradoxes of everyday life, poverty, and the *nouveaux riches'* idiosyncratic consumption tastes seems to best characterize the artistic expression of this postcommunist culture of despair. Many other musical groups address satirical texts to present Romanian politics and everyday life, among which are *"Divertis," "Vama Veche"* (Old Customs), *"Vacanţa Mare"* (Great Holidays), and *"Timpuri Noi"* (New Times).

Another musical genre that has gained much popularity in postcommunism is the one called *"manea"* (plural *"manele"*). *Manea* represents an eclectic style. It combines Oriental—reminiscent of Turkish-Phanariot cultures[32]—with Roma cultural influences, and rarefied forms of Romanian folklore or suburban styles. *Manea* is also controversial in many musical quarters; it is called by its foes a type of music "from the periphery" or plain kitsch. There may be an underlying anti-Roma feeling expressed in this controversy about *manele/"Gypsy pop."*

Whatever the case, *manele* is highly consumed in the rural and (sub)urban Romanian environment today, and, despite its detractors, *manele* can represent a musical genre in its own right, responding to present postcommunist tastes and social realities, no matter how aesthetically "illegitimate"—in Bourdieu's sense. Some of the most famous interpreters of *manele* are *"Naşu"* (the Godfather) and *"Adrian Copilul Minune"* (Adrian the Wonder Boy).

As both *muzica uşoară* and rock are fading away under the new influence of rap, hip-hop, and *manele*, the political message also shifts toward these musical subgenres and their associated symbolic universe. In other words, as a means of communicating political messages, rap and hip-hop have replaced rock, without leaving the Romanian artistic stage barren of political satire and the subversive, as the devaluation of rock in postcommunism might seem to suggest. The only other comparable transfer of emotional investment, thus paralleling the replacement of rock with rap, is the Latin American tearjerker "telenovela," which is hugely popular with Romanian housewives, thus ending the decades-long Hollywoodian escapist dream nurtured under communism.

On the other hand, these new musical genres indicate a high, gendered, sexualization of youth within a booming show business industry that, although highly imitative of its Western counterpart, responds to the realities of postcommunist Romania: from young, seminaked female bodies exposed on the stage and TV shows, to the newly published Romanian versions of *Playboy* and *Hustler*.

Finally, other songs deplore the political condition of Romanians today as denizens of the Balkans, who, as described by Maria Todorova, perceive themselves through a complex of inferiority.[33] This is also the message conveyed by the rock band *"Holograf,"* which sings an inspired tragicomic text called *"Sunt un balcanic"* (I Am a Balkanic) and enumerates the Western and Eastern European internalized stereotypes regarding a so-called "Balkanic temperament":

Sunt un balcanic (I am a Balkanic),
Iremediabil sunt pierdut (I am irremediably lost),
Sunt un balcanic (I am a Balkanic),
Nu termin ce am început (I do not finish what I start),
Sunt un balcanic (I am a Balkanic).
Nu sunt capabil să durez ceva mai trainic (I am incapable of building some-thing more durable)
Şi mă scufund mai glorios ca un TITANIC (And I sink more gloriously than a Titanic)
Sunt neserios, dar nu-i nimic, căci sunt balcanic (I am not honest, but that's OK, since I am Balkanic). . . .
Îmi fierbe sângele în venă (The blood boils in my veins), . . .
 Mă supăr foarte tare, dar îmi trece grabnic (I get angry very bad, but I get over it quickly),
Ireconciliabil sunt, dar sunt şi paşnic (I am irreconcilable, but I am also peaceful)
Sunt mincinos politician şi nu sunt harnic (I am a lying politician and I am not

hardworking).
Temperament vulcanic am, deci sunt balcanic (I have a volcanic temperament,
thus I am Balkanic). . . .
Deci sunt gelos şi sigur mă oftic amarnic (Thus I am jealous and I get badly
angry, for sure).
Şi nu mizaţi nicicând pe calmul meu britanic (And never bet on my British stiff
upper lip). . . .
Sunt un balcanic (I am a Balkanic).[34]

In the end, youth remains a liminal category at the borders of social,
economic, and political integration/exclusion. To be a youth in postcommunist
Romania, a country where subject-formative experiences are largely framed not
only by practices conveyed by market and democratic transformation, but also
by patriarchy, sexism, nationalist rhetoric, and gerontocracy (versus merit
system), means today to be a producer and consumer of a popular culture headed
by Western symbols and icons, local political satires, or more rural, traditionalist
codes. It also means to walk as a passive political actor, or a marginalized
category—such as are elderly people, women, children, and the disabled—through
the metaphoric *city* which postcommunism is, a situation that perhaps can sadly but
truly be summarized under the provoking title of an inspired recent newspaper article
titled *"Adolescent într-o Românie bătrână"* (Adolescent in an Old Romania).[35]

4.1 An Internet café on *Calea Victoriei* at *Piaţa Amzei* Street, and its two young
attendants.

4.2 Magazine article about rap and hip-hop singer "Marijuana": Interview by Ioana Maximilian, "Primul dans cu Marijuana" (The First Dance with Marijuana), *CSVD: Revista peste media*, no. 38, 19 June 2000: 12-3. Posters with "Valachia," "Latin Express," and "Angels," in *Fan: Hits and Posters*, no. 0, July 2000. The hip-hop group "B.U.G. Mafia," the *manele* singer "Naşu," the singer Cătălina Toma, and the pop group "Gaz pe foc" (Gas on Fire)—all in *Fan: Hits and Posters*, no. 0, July 2000.

4.3 Pop magazines such as *CSVD: Revista peste media* no. 38, 19 June 2000, and *Fan: Hits and Posters*, no. 0, July 2000; and the Romanian version of the American *Playboy*, June 2000.

4.4 Collection of women's and young girls' magazines. Some are Romanian versions of their Western counterparts, such as *Cosmopolitan* or *Madame*. Others are local, such as *Ioana, Lumea Femeilor* (Women's World), *Avantaje* (Advantages), or *Super*.

Notes

1. C. Banc and Alan Dundes, eds., *You Call This Living? A Collection of East European Political Jokes* (Athens: The University of Georgia Press, 1990), 69.

2. Pierre Bourdieu, *Distinction: A Social Critique of the Judgement of Taste,* trans. Richard Nice (Cambridge: Harvard University Press, 1984), 370-1.

3. Lawrence Grossberg, *We Gotta Get Out of This Place: Popular Conservatism and Postmodern Culture* (New York: Routledge, 1992), 171.

4. Grossberg, *We Gotta Get Out,* 171.

5. Grossberg, *We Gotta Get Out,* 175.

6. Michel Foucault, *Discipline and Punish: The Birth of the Prison,* trans. Alan Sheridan (New York: Vintage Books, 1995), 135; Grossberg, *We Gotta Get Out,* 176.

7. Grossberg, *We Gotta Get Out,* 178.

8. Grossberg, *We Gotta Get Out,* 178.

9. Another level of "performative politics" can consider, for example, the discursive, gendered construction of the sexed body. See Judith Butler, *Gender Trouble: Feminism and the Subversion of Identity* (New York: Routledge, 1990) and, in this book, chapter 7 on queer.

10. Dick Hebdige, "Posing . . . Threats, Striking . . . Poses: Youth, Surveillance and Display," *Substance,* no. 37/38 (1983): 68-88, quoted in Grossberg, *We Gotta Get Out,* 178.

11. Grossberg, *We Gotta Get Out,* 179.

12. Luigi Tomasi, "The New Europe and the Value Orientations of Young People: East-West Comparisons," in *Politics and Religion in Central and Eastern Europe: Traditions and Transformations,* ed. William H. Swatos Jr. (Westport: Praeger, 1994), 55.

13. Tomasi, "The New Europe," 55.

14. For a comparative analysis of the post-Soviet youth, see Hilary Pilkington, "'The Future Is Ours': Youth Culture in Russia, 1953 to the Present," in *Russian Cultural Studies: An Introduction,* ed. Catriona Kelly and David Shepherd (Oxford: Oxford University Press, 1998), 368-86. On a comparative analysis of postcommunist Serbian youth, see Eric Gordy, "'Turbasi' and 'Rockeri' as Windows into Serbia's Social Divide," *Balkanologie* IV, no. 1 (2000): 55-81.

15. Tomasi, "The New Europe," 63.

16. Timothy W. Ryback, *Rock around the Bloc: A History of Rock Music in Eastern Europe and the Soviet Union* (New York: Oxford University Press, 1990), 128; Sabrina P. Ramet, ed., *Rocking the State: Rock Music and Politics in Eastern Europe and Russia* (Boulder: Westview Press, 1994), 8-9.

17. Foucault, *Discipline and Punish,* 200.

18. Grossberg, *We Gotta Get Out,* 180.

19. Grossberg, *We Gotta Get Out,* 180.

20. See Ramet, *Rocking the State,* 243.

21. Political jokes proved an unprecedented flourishing under communism despite its alleged muscular ideological arm. See the scintillating collection of annotated Eastern European political jokes edited by Banc and Dundes, *You Call This Living?*

22. See Michel de Certeau, *The Practice of Everyday Life*, trans. Steven F. Rendall (Berkeley: University of California Press, 1984); and John Fiske, *Understanding Popular Culture* (New York: Routledge, 1991), 32.

23. From a comparative perspective of generational experiences of subjectification, I can note that the "Blue Jeans Generation" of Romanian urban youth born between the early sixties and mid-seventies, and attaining the age of adolescence in the mid-seventies to late eighties, has a counterpart that is usually referred to as the American "Generation X" (also born between the early sixties to mid-seventies), a concept introduced by Douglas Coupland in his book *Generation X: Tales for an Accelerated Culture* (New York: St. Martin's Press, 1992).

24. Daniela Caraman Fotea, *Meridianele Cîntecului* [The Song's Meridians] (Bucharest: Editura Muzicală, 1989), 270-1. Romanian artists were able to perform abroad and their contracts were supervised by the Bucharest-based "*Agenția Română de Impresariat Artistic*" (the Romanian Artistic Impresario Agency), *ARIA*, an institution that undoubtedly deserves a separate study. *ARIA* constituted in fact another venue to bring in hard currency to the Romanian state. According to their contracts, Romanian artists had to provide *ARIA* with up to half of their foreign revenues in exchange for their privileged right to perform abroad, many times in underpaid situations and with no health insurance.

25. See also Ryback, *Rock around the Bloc*, 124.

26. As a teenager, this author was in the audience of "Smokey's" concert in Bucharest.

27. On the escapist imaginary conveyed by the Hollywoodian productions as a cultural genre, see Richard Dyer, "Entertainment and Utopia," in *The Cultural Studies Reader*, ed. Simon During, 2nd ed. (New York: Routledge, 1999), 371-81.

28. As a teenager, this author was also in the audience of Pittiş's rock show, which was ultimately banned before the mid-eighties.

29. On "Pop Club," see also Ryback, *Rock around the Bloc*, 122-3.

30. Sarmale Reci (Mihai Iordache and Florin Dumitrescu), "Prostia-i la putere," in *Răpirea din Serai* (Bucharest: Media Pro Music, 1998).

31. Ada Milea, "Perspectiva," in *Republica Mioritică România* (Bucharest: Intercont Music, 1999).

32. Miron Manega, "Cui îi este frică de manele?" [Who Fears Manele?], *Național*, 27 January 2001, <http://www.nationalpress.ro/> (28 January 2001).

33. Maria Todorova, *Imagining the Balkans* (New York: Oxford University Press, 1997).

34. Holograf, "Sunt un Balcanic," in *Holografica* (Bucharest: Media Pro Music, 2000).

35. Dănuţ Ungureanu, "Adolescent într-o Românie bătrână," *Curentul*, 15 May 2001, <http://www.curentul.ro/curentul.php> (16 May 2001).

Chapter Five

Popular Culture and the Discourse of Hate: The Case of Anti-Semitism[1]

Somewhere on an island with sun and shade, in the midst of peace, security, and
happiness, I would in the end be indifferent to whether I was or was not Jewish.
But here and now I cannot be anything else. Nor do I think I want to be.
— Mihail Sebastian, *Journal*[2]

- How are things in Romania under communist rule?
- Wonderful. We live on permanent Yom Tov.
- What do you mean?
- Well, you see, we dress like on Purim, are housed like on Sukkot, and eat like
on Yom Kippur.
— East European political joke[3]

As a form of *hate speech*, a *discourse*, a *representation*, and an *experience of*
subjectification, anti-Semitism is more prevalent in the postcommunist
Romanian discursive practices than the actual existence of a Jewish minority
and organized Jewish identity politics. As we enter the third millennium and in
light of the Jewish people's history in this part of the world—a history marked
by assimilation and inclusion, or by exclusion, Holocaust, and national-commu-

75

nism—Jewish politics is almost nonexistent today in Romania compared with precommunist times,[4] a situation that can be correlated with this minority's present scant number of members, which in turn is the result of intolerance, assimilation, and emigration.[5] But the discussion about anti-Semitism is worth placing here due to the striking pervasiveness of this discourse in postcommunism and popular culture as well as the symbolically charged representation that accompanies such a form of hate speech *even in the absence of a significant Jewish minority*. Finally, as a form of hate speech, anti-Semitism brings popular culture to one of its most significant intersections, namely with politics. Thus, in this chapter, anti-Semitism will be analyzed solely as a discourse in postcommunism—as opposed to, for example, institutional anti-Semitism such as extremist political parties or organizations—and as a matter of popular culture—as opposed to intellectual anti-Semitism or anti-Semitism in the Romanian culture in general.[6]

As presented in the introduction to this book, a genuine discussion about Jewish identity and the politics of a Jewish movement today does not have enough empirical grounds in Romania. Similar to the absence of feminist, queer, or youth political identities mentioned throughout this book—but in the presence of experiences, discourses, and practices of subjectification as women, youth, queer, or aesthetic subjects—anti-Semitism as a discourse can function *in the absence* of a significantly synchronic Jewish entity, organized minority, and subsequent Jewish politics.[7] Nevertheless, what makes the analysis of anti-Semitism as a *discourse* in popular culture different from an analysis of youth, women, and queer as *subjectivities* is the *indirect* character of the former and the *direct* nature of the latter. Thus, while women, queer, and youth prove to have a material existence within various *subject-formative* experiences, irrespective of an absence of a correlated identity politics (be it feminist, queer, or youth), as a discourse—moreover, as a discourse *about* the Jewish minority—anti-Semitism functions as a mirror, an oblique experience that *reflects* the Jewish being—past and present—in the imaginary of a non-Jewish majority, as is the case here. I have thus called this mediated, discursive experience a *subject-reflected experience*. This means that it is not the Jewish entity itself that is going to be present in this research through what would otherwise be an analysis of the *subject-formative experiences* of a postcommunist Jewish subjectivity and corresponding identity/ethnic politics. Such a direct analysis would have to take into consideration, for example, not only the Holocaust legacy, or national-communism, but also the general social, political, economic, cultural, and scientific integration of this minority into the life of Romania, as well as a gender-based, inter-ethnic, or cross-subjectivity analysis. Instead of presenting the subject-formative experiences of the Jewish minority, I have decided to focus on its *subject-reflected* reality, which the discourse of anti-Semitism is. In this sense, I was motivated by the otherwise inexplicable preponderance of the latter (a discourse) over the former (a subjectivity, or an entity) in some Romanian postcommunist discursive spaces. This type of direct or indirect, primary or mediated analysis is also what Feminist Theory—which, as explained in chapter 2, stands as one of the methodological pillars of this book—presents as the concept of "standpoint."[8] Thus, here I have displaced the epistemological standpoints that ground the analysis of various subjectivities and, while I discuss women, queer, youth, and aesthetic subjects from their inner subject-formative standpoints—in other words, from the point of view of their *own* experiences—I have displaced the epistemological standpoint in the case of the Jewish identity and have located it in *another* entity's subject-formative experiences—a non-Jewish majority for the case here—and which ultimately makes the discourse of anti-Semitism a case of a Jewish *subject-reflected* experience.

Finally, the notion that anti-Semitism can be explained here, as expressed, as a point of disjuncture between reality (the existence or not of a Jewish minority) and a discourse (anti-Semitism) that nuancedly characterizes some Romanian discourses today, enables one to understand the dynamic of the anti-Semitic discourse by eschewing the regulatory idea concomitant with a Western understanding of minority/identity politics that anti-Semitism must be linked to a correspondingly synchronic Jewish identity. In other words, in the anatomy and symbolism of postcommunism—understood, as explained earlier, as a conflicting set of recirculated precommunist and communist symbolic systems—discursive practices of identification do not require corresponding entities, organized minorities, political identities, or social movements in order to function as *representations* and *discourses*—which would otherwise be associated with a Western understanding of vocal grassroots politics and identities.

Analyzed here as a discourse, a representation, and a subject-reflected practice of identification, anti-Semitism is as integral to a general concept of hate speech as are other derogatory discourses that target other ethnicities and cultural minorities such as Hungarians, Roma, women, and subjects with different sexual orientations. As this chapter introduces it, postcommunist discursive anti-Semitism conveys an entire postcommunist mythology, which constructs "the Jew" as a "mythical" fantasy, a representation symbolized by the idea of an *epicenter of international conspiracy against the nation.*

Within what has already become a mark for the anti-Semitism of postcommunist Europe—"anti-Semitism without Jews"[9]—this chapter introduces a particular form of anti-Semitism based on what Leon Volovici calls "the mythical Jew."[10] This representation constitutes a post-Holocaust, postcommunist form of hate speech specific for those Eastern European societies where the number of Jewish communities was drastically reduced either by fascist extermination or by assimilation, or through emigration under communism and postcommunism.

It can be said that, in light of the last decade of rereadings and rewritings of the past, postcommunism appears as a pervasively nostalgic landscape, while everyday life becomes a "topography of memory," understood as "collective frameworks of memory" that construct "nostalgic re-creations of the past,"[11] perceived as the lost Eden. The narrative of "the mythical Jew" could be said to transpire on this complex background that includes: nostalgia, conspiracy theories, and scapegoatism; self-perception as the "victimized majority," whereby a "majority may feel itself to be the victim" of various imagined or real internal and external perils;[12] and a positively revived interwar fascist mythology intertwined with a fantasized representation of Romania's interwar *belle époque*, and coupled with ideas of a *mythical savior*.[13] Romanian historian Lucian Boia has inspiringly expressed this last Romanian myth as:

> The conviction . . . that some "chosen" ones can stand beyond the normal human condition, ensuring the relationship between the earthly and divine register, or, in the secularized version, between community and history, between us and an idea higher than the banal quotidian existence. . . . Thus, one can explain the exceptional career of the providential character in Romanian society. Confronted with a fluid and uncertain history, Romanians have constantly felt the need for some stable markers, particularly the need for some qualified "guides," who should take them on the hazy paths of history and finally deliver them to an end. The process of mythification has infallibly worked, being applied to a variety of diverse personalities with unequal merits—yet, it is not the merit that counts, but the transfiguration, spontaneous or programmed, that takes place in the social imaginary. The greater the social expectation is the greater a personality becomes, and the saviors show up, undoubtedly, when it seems that they are needed.[14]

A tormented postcommunist socioeconomic transformation and its correlative cultures of despair can also be added to the above.[15]

Since 1989, anti-Semitism has become not only a matter of the newly emerging nationalist organizations and parties, but it has also resurfaced in popular culture—the focus of this chapter—as well as in various intellectual spaces. This resurgence of anti-Semitism has brought with it new forms of discursive chauvinism and hate speech. Most of them are prevalent in the pages of some mainstream newspapers or limited series journals. In the first decade of postcommunism, these included: *România Mare* (Greater Romania) and *Politica* (Politics) (both published by Corneliu Vadim Tudor), *Atac la persoană* (Personal Attack) (published by Dragoş Dumitriu), *Noua Dreaptă* (The New Right) (published by Radu Sorescu), *Puncte Cardinale* (Cardinal Points) (published by Gabriel Constantinescu), the neolegionary[16] *Gazeta de vest* (Western Gazette) (published by Ovidiu Guleş), *Mişcarea* (The Movement) (published by Marian Munteanu), *Permanenţe* (Permanences) (published by Mircea Nicolau), *Vremea dreptei naţional-creştine* (The Time of the National-Christian Right) (published by Nicolae Henegariu), *Naţiunea* (The Nation) and *Renaşterea bănăţeană* (The Banat Revival)—the last two under the patronage of Iosif Constantin Drăgan, an Italian businessman and a former legionary who, according to Romanian public knowledge, was a friend of the defunct Romanian dictator Ceauşescu.[17] As a discourse of hate, anti-Semitism was present during the first decade of postcommunism in daily polemics (exhibited mainly in the press), public statements or parliamentary discourses, religious articles, books, and, more recently, in graffiti (representing mainly the Star of David) or posters advertising "neo-Christian" youth political organizations, which could be encountered in Bucharest's subway stations, for example. Strolling through postcommunist Bucharest, one could notice that *The Protocols of the Learned Elders of Zion*, translated by Ioan Moţa and published in 1999 by Samizdat publishing house, an uncritical version of Hitler's *Mein Kampf* published in 1997 by the Craiova-based Beladi publishing house, and Roger Garaudy's *Miturile fondatoare ale politicii israeliene* (The Founding Myths of Israeli Politics), published by Alma Tip publishing house in 1998, were sold freely in the streets. Finally, in 1996, a small, green ad in the basement of the Faculty of Law in Bucharest advertised the nearby opening of a legionary bookstore.

In terms of an intersection of anti-Semitism with popular culture and what I call *cyber-postcommunism*, one notices the existence of booming hate cyber-communities.[18] Thus, one can find transnational websites, among which is the extremist, London-based "International Third Position" (ITP), with its motto taken from Corneliu Zelea Codreanu and its links to the "Romanian Legionary Third Position."[19] Among its declaration of principles—translated and posted on its website in English, French, Spanish, Portuguese, Romanian, and Serbo-Croatian—the ITP declares the primacy of Spirit over Matter, "opposition to materialist philosophies including Freemasonry, Liberalism, Capitalism, Socialism, Marxism, Imperialism, Anarchism, Modernism and the New Age," and "opposition to Zionism in all its manifestations." ITP also acknowledges that the hardcopy version of its nationalist fan magazine ("fanzine") is regularly published in English and Romanian; its 8 July 2002 electronic issue ("e-zine") introduces as a prize an oil painting representing Codreanu and advertises the opening of a legionary bookshop in Romania. ITP's online bookstore sells a number of books by Codreanu and Horia Sima, books published by the Legionary Press. Its *port-parole* in Romania is the Timişoara-based journal *Gazeta de vest*, which displays the legionary symbol. There are also native Romanian hate sites, mainly neolegionary, such as the one of neolegionary Şerban Suru, a leader of the legionary "*cuib*" (nest) "*Fapta*" (the Deed),[20] "*db Jurnal: Revista Online a Mişcării Legionare din România*" (db Journal: The Online Journal of the Romanian Legionary Movement),[21] and "*Noua Dreaptă* (the New Right), a formation that wishes to solve "the Gypsy question" and, considering homosexuality a vice, wishes to reincriminate it.[22] There is also the American-based legionary website *Pagina României Naţionaliste* (The Page of Nationalist Romania), which, with a very appealing and sophisticated web design, presents dozens of images from the Bucharest legionary mass manifestations from the Fall of 1940, including legionary books, poems, songs, and photos, claiming as part of the legionary heritage famous interwar Romanian intellectuals such as Mircea Eliade, Constantin Noica, and Emil

Cioran.[23] As part of the postcommunist popular culture, Internet as cyber-postcommunism is not that difficult to access: As introduced in chapter 1, there are many urban Internet cafés, schools and universities are acquiring new technology, and there is ample Western humanitarian support for new publications and websites. Thus, as expressed in chapter 4, the profile of the average Romanian consumer of cyberspace could be summarized as young, urban, with a relatively good knowledge of the English language, and an attraction to Western popular culture. Those accessing hate websites may also be linked to a nationalist ethos. It could be argued that, at first, many international hate websites enter Romanian postcommunist popular culture through this valorizing of Western popular culture, in which underlying political messages eventually come to dominate some local youth communities.

A brief summary of the contexts that harbor anti-Semitic discourses in postcommunism—and, while pervading popular culture have directly linked it to politics—would have to include the following. First, there is the alleged Jewish contribution to the establishment of communism in Romania—"the Gulag" as a Jewish creation, or the "Judeo-Bolshevik" thesis—an issue otherwise historically and critically explained by Robert R. King's history of the Romanian Communist Party (RCP).[24] Second, the Jews and the Holocaust are also considered uncomfortable testimonies in the present debate over rewriting national history and culture, this within a national gallery of resurrected pro-Nazi interwar statesmen and political leaders, such as Marshall Ion Antonescu[25] and prominent figures from the Iron Guard, such as *Căpitanul* Corneliu Zelea Codreanu.[26] And, although the Holocaust in Romania was mystified in Romanian communist textbooks,[27] in postcommunism significant changes mark the new alternative history textbooks, some of which devote text and pictures to the Holocaust and even include quotations from Sebastian's *Journal* (see, for example, the alternative history textbooks for the seventh grade published in 1999 by the Humanitas, Nemira, and Corint publishing houses). Finally, with regards to the Holocaust, the Romanian government has recently passed the Emergency Ordinance no. 31, published in *Monitorul Oficial* (the Romanian Official Gazette) no. 214 from 28 March 2002, penalizing and forbidding intolerant and extremist organizations and discourses, including forms of anti-Semitism and public Holocaust denial. This last regulation and, before it, the existence of a European legislation forbidding forms of Holocaust denial, such as the French Law Fabius-Gayssot passed in 1990, have stirred various discussions in the Romanian intellectual spaces, debates that sought to emphasize the fundamental right of "freedom of speech" against such statutes that interdict public Holocaust denial, even in the case of Roger Garaudy and his indictment for negating the Jewish Holocaust in his *Les mythes fondateurs de la politique israelienne*.[28] Nevertheless, what transpired from these narratives was a total misunderstanding of the connection between such Holocaust revisionism and the precise anti-Semitic interests of its supporters; in other words, the fact that such negations are usually used precisely as forms of anti-Semitism, which, in the case of Romanian postcommunism, is exemplified by the legitimacy given to the cult of Antonescu.

The third context of anti-Semitic discourse worth mentioning here—and here popular culture intersects with high culture—involves the Criterion Generation, the most prominent generation of intellectuals in twentieth-century Romania, who are all linked—in a way that Leon Volovici considers more spiritual, ethical, and mystical—to the interwar legionary movement.[29] This group included professor of logic Nae Ionescu, the brilliant mythologist Mircea Eliade, and philosophers Emil Cioran and Constantin Noica. The fourth context—and in stark contrast to the first point above, thus underlining the irrational nature of anti-Semitism—is the communist/ultranationalist argument that the Jews are responsible for the collapse of communism, within an overall scenario whereby Romania lurches toward new forms of destabilization. Here, the statement refers both to the Jew as an "enemy from within," but also as an "enemy from without," portraying the Jews as leading the world in the occult form of "Judeo-Masonry"—also referred to as "the global Jewish government" or "conspiracy"—through such organizations as the UN, the IMF, and even through U.S. and Western capitalism.[30] Fifth are the allegations of Jewish "parasitism" that can also be found within postcommunist popular culture. These are based on that all too familiar characterization of Jews and their so-called "fraudulent" wealth, a supposition grounded in essentialist character features. Not coincidentally, this (mythical) instrument of accusation came into force from popular culture into high politics at the very moment when certain groups began pressuring the 1990-1996 governments on the issue of restituting Jewish patrimonial properties. Ultimately, this accusation was correlative with another one, which transcended ethnic boundaries, and made reference to the "boyars" and "*chiaburi*" when decommunization and the restitution of real estate first became a discursive and material issue in postcommunist Romania. Finally, anti-Semitism operates within the recirculation of the Christian theological position regarding Judaism, disseminating old controversies about such notions as "chosen people" and the issue of deicide. *România Mare* was abundant in such hateful statements: "It is their paranoid thirst for domination, subjugation, for blackmail, and for illustrating the world's first fascist slogan: *The Jews are God's chosen people*. What are the merits or missions for which they were chosen? For having slapped, spit, whipped, and crucified the *Savior*?"[31] And, as a reminder, *Atac la persoană* published an article on 7 September 1998 titled "Swastika," expressing that there were too many "potential soap" people "from Tel Aviv" on Bucharest's streets, regretting that Romania's transitional economic "penury" did not provide sufficient amounts of "barbed wire and Zyklon-B gas" as a solution to this problem.[32]

It can be seen, then, that the vanishing of Jews from Romanian society did not bring about the disappearance of anti-Semitism.[33] On the contrary, this shift revealed a special form of popular anti-Semitism based on, as was presented before, "the mythical Jew." While linking popular culture with high politics and with some intellectual spaces such as the press, this concept stresses the mythical and, at the same time, discursive imagery of the Jew in the Romanian symbolic system. Thus, it is no longer the Jews' perceived character or physical appearance that is the object of anti-Semitism, but an abstraction, a representation, and an image; this, like other myths, is a matter of syncretism, mixing elements of the past—in the form of prejudice—with frustrations of the present postcommunist transformation. The irrational, mythical component of the anti-Semitic stereotype dominates this abstraction, and, in the context of an absence of the very Jewish entity, it can broadly be said that today a mythology has replaced a stereotype. Since in the anti-Semitic imagery the Jews' real, actual presence is no longer relevant or necessary, the object of the new form of anti-Semitism becomes the invisible, so-called "Jewish conspiracy." On a Romanian background of an overwhelming peasantist cultural past combined with urban milieus of "bourgeois" European culture—as explained in the previous chapters—the image of "the mythical Jew" is also promoted by more popular-peasantist forms of anti-Semitism persistent in religious tradition and folklore and urban-intellectual forms of an European anti-Semitic heritage. Moreover, this figment of imagination is inserted into daily, mundane speech, due to present, common fantasies in turn based on the destabilized realities and fragmented identities that characterize postcommunist Romanian society overall.

By being more discursively imagined than materially present—but not as a result more tolerant—"the mythical Jew" encapsulates various other representations. As expressed before, in postcommunism this discursive image functions on many levels: on a horizontally dispersed form of popular culture anti-Semitism and on a vertically assimilated, intellectual, and political anti-Semitism—although their boundaries are fluid. In the former, the popular imagination has traditionally retained some essentialist characteristics of the Jews, stereotypes with widespread European roots.[34] In his seminal study, *Imaginea evreului în cultura română* (The Image of the Jew in Romanian Culture), Andrei Oişteanu has gathered some of the most historically pervasive stereotypes that have animated—as a subject-reflected experience and a discourse—the Romanian popular imagery of the Jewish ethnic:[35] elements of "physiognomy and anthropology," from cleanness and "freckled" or "red people," to the "beautiful, elegant Jewess"[36]; professions such as "merchant" or "lender"[37]; "intellectual and moral profiles" such as "intelligence" but also "cunningness," or cowardliness[38]; "magic and mythical" features such as the "wandering Jew" or the "sorcerer Jew"[39]; and "deicide" and "ritual infanticide."[40]

Bordering popular culture, there is also a form of intellectual anti-Semitism—usually connected to a nationalist ethos and to more European traditional forms of anti-Semitism—that can become overtly political. Such a form is active and conscious, assimilating elements from the popular imagery. In most of these cases, the references regard not only such urban occupations of the Jews as businesspersons or bankers, industrialists, or intellectuals—and, in postcommunism, their ownership of many recently opened casinos and restaurants—but also an alleged international dimension of conspiracy coupled with their perceived *alienness*. Other times, as presented before, popular culture intersects with high culture and politics, the references then gesturing toward icons of Romanian culture such as the Criterion Generation of Romanian intellectuals, Marshall Ion Antonescu, and the fascist leader Corneliu Zelea Codreanu. These present topics bear uncomfortable correlations with legionarism, the Holocaust, and the nature of Romania's participation to WWII. And, although many Romanian intellectuals have expressed their intentions of discussing not only the "decommunization" but also the "defascization" of Romanian postcommunist society, there are also the accusations of a Jewish-induced communist regime— the "Judeo-Bolshevik" thesis, as discussed earlier—and the abstract, decontextualized, and dehistoricized claim of equivalence between the Holocaust and the communist Gulag, with the further circular accusation that, while victims of the Holocaust, the Jews were chief perpetrators of the Gulag.[41] In postcommunism, intellectual and political anti-Semitism, although not coming solely from the ultranationalist camp, has also targeted Jewish journalists, writers, ideologues, professors, and politicians, more often than not highlighting them as uncomfortable and alien voices linked to the communist past—voices that include Silviu Brucan, the late Chief-Rabbi, Dr. Moses Rosen, and politician Petre Roman. Other times, intellectuals of various political persuasions have employed not only *The Protocols of the Learned Elders of Zion*, but also Roger Garaudy's *Les mythes fondateurs de la politique israelienne* and Norman Finkelstein's controversial *The Holocaust Industry*[42] as a reference and a basis to discuss Jewish identity, anti-Semitism, the Holocaust, and the vexed relationship between interwar Romanian stellar intellectuals, Jewish identity, and Romanian fascism.[43] Finally, although not usually employing an anti-Semitic stance, hostility toward active ethnic and cultural politics, toward politicized democratic identities, and social movements within a vibrant civil society, comes as a defense of Romanian *authenticity* and *tradition* simultaneous with an attack on *multiculturalism*[44] and its main representative, the American society. In this context, multiculturalism is regarded as a theory of aggressive minorities, which reminds one of the discourses uttered today, in a context of tensed European integration and expansion, by French Jean-Marie Le Pen, Austrian Jorg Haider, Italian Umberto Bossi, the late Dutch Pim Fortuyn, and Denmark's Pia Kjaersgaard. In Romania, the attacks on multiculturalism come in spite of historical evidence that attests to the existence of many national minorities, and of practices of exclusion that include the Holocaust, and Roma and queer discrimination for example—practices that were selectively embedded in both governmental and social agency of precommunism, national-communism, and postcommunism. Such attacks on notions of inclusive democracy come not only from the ultranationalists, but also from liberal and conservative-libertarian quarters. As with many other postcommunist notions of Western descent, flawed accounts of multiculturalism have permeated Romanian discursive spaces, being published in nonpeer-reviewed volumes and journals, and usually presented in a derogatory way as an abstract, chimerical notion, and as an attack on classical European culture and identity. This contempt toward multiculturalism reminds one of Constantin Noica's conservative rejection of the 1960s and 1970s European social movements in particular and minority identity politics in general (as discussed in chapter 3), as well as his more general negation of Michel Foucault's work as a philosophy of *ressentiment*, and an obsession with "marginality."[45] However, volumes that approach the notion of multiculturalism in scholarly fashion and as an empowering politics—such as *Altera*,[46] published by *Liga Pro Europa*—do exist, yet their availability to the average Romanian reader, compared with the journalistic press, is unclear at the time this book is being written.

The problem is that, at certain times of political unrest, intellectual anti-Semitism re-enters the popular imagination through a feedback relationship. Yet, what is being changed is the new, consciously ideological, mobilizing character that accompanies this shift. And, although popular anti-Semitism is "latent" and intellectual anti-Semitism is already "militant,"[47] one concludes that, occasionally, the line between the two is blurred.

But what does the paradigm of "the mythical Jew" mean in the context of postcommunism, and how does it function concretely at the intersection between popular culture and politics? Symbolically speaking, various phenomena are worth noting. First, a discursive translation seems to be occurring within the structure of anti-Semitism as a semiotic *sign*, a translation of meaning from national to international context. Thus, once the physical presence of the national Jew is no longer a tangible fact, then the negative representation of the Jew is meshing with the perception of a post-1989 national and international threat and destabilization. What this equation creates then is a new form of popular anti-Semitism: "the mythical Jew," which, as expressed before, is considered the *epicenter of international conspiracy against the nation.* I must note that the nation, as the master-symbol, master-narrative, or myth in the Romanian symbolic order, is counterpoised to this new interpretation of the Jew who, from a mere ethno-religious, internal "other" becomes the equal of the nation but in its paramount international negative incarnation. The alleged "Jewish" or "Mason plot" with its derivative in an "international Jewish power" is a seduction in most former communist countries, which, in the absence of rational political cultures, are living in a fantasized reality—that of myth.

Another feature of the mythical Jew comes from the discursive clashing of meanings between the symbol of the mythical Jew and that of the gentile "other." According to Leon Volovici, the product is non-Jewish: the "crypto-Jew." That is, any incriminated "other" becomes in this form of hate speech a

Jew (other times a Hungarian or a "Gypsy").[48] Hence, today it is not that "every Jew is an enemy," but that "every enemy has become ipso facto a Jew."[49] Katherine Verdery noticed in the same vein that since "the other" as class enemy under communism has vanished after 1989, its meaning had to be quickly replaced in the process of building a new Romanian identity based on the binary opposition *us* versus *them*.[50] The easiest identification of otherness is the ethnic, which is where the concept of "the mythical Jew" plays a major role. Correlatively, one could argue that, in regards to the very word "kike" (*jidan*), this notion faces today some linguistic erosion in the daily speech, although it has not discarded its anti-Semitic foundation. The notion of the "crypto-Jew," as addressed above, might also explain those situations when a person, if perceived as unpleasant in any way, immediately becomes a "kike" (or, interchangeably, a "Gypsy," or a Hungarian). Other times, meanings begin to overlap in the construction of various hate speech representations. For instance, under the perception of a threat from the Hungarians or Roma, "the other" becomes the "Judeo-Hungarian" or "Judeo-Gypsy," apparently antagonizing the entire gamut of otherness from popular culture against the Romanian ethnic.

Furthermore, it is important to note that "the mythical Jew" has a particular location within a broader universe of a perceived "other." As explained in the beginning of this chapter, in some present Romanian popular, intellectual, and political derogatory discourses, "the other" is considered—ethno-religiously speaking—to be the Hungarian, the Roma, or the Jew, not to mention some ethico-cultural criteria producing other marginalized or plainly discriminated categories like women or queer. But, expressing significantly numerous entities and subject-formative experiences—compared with the present Jewish minority—Hungarian or Roma, gender or queer politics are not "mythical" political issues in postcommunism. Thus, the type of hyperbolic representations conveyed by "the mythical Jew" are not found in the cases of these other—non-Jewish—identities, for whom an activism responds to stringent, real problems claimed by their represented groups.

On a more fundamental level, I argue that the issue of "the mythical Jew" in postcommunist popular culture also reflects some levels of dissolution of this very representation. A good proof of this is "the mythical Jew" issue itself, since it represents the decomposition phase of a process of perceptual, physical, and juridical extermination of the Jews started long ago. The case with the Israeli investors in Romania after 1989 and also with the couple of thousand Romanians employed in the construction industry in Israel since 1993-1994 are possible indications of this dissolution phase. Although there were complaints in the Romanian press and televised talk shows over the working conditions of the Romanian workers in Israel, there was little, if any, anti-Semitism in conjunction with these issues. For example, a 1996 televised documentary on economic issues developed an investigative report as a result of one of its anchor's field trips to Israel. The documentary thus showed the Romanian public that the working and living conditions of the Romanian workers in Israel were not different from those of other foreign workers in that country, although not excellent. According to their public statements, many Romanian workers were satisfied with their salaries and Israeli employers. "The mythical Jew" simply could not work in these cases. This means that, if anti-Semitism is present today in Romanian popular culture in the discursive form of "the mythical Jew," it is a matter of an anti-Semitic representation grounded in past, diachronic discourses and in sheer fantasy. In other words, this one is not a form of anti-Semitism as a reflection of a correlated, synchronic Jewish entity. However, due to the international character expressed in the symbolism conveyed by "the mythical Jew" in postcommunism, and since Romania faces today issues related to European and transatlantic integration, anti-Semitism presently fluctuates among popular, intellectual, and political discourses.

Finally, to counterbalance the existing anti-Semitism—"the mythical Jew"—at least the one that discursively transpires from the press, the Federation of Jewish Communities from Romania and its President, Dr. Nicolae Cajal, have expressed the Federation's preoccupation with introducing the concept of "Real Semitism." This new concept seeks to explain the historically substantial contribution of the Jewish minority to the socioeconomic and cultural development of Romania. In this sense, some of the books published by the Federation's publishing house, Hasefer, and presenting the Jewish intellectual contribution to a common Jewish-Romanian history discuss such issues as Judaism as philosophy and religion (Henri Wald),[51] Romanian songs written by Jewish composers (Mişu Iancu),[52] the Jewish press from Bucharest in the late nineteenth and twentieth centuries (Harry Kuller),[53] Jewish-Romanian linguists and philologists (Lucia Wald),[54] Jewish-Romanian musicians (Iosif Sava),[55] Jewish customs (Victor Rusu),[56] and literature (Mihail Sebastian).[57]

As discourses, representations, and practices of identification, myths are fundamental structures grounding the political culture of national identity and statehood in Romania. Within this nation building framework, the real "Jewish question" once occupied an important place in the panoply of a perceived otherness from within. The proofs are at least such movements of modernity expressed in nationalist romanticism and radical-fascistic ethos of uncertain interwar times. Today, times in Romania are again uncertain. Within a general crisis of identity, once the constructed symbolic order of the communist ideology has collapsed, the predisposition toward "salvation myths"[58] constitutes the imaginary background through which reality is filtered. For example, in the November-December 2000 parliamentary and presidential elections, Corneliu Vadim Tudor, the ultranationalist (anti-Semitic, anti-Hungarian, anti-Roma, and anti-queer) leader of *Partidul România Mare* (Greater Romania Party), PRM, managed to gather couple of million votes or almost one-third of the Romanian electorate. In the current legislature, 2000-2004, PRM's parliamentary representation is at twenty-one percent.[59] And although anti-Semitism was considered marginal as a stimulant in electoral politics, the result of these elections suggests that there is a broader social capacity to absorb surrogate solutions based on ethnic hostility. If, in the early 1990s, James P. Niessen was asserting that "fervent nationalism appears, at the end of 1992, to have only limited popular appeal" in Romania,[60] this is not the case today, particularly in light of the 2000 elections. Although the percentage obtained by the PRM and its leader in the 2000 electoral results might point toward a strengthening of "mythical" anti-Semitism (as a form of conspiracy theory and scapegoatism), the situation is more complex, irreducible solely to Jewish or ethnic politics, and involving larger social, economic, and other political and international phenomena in the context of postcommunist transformation and admission to European and transatlantic multilateral institutions.

Ultimately, within present Romanian discourses, "the mythical Jew" constitutes today a disarticulated, volatile, and I would say anachronistic subject-reflected experience grounded in past representations, yet recirculated as a residue with new ramifications brought by transnational politics, and varying from popular culture, to intellectual, and political spaces—a situation that, comparatively speaking, by no means constitutes an exception in the region. Such a postcommunist representation expresses a popular, political, and cultural discourse that has to deal today with the change of entire precommunist and national-communist symbolic systems framed by disjunctive "limits of the *sayable*," and "final vocabularies" regarding acceptance of otherness.

Notes

1. My use of the notion anti-Semitism here follows its general, current use in the American discourse: "anti-Semitism." Nevertheless, I would like to mention that, according to the policy promoted by the Vidal Sassoon International Center for the Study of Antisemitism, at the Hebrew University of Jerusalem, the spelling of this notion should be "antisemitism." According to the Center, since there is no "Semitism" as an ideology, there is no "anti-semitism" as a counter-ideology, but only "antisemitism" as an ideology, which from the beginning referred to the ethno-religious antagonism toward Jews.

2. Mihail Sebastian. *Journal 1935-1944: The Fascist Years*, trans. Patrick Camiller, Introduction and notes Radu Ioanid (Chicago: Ivan R. Dee, 2000. Published in association with the United States Holocaust Memorial Museum), 452. Sebastian's *Journal* was first published in Romania in 1996, at the Humanitas Publishing House in Bucharest, with Professor Leon Volovici from the Vidal Sassoon International Center for the Study of Antisemitism signing the Preface and notes, and with Gabriela Omăt as text editor. Then, the volume was translated into French by Alan Paruit and was published in Paris in 1998 by Stock, with a preface by Edgar Reichmann. The fragment cited here and dated Wednesday, 17 December 1941, indicates Sebastian's internal struggle with his own identity under Romanian fascism and subsequent persecution of the Jews.

3. C. Banc and Alan Dundes, eds., *You Call This Living? A Collection of East European Political Jokes* (Athens: The University of Georgia Press, 1990), 67. As also explained by Dundes, "Yom Tov" means holiday in Hebrew. The references to the traditional Jewish holidays of "Purim," "Sukkot," and "Yom Kippur" indicate carnival, hut, and fast, respectively.

4. However, in postcommunism, the writer Dorel Dorian stands as the Jewish minority's MP in the Romanian Parliament.

5. According to the preliminary results of the 2002 census, today there are some 5,870 Jews, that is less than 0.1 percent of a total population of some 21.7 million, compared with 9,107 Jews (0.3 percent of a total population of some 23 million) in 1992. For the 2002 data, see *Recensământ 2002* [Census 2002], <http://www.recensamant.ro/> (17 July 2002); and for the 1992 data, see Irina Moroianu-Zlătescu and Ioan Oancea, *The Legislative and Institutional Framework for National Minorities from Romania* (Bucharest: The Romanian Government—The Council for Ethnic Minorities, 1994), 7-8. Before WWII, there were around 757,000 Jews living in Romania (i.e., 4.2 percent out of a total population of 18 million)—both Ashkenazi and Sephardic Jews. In 1941, there were only some 375,000 Jews left; and in 1942, 295,000. In 1945, the Jewish population gathered some 355,000 people (i.e., 2.1 percent out of a total population of 17 million). See Radu Ioanid, *The Holocaust in Romania: The Destruction of Jews and Gypsies under the Antonescu Regime, 1940-1944* (Chicago: Ivan R. Dee, 2000), xix, xxi.

6. For an analysis of institutional anti-Semitism (political parties and organizations) in postcommunism, see Michael Shafir, "The Mind of Romania's Radical Right," in Sabrina P. Ramet, ed., *The Radical Right in Central and Eastern Europe Since 1989* (University Park: The Pennsylvania State University, 1999), 213-32. On intellectual anti-Semitism in postcommunism, see Michael Shafir, "The Man They Love to Hate: Norman Manea's 'Snail House' between Holocaust and Gulag," *East European Jewish Affairs* 30, no. 1 (2000): 60-81; Denise Rosenthal, "The Mythical Jew: Anti-Semitism, Intellectuals, and Democracy in Post-Communist Romania," *Nationalities Papers* 29, no. 3 (2001): 419-439; and the London-based Institute for Jewish Policy Research Online Report, "Antisemitism and Xenophobia Today: Romania," <http://www.axt.orh.uk/antisem/countries/romania/index.html> (8 July 2002). For an analysis of anti-Semitism in general in the Romanian culture, see Leon Volovici, *Nationalist Ideology and Antisemitism: The Case of the Romanian Intellectuals in the 1930s*, trans. Charles Kormos (Oxford: Pergamon Press, 1991); Andrei Oişteanu, *Imaginea evreului în cultura română* [The Image of the Jew in Romanian Culture] (Bucharest: Humanitas, 2001); Radu Ioanid, *The Holocaust in Romania*; and Teşu Solomovici, *România Iudaica: O istorie neconvenţională a evreilor din România. 2000 ani de existenţă continuă* [Romania Judaica: An Unconventional History of the Jews from Romania. 2000 Years of Continuous Existence], vols. I and II (Bucharest: Teşu Publishing House, 2001).

7. On a similar topic, see Bernard Glassman, *Anti-Semitic Stereotypes without Jews: Images of The Jews in England, 1290-1700* (Detroit: Wayne State University Press, 1975).

8. Sandra Harding, "Feminism, Science, and the Anti-Enlightenment Critiques," in *Feminism/Postmodernism*, ed. Linda J. Nicholson (New York: Routledge, 1990), 83-106 and "Rethinking Standpoint Epistemology: What Is 'Strong Objectivity'?," in *Feminist Epistemologies*, ed. Linda Alcoff and Elizabeth Potter (New York: Routledge, 1993), 49-82; and Nancy C. M. Hartsock, "The Feminist Standpoint: Developing the Ground for a

Specifically Feminist Historical Materialism," in *Feminist Social Thought: A Reader*, ed. Diana T. Meyers (New York: Routledge, 1997), 461-83.

9. Paul Lendvai, *Anti-Semitism without Jews: Communist Eastern Europe* (Garden City: Doubleday, 1971), quoted in Michael Shafir, "Radical Politics in East-Central Europe. Part III: X-Raying Postcommunist 'Radical Minds'. Conspiracy Theories and Anti-Semitism," *East European Perspectives* 2, no. 1 (January 2000), <http://www.rferl.org/eepreport/2000/01/01-120100.html> (24 July 2002); and Michael Shafir, "Anti-Semitism without Jews in Romania," *Report on Eastern Europe* 2, no. 26 (1991): 20-32.

10. Leon Volovici, *Antisemitism in Post-Communist Eastern Europe: A Marginal or Central Issue? ACTA no. 5* (Jerusalem: The Vidal Sassoon International Center for the Study of Antisemitism—The Hebrew University of Jerusalem, 1994), 4, excerpts translated by Louis Ulrich as "Mit şi realitate" [Myth and Reality], *Sfera Politicii*, no. 32 (1995): 4-8.

11. Svetlana Boym, "From the Toilet to the Museum: Memory and Metamorphosis of Soviet Trash," in *Consuming Russia: Popular Culture, Sex, and Society Since Gorbachev*, ed. Adele M. Barker (Durham: Duke University Press, 1999), 384-385. On *the past* as a pervasive condition in postcommunism, see also Katherine Verdery, *The Political Lives of Dead Bodies: Reburial and Postsocialist Change* (New York: Columbia University Press, 1999).

12. Aurel Braun, "The Incomplete Revolutions: The Rise of Extremism in East-Central Europe and the Former Soviet Union," in *The Extreme Right: Freedom and Security at Risk*, ed. Aurel Braun and Stephen Scheinberg (Boulder: Westview Press, 1997), 150.

13. See also Lucian Boia, *Istorie şi mit în conştiinţa românească* [History and Myth in Romanian Consciousness] (Bucharest: Humanitas, 1997), 290.

14. Lucian Boia, "Iluzia 'Salvatorului'" [The Savior's Illusion], *Curentul*, 12 March 1999, <http://www.curentul.ro/curentul.php> (12 March 1999).

15. See also Catherine Durandin, "Cred că a fost supraevaluată capacitatea de ideal a Estului" [I Believe That We Have Overestimated the East's Capacity for Ideal], in *Fin de siècle: Un nou început* [Fin de siècle: A New Beginning], ed. Petre Răileanu (Bucharest: Atlas, 1999), 32-42.

16. Legionarism was the Romanian fascist ideology during interwar times and WWII. See Irina Livezeanu, *Cultural Politics in Greater Romania: Regionalism, Nation Building, and Ethnic Struggle, 1918-1930* (Ithaca: Cornell University Press, 1995); Ioanid, *The Holocaust in Romania*; and Volovici, *Nationalist Ideology and Antisemitism*.

17. For a detailed account of Romanian postcommunist extremist publications, see George Voicu, "Teme antisemite în discursul public. II" [Anti-Semite Themes in Public Discourse. II], *Sfera Politicii*, no. 81 (2000): 52-8.

18. For an analysis of anti-Semitism and hate speech on the Internet, see also Victor Eskenasy, "Antisemitic Rhetoric and Propaganda on the Web," *Der Fall Antonescu—Cazul Antonescu*, ed. William Totok, 9 January 2001, <http://home.t-online.de home/ totok/ ion2f.htm> (27 January 2001).

19. "International Third Position," <http://dspace.dial.pipex.com/third-position/in dex.html> (8 July 2002).

20. *Mişcarea legionară* [The Legionary Movement], <www.miscarea-legionara.com> (8 July 2002).

21. *db Jurnal. Revista Online a Mişcării Legionare din România*, <http://dbjurnal. hypermart.net> (8 July 2002).

22. *Noua Dreaptă*, <http://www.nouadreapta.org/> (8 July 2002).

23. *Pagina României Naţionaliste*, <http://pages.prodigy.net/nnita/> (8 July 2002) and currently connected to <www.miscarea-legionara.com>.

24. See Robert R. King, *A History of the Romanian Communist Party* (Stanford: Hoover Institution Press—Stanford University, 1980), 33-8, particularly the description of the relationship between the RCP and minorities.

25. On the postcommunist revaluation of Ion Antonescu, see Randolph L. Braham, *Romanian Nationalists and the Holocaust: The Political Exploitation of Unfounded Rescue Accounts* (New York: The Rosenthal Institute for Holocaust Studies—The City University of New York, 1998), 61-70; and Ioanid, *The Holocaust in Romania*, xxii.

26. For example, in early December 1997, the Museum of the Romanian Peasant dedicated an homage day to Corneliu Zelea Codreanu during a festivity that was intended to celebrate the 1950s' Romanian anticommunist resistance.

27. On the Holocaust representation in Romanian communist textbooks or historiography, see Alexandru Florian, "The Holocaust in Romanian Textbooks," *The Tragedy of Romanian Jewry*, ed. Randolph L. Braham (New York: The Rosenthal Institute for Holocaust Studies—The City University of New York, 1994), 237-85; and Volovici, "Antisemitism in Post-Communist Eastern Europe," 13.

28. On this debate, see Shafir, "The Man They Love to Hate." With regards to the governmental emergency ordinance no. 31/2002, see the open letter of protest addressed in the name of "freedom of speech" by one leader of the Romanian Legionary Movement, Şerban Suru, in April 2002, <http://www.miscarea-legionara.com/ protest.htm> (25 July 2002).

29. Regarding the spiritual and ethico-mystical affiliation of Mircea Eliade, Emil Cioran, and Constantin Noica to the legionary movement, see Volovici, *Nationalist Ideology and Antisemitism*, 134-37.

30. See also George Voicu, "Rechizitoriu cu tîlc" [Inquiry with a Twisted Meaning], *Sfera Politicii*, no. 32 (1995), 15-7.

31. Corneliu Vadim Tudor quoted in Voicu, "Rechizitoriu cu tîlc," 16. Emphasis in the original.

32. *Atac la persoană* quoted in the Institute for Jewish Policy Research, "Antisemitism and Xenophobia Today: Romania."

33. See also Radu Florian, *Criza unei lumi in schimbare* [The Crisis of a Changing World] (Bucharest: Editura Noua Alternativă, 1994), 118-29.

34. See, for example, Hannah Arendt, *Antisemitism. Part One of the Origins of Totalitarianism* (New York: Harcourt Brace & Company, 1958); and Frank Felsenstein, *Anti-Semitic Stereotypes: A Paradigm of Otherness in English Popular Culture, 1660-1830* (Baltimore: Johns Hopkins University Press, 1995).

35. See also Andrei Oişteanu, "'Evreul imaginar' versus 'evreul real'" [Imaginary Jew versus Real Jew], *Sfera Politicii*, no. 60 (1998): 34-40 and "'Imaginary Jew' Versus 'Real Jew' in Romanian Folklore and Mythology," in *Identitate/alteritate în spaţiul cultural românesc* [Identity/Alterity in the Romanian Cultural Space], ed. Al. Zub (Iaşi: Editura Universităţii "Alexandru Ioan Cuza," 1996), 266-92.

36. Oişteanu, *Imaginea evreului*, 60-106.

37. Oişteanu, *Imaginea evreului*, 127-63.

38. Oişteanu, *Imaginea evreului*, 201-35.

39. Oişteanu, *Imaginea evreului*, 272-315.

40. Oişteanu, *Imaginea evreului*, 336-93.

41. See Alexandra Laignel-Lavastine, "Fascisme et communisme en Roumanie: enjeux et usage d'une comparaison," in *Stalinisme et nazisme: Histoire et mémoire comparées*, ed. Henry Rousso (Bruxelles: Éditions Complexe, 1999), 201-54; George Voicu, "Un text din Le Monde şi replici la el. IV: Indecenţa comparativă" [A Text from *Le Monde* and Reactions to It. IV: The Comparative Indecency], *22*, no. 11 (2000), <http://www.dntb.ro/22/2000/11/7voicu.html> (30 March 2000); and William Totok, "Prolog, " in *Der Fall Antonescu—Cazul Antonescu*, ed. William Totok, 21 August 2000, <http://home.t-online.de/home/totok/ion2c.htm#PROLOG> (27 January 2001).

42. Norman G. Finkelstein, *The Holocaust Industry: Reflections on the Exploitation of Jewish Suffering* (New York: Verso, 2000).

43. On these controversial situations, see most recently George Voicu, "*Ravelstein*: Text şi Pretext" [*Ravelstein*: Text and Pretext], *22*, no. 42 (2001), <http://home.t-online.de/home/totok/ion2i.htm#Ravelstein> (31 July 2002).

44. On theories of multiculturalism in North American society, see Will Kymlicka, *Multicultural Citizenship* (Oxford: Clarendon Press, 1995) and the contributions of Charles Taylor, Jürgen Habermas, K. Anthony Appiah, Steven C. Rockefeller, Michael Walzer, Susan Wolf, and Amy Gutmann in *Multiculturalism*, ed. Amy Gutmann (Princeton: Princeton University Press, 1994). Finally, Canada is the first country to introduce multiculturalism as an official policy in 1971; in 1988, the *Canadian Multiculturalism Act* was passed. Also, the 1982 Canadian Charter of Rights and Freedoms, which is part of the Canadian Constitution, supports equality provisions—section 15 (1) and (2)—consistent with multiculturalism. Government of Canada, *Canadian Multiculturalism Act*, <http://lois.justice.gc.ca/en/C-18.7/29236.html> (25 July 2002).

45. Gabriel Liiceanu, *The Păltiniş Diary: A Paideic Model in Humanist Culture*, trans. James Christian Brown (Budapest: Central European University Press, 2000), 24, 62.

46. *Altera*, <http://www1.proeuropa.ro/ALTERA/altera.htm> (30 July 2002).

47. On "latent" and "militant" anti-Semitism, see also Leon Volovici, "Discussion: Notes on 'Latent Antisemitism,'" *Annual Report* (The Vidal Sassoon International Center for the Study of Antisemitism—The Hebrew University of Jerusalem) (1997): 16-8.

48. Volovici, "Antisemitism in Post-Communist Eastern Europe," 7-8 and "Mit şi realitate," 6.

49. Volovici, "Antisemitism in Post-Communist Eastern Europe," 8 and "Mit şi realitate," 6.

50. See Katherine Verdery, *What Was Socialism, and What Comes Next?* (Princeton: Princeton University Press, 1996).

51. Henri Wald, *Înţelesuri Iudaice* [Judaic Meanings] (Bucharest: Hasefer, 1995).

52. Mişu Iancu, ed., *Cântece, cântece, cântece ale unor compozitori evrei din România* [Songs, Songs, Songs of Some Jewish Composers from Romania] (Bucharest: Hasefer, 1996).

53. Harry Kuller, *Presa evreiască bucureşteană 1857-1994* [The Bucharestian Jewish Press 1857-1994] (Bucharest: Hasefer, 1996).

54. Lucia Wald, ed., *Lingviști și filologi evrei din România* [Jewish Linguists and Philologists from Romania] (Bucharest: Hasefer, 1996).

55. Iosif Sava, *Harpiștii Regelui David* [King David's Harpists] (Bucharest: Hasefer, 1998).

56. Victor Rusu, *Iţic şi lumea lui* [Iţic and His World] (Bucharest: Hasefer, 2000).

57. Mihail Sebastian, *De două mii de ani* [For Two Thousand Years] and *Cum am devenit huligan* [How I Became a Hooligan] (Bucharest: Hasefer, 2000).

58. See Vladimir Tismaneanu, *Fantasies of Salvation Democracy, Nationalism, and Myth in Post-Communist Europe* (Princeton: Princeton University Press, 1998).

59. See Michael Shafir, "Romanians Vote for the Past and for Extremists," *RFE/RL Newsline*, 27 November 2000, <http://www.rferl.org/newsline/2000/11/271100.asp> (28 Dec. 2000).

60. James P. Niessen, "Romanian Nationalism: An Ideology of Integration and Mobilization," in *Eastern European Nationalism in the Twentieth Century*, ed. Peter F. Sugar (Washington: The American University Press, 1995), 273-304.

PART THREE
GENDER AND SEXUALITY

Chapter Six

The Postcommunist Feminine Mystique[1]: *Women as Subjects, Women and Politics*

Years and years later, I will remember every detail of how beautiful she was at
that moment, a magician who created beauty out of nothing.
She ignored reality, the fact that there was no choice, fighting it with the old
beauty recipes that she had learned from her mother and grandmother.
After all, one could always make a peeling mask out of cornflour, use olive oil
for sun-tanning or as a dry hair treatment, or give a deep brown tone to the
hair with strong black tea.

— Slavenka Drakulić, *How We Survived Communism and Even Laughed*[2]

Romanian feminist philosopher Mihaela Miroiu has termed postcommunist
Romania a "society of survival"[3] where, like in other Eastern European
countries, present market and democratic changes indicate an uneven transformation.[4] According to the World Bank, this postcommunist transformation is
often marred by poverty and underdevelopment (mainly in rural areas).[5] After
1989, with the resurrection of precommunist, interwar, and nineteenth century
traditional cultural, political, and subjectification patterns, which are added to
the legacy of communism and contemporaneous Western influences, it seems

that women[6]—who, according to the 2002 Census preliminary results, represent 51.2 percent of the total population[7]—are relegated under postcommunist patriarchy to the status of what Miroiu calls "second-class citizens."[8]

When analyzing the general condition of Romanian women during the last twelve years of postcommunism, one notes that the identity construction of women operates in a complex of inferiority, corresponding to various levels of social, economic, and political marginalization. In terms of practices of (self-) identification, there exists what Miroiu calls a "minimalist citizen" mentality which, having a heritage relationship with communism, represents a consequence of entrenched disrespectful and cynical bureaucratic practices, and has an expression of a low self-esteem, distrust for institutions and the law, fear of public servants, and a tendency to suffer from "a persecution complex regarding hierarchical inferiority"; this prototype of citizen is unaware of the language of contractualist democracies—rights and liberties—and her or his only wish is to live invisibly.[9] This "second-class citizen" experience of subjectification is complexified by ethno-religious, age, gender, sexuality, or ableness cross-identifications—and to some of these the present chapter will make reference.

The communist legacy of the double, triple, or quadruple burden for women—public job, household, bearing children, and coping with simplistic technology at home—has already been brought up in the relevant literature on gender, communism, and postcommunism in Romania.[10] Another correlated condition came from the fact that, as proletarians and irrespective of their gender, all Romanian citizens attaining the suffrage age of eighteen had the legal obligation to work in the public sphere under the threat of indictment for "parasitism." Thus, devoid of its positive, assertive connotation symbolized by the right to choose between taking a public job or remaining in the private sphere as a housewife, during communism women's identity construction was, according to the official ideology, supposed to be molded on the blueprint of the proletarian worker, being thus reduced to the mandatory obligation to work in the public sphere. Although working patterns per se are not the topic of this book, I will note that, against this official model and at the level of everyday life, the situation was more complex. The notion of "fractality"—of work patterns in this case—introduced by Susan Gal and Gail Kligman[11] might provide a good start to understand the myriad of activities, public and private, that constructed, from the quotidian point of view, the revenues of the Romanian citizens, from the rural and urban milieus, from the official economy of shortages and the second economy during communism.

Since the fall of the communist regulatory state atheist ethic in 1989, a morality of a precommunist, religious nature has become very prominent in Romania, as it has in the rest of postcommunist Eastern Europe. Today, the rise of religion in general and fundamentalism in particular, coupled with a mixture of rural and urban values and a provocative "feminine mystique" of older, precommunist, "bourgeois," or more recent, Western, popular culture origins stressing beauty as a paramount goal—all with their particular subject-formative prescriptive ideals, including gender—make Romanian *adult women in general more conservative than men*; indeed, they reject feminism. Hence, the way Romanian women in postcommunism construct their selves based on gendered subjectivities is highly antifeminist. As is the case with other postcommunist countries, such a reaction can be briefly explained by the desire to reject the *communist freedom*, which, as explained, meant the duty to take a public job, extreme fatigue resulting from the double and triple burden, and often a sense of desperation regarding transformation and the post-1989 sociopolitical and economic turmoil. From this it follows that, as few as they are, Romanian feminists[12] hold dramatically different ideas about emancipation than their average compatriots. If, for feminists following the Western model, emancipation means autonomy and taking a public job—or, at least the right to choose between the private and public sphere—for many Romanian women, emancipation means dependency and the newly gained right to be a housewife, thus a return to the private sphere; yet, for those many more who do take a job in the public sphere, this move, as explained in this chapter, is not identified with a feminist empowering gesture, but a survival issue under the postcommunist feminization of poverty.

Competing Femininities

As noted before, in postcommunism the identity construction of woman is conditioned by the revival of traditional, precommunist patriarchal values—both rural peasantist and urban "bourgeois"—intertwined with communist symbolic gender constructions.[13] As well, though, more recent Western notions are increasingly having an impact on the formation of women's subjectivities and political identities.

With regards to the influence of the rural milieu on the formation of women as subjects, woman's subjectivity comes to be symbolized by the Romanian peasant woman.[14] And, until now, the literature in the field has identified the Romanian peasant woman as submissive, dedicated to her household, reserved, and brought up in a culture of self-sacrifice to her man, family, and, occasionally, to her country;[15] the peasantist, semi-feudal symbol of the Virgin Mary is considered to epitomize this identification.[16] Nevertheless, as the anthropologist Andrei Simić explains, common for the Balkan basin of civilization is also the notion of private "cryptomatriarchy," which stands as a parallel to public patriarchy.[17] Simić notes that, in terms of family patterns in which generational (as opposed to nuclear) extended family kinship dominates, older women in the Balkan rural area are by tradition extremely powerful in the private sphere, and they also gain positions of public authority in the public sphere of expressly patriarchal societies through their sons. As Simić says, this conflict between patriarchy in the public sphere and "cryptomatriarchy" in the private sphere is resolved by segregation of public versus private activities[18]—a condition which Gal and Kligman would call "fractality." Finally, as Simić also concludes, this cryptomatriarchy, this mother-cult, is in a fact a tradition with deeper roots in the Balkan (and ancient Mediterranean) cult of, as expressed before, "martyred and self-sacrificing mothers"[19] or goddesses of fertility-based matriarchies. In this sense—although such an analysis transcends the scope of this book—the differentiated, comparative use of the notion "cryptomatriarchy" for the Romanian case could possibly serve future studies in their endeavor to deepen their understanding—beyond simplistic yet readily available notions that relegate peasant women to submissiveness—of the way gender conditions the relationship between public and private spheres in the rural and rural-urbanized areas, as well as of the way gender is conditioned by these spheres' interaction and shifting boundaries.

Under communism, women's identity construction in general followed the Bolshevik woman-proletarian model, apparently an embodiment of nonsexuality and nonfemininity, usually identified in Romania with Ana Pauker (one of the first communist women-leaders and a symbol of austerity, she was purged by subsequent national-communist elites in conjunction with her Jewish origins),[20] Suzana Gîdea (deputy secretary for culture and education under Ceauşescu), and Elena Ceauşescu (Ceauşescu's wife, number two—often one—in the communist hierarchy of power). The idea of self-sacrifice for the party and the regime, although different from the peasantist model, was an enduring feature of identification under communism, dissolving the person with her individuality and body. Proletarian self-sacrifice meant a "supererogatory" practice of identification, defined as acts going beyond the bounds of duty, saintly and heroic acts, in this case of the New Socialist Being.[21] However, in line with the discussion of the New Socialist Being introduced in chapter 2 by Catriona Kelly, Hilary Pilkington, David Shepherd, and Vadim Volkov,[22] and following the context of subjectification (of youth, women, queer, and aesthetic subjects) provided in this book, I wish to express doubts that such a fictitious supererogatory being was actually exacted in practice, let alone internalized as a behavioral code or subjectivity, by the average Romanian citizen—at least the one who, of interest for this book, inhabited urban Romania, mainly Bucharest, in the 1980s. Comparatively, Andrei Simić reaches similar conclusions when asserting that:

> the generally particularistic and personalistic nature of Balkan culture did not significantly diminish under the impact of Marxism, economic development, and modernization. Thus, the system of intense reciprocal ties linking family members and kin (and, by extension of the same principle, fictive kin and close friends) continues to provide the individual in today's Yugoslavia with what is probably his or her most vital resource in the struggle for success or simple survival."[23]

As expressed before, individuals under Romanian communism had developed various practices of survival—even if unconscious—such as subversion, manipulation, and dissimulation, thus an empowering concept of *resistance-duplicity*. The average citizen had indeed generated a notion of everyday life unfolding in opposition to imposed identitary models that were not only loosened, displaced, or circumvented through a semiconscious reflex of survival but were not even taken seriously by such people more pragmatically interested in the practicality (not even politics) of the quotidian existence and its trivial life details. This may be the victorious sense that transpires from Slavenka Drakulić's paradigm—often used in this book—"how we survived communism and even laughed."[24]

Finally, besides such models of (un)femininity as the peasantist "Virgin Mary" and communist "Bolshevik proletarian woman," the urban milieu had also managed to preserve some elusive, yet always present private spaces of precommunist "bourgeois" subject-formative practices of femininity. Under communism, some women, mainly women-intellectuals (teachers, professors, doctors, lawyers, economists, and engineers), women-artists, and teenager girls in the urban milieu were well acquainted with what was otherwise considered "bourgeois" femininity. This refers to a European-based rule of the chic, which, while following a Parisian lifestyle, has had a long tradition in precommunist urban Romania—as attested for example by Countess Waldeck's depictions of interwar social life in Bucharest.[25] A separate, more comprehensive study of such precommunist lifestyles would be a real gain for the knowledge of urban Romania's social history; nevertheless, I can recall here how the Bucharestians of the late nineteenth and early twentieth centuries enjoyed a tumultuous coffeehouse bohemian subculture, which mingled the middle and upper bourgeoisies, aristocracy, dandies, artists, bankrupts, foreigners, politicians, radicals, and high-class prostitutes, and which included Western-based (mainly Parisian) fashion, behaviors, literary, and even infatuation styles. This subculture was epitomized by the *Capşa* restaurant, hotel, and cafeteria.[26] Bucharest also knew the aristocratic salon culture, with the two most reputable Bucharestian salons led by two women, Mrs. Oteleşanu and Princess Irina Grigore Şuţu.[27] Also, there existed the rules of the *"Chic Bucarestois,"* the code of manners of the Bucharestian dandy, which followed Western fashion and *"savoir vivre,"*[28] and which become so lively for example in the descriptions of Mihail Sebastian's *Journal*.[29] This heritage of a "bourgeois" subculture that had survived in very inconspicuous yet undeterred private spaces under communism had influenced its subsequent generations—all of which had at least a parent or grandparent who had witnessed the times of the interwar *"gens du monde."*[30] To this situation one can also add, as was explained in chapter 4, the continuous leaking of Western popular culture into Romania's urban milieus. Thus, in the case of a construction of femininity as subjectivity under communism and at the intersection of public and private spheres, one notices that these precommunist "bourgeois" and Western popular culture influences conveyed not only dressing codes that followed Western fashion of yore and of present—from high heels, a modern hairdo, and elaborate dresses, including miniskirts for teenager girls, or lace gloves for older women—but also practices that are usually associated with behaviors in more affluent societies, such as dieting or skin and body care. In the 1980s, the student girls from the Bucharest high schools "Ion Creangă," "Gheorghe Şincai," "Dimitrie Cantemir," "Nicolae Bălcescu," or "Gheorghe Lazăr" were heavily dieting, and slimming was one of the main topics of private discussions for such adolescents who were discovering Western fashion, rock 'n' roll, and their bodies. My discussion with various alumni of such high schools has revealed that, as adolescents under communism, and while seeking to gain ideas and images about their female body and sexual desirability, some of them had even experienced *anorexia nervosa* and *bulimia*, eating disorders that are usually associated with youth behaviors in Western societies.[31] Their feminine ideal was—as it still is today across Europe in counter-distinction with the North American, post-Second Wave feminist model of "fitness" femininity—the extremely slim French type commonly referred to by these categories of urban Romanians as the *"midinette."* Also, in communist Bucharest, in other big cities, and along the seaside resorts, cosmetic, body, and hair care were quite well developed under the networks *"Igiena"* (Hygiene). One such example was the Bucharest skin and body care center *"Iris,"* which performed skin care, body massage, sauna, and body wax-shaving.[32] As explained, this too was a means to semiconsciously construct counter-subjectivities based on alternative identitary models and on a politics of everyday life resistance—true, for those urbanites who could afford these services. But what is crucial here is that such services existed, and this conveys a notion of diverse lifestyles that, despite the scarcity within the regime, did exist under Romanian communism. Through its dispersal, such a politics of the quotidian would resist its encapsulation into state ideological discourses and would thus valorize multiple synchronic (Western) and diachronic ("bourgeois") experiences creative of subjectivities, which did exist under communism, itself a matter of discursive syncretism.

As explained in the previous chapters, in postcommunism new Western fashions and behaviors integral in popular culture influence the construction of femininity for women and youth, at whose intersection as subjectivities *young girls* are of interest here due to their revalorization of the body. In terms of the (re)appropriation of one's own body—in terms of pop culture body practices— one notices not only the colorful makeup, hairdos, or tight dressing, but also the new drug subculture that shatters the urban youth communities today, the new youth tattooing fashion—which was previously associated only with prostitutes, sailors, and the underworld[33]—and even body piercing (ear and eyebrow are most common).[34] Youth's reappropriation of the body is a sign of sexual liberalization and at least an intention of a personal politics based on popular culture, the practices of everyday life, and, as Joan Jacobs Brumberg calls it, the body as a "message board."[35]

The Feminization of the Postcommunist Transformation

In terms of work practices, the construction of women's identity in postcommunist Romania generally rests on rural (mainly agricultural) or urban (industrial, entrepreneurial, or professional) gendered labor practices—many times underpaid and occasionally based on flexible, part-time routines.

With the collapse of communism and an International Monetary Fund (IMF)-led transformation in a world of globalization, Romania was not spared the intensification of the feminization of poverty. Unemployment is the main vulnerability experienced by Romanian women under democratization and marketization.[36] Women are working mainly in underpaid areas (education, trade, health, and social assistance) while the number of women-led single parent families, particularly poor ones, is growing. Nevertheless, Romania has recently been shown to have the highest Eastern European rate of self-employment: In 1997, 45 percent women and 35 percent men were self-employed in Romania, statistics followed only by Poland with 27 percent women.[37] For the Romanian case one explanation is the importance of the family farm, a sector reemerging in postcommunism. At the same time, Romania is also experiencing the feminization of agriculture: In 1997, 90 percent of Romanian women were self-employed in agriculture.[38] This means that women's self-employment tends to get lost in the income of a reemerging "semifeudal," "patriarchal family unit" as "the rural economic unit in the newly marketized societies."[39] Nevertheless, women entrepreneurs dominate the new private business sector, mainly small business.[40] One explanation for this situation is the feminization of low productivity sectors, while, as elsewhere in the postcommunist perimeter, the *apparatchiks* (first and second echelons of former communists) dominate big business. Another explanation could be that women have come out of the double and triple burden already prepared for the vicissitudes and instability of a novel lifestyle based on a market economy that, in some ways, requires efforts that seem to be contiguous with their previous volatile living under communism; thus, they feel eager and ready to take initiative. Finally, one cannot forget that the current generations of adults are highly educated and skilled,[41] which is also an important factor enabling their accommodation, even if gender-differentiated, to the personal and professional requirements of the postcommunist transformation.

Also, Romania has the highest rate of part-time jobs (18 percent),[42] and the causes must be sought in the new labor market structure imposed by the economic transformation and the fact that this increasing flexibility of work seems to better suit disempowered women living in the liminal, "fractal" space of the private/public threshold.[43]

With regards to the gender pay ratio during the last decade of postcommunism, the trend toward an increasing gender wage gap is already visible. This can be explained in terms of gendering occupational patterns, education, types of employment (full or part time), and job structure by age groups. Nevertheless, the gender wage gap is not unusual for Eastern Europe. For example, Romanian women's monthly wages were 78.6 percent of those of men in 1994, decreasing to 76.2 percent in 1997. Comparatively, Azerbaijan has the lowest rate, 52.6 percent (1995), while in East-Central Europe, in countries such as the Czech Republic, Slovakia, Poland, and Hungary, women are catching up with men's wages.[44]

On a different plane, the way women in postcommunist Romania relate to their health and issues of family planning expresses a dramatic situation and an important feature of identification through absence and neglect.

The share of sexually active Romanian women who generally use traditional contraception and are in need of better or modern contraceptives is highly uneven (20 percent in the 15-24 age group, 57 percent in the 25-34 age group, and 45 percent in the 35-44 age group).[45] Generally, urban, educated, wealthier women tend to use modern contraceptives more than uneducated, rural or suburban, often poor women. Still, the use of traditional methods of contraception represents the main trend, although women in postcommunist Romania show a preference for abortion, which is cheap, as a mode of contraception. This preference for abortion must be understood—as explained by Gail Kligman[46]—as a consequence of Ceaușescu's pro-natalist, antiabortion politics, which, for some twenty-four years of communism (starting with 1966, when abortion was generally banned), had succeeded to limit women's freedom of choice and the individual's ability to sexually control her own body and life, thus pushing her toward subversive practices of body resistance through illicit abortions or more traditional contraceptive techniques. This is why, differently from other postcommunist countries, Romanian women perceive their newly recovered right to abortion—legalized immediately after the 1989 revolution and for which they had to pay with mutilations and deaths caused by illegal and archaic abortion techniques—as a sign of liberation, making the activity of any pro-life groups futile.[47] In 1997, there were 150 legal abortions per 100 live births (compared with only 50 legal abortions per 100 live births in 1989), which placed Romania in the fourth place after Russia, Belarus, and Estonia.[48] In conjunction with the unsafe illicit abortions practiced under communism, in 1989 Romanian women suffered the highest maternal mortality rate in Eastern Europe (169 per 100,000 live births), which, by 1997, had considerably decreased to 40—not unusual for the region, but still above the East Central European average.[49] Without education about female-related sexual diseases or AIDS, and with a lack of clinics and a technology comprehensive enough to address such problems, Romanian women's health is at high risk: For example, they have the highest incidence of uterus cancer in Europe.[50]

Generally, awareness about sexual health, family planning, and sexuality rises with educational and professional status as well as location within urban boundaries. This can be explained by the predominantly traditional-conservative knowledge about reproductive practices that still dominates rural areas—including, for example, the idea that contraceptives encourage infidelity—while the city holds a progressive role as promoter of Western ideas about sexual politics. The British network of birth control clinics *Marie Stopes*—founded in Bucharest in the early 1990s and extending its activity in other major Romanian cities—represents such an empowering example.

Finally, sexuality in general is still considered as *libertinage*, or an inimical Western sophistication. The rule of thumb is that both marriage and sexuality obey the cult of motherhood, which is perceived as a duty, while marriage is seen as a contractual basis for procreation. Nevertheless, this does not discard other more sophisticated lifestyles and sexual practices that, as the next chapter on queer subjectivity will show, have always existed at various levels and in various milieus in Romania.

Changing perspectives, violence—be it physical, verbal, sexual harassment, or human trafficking—is an important yet disturbing feature of postcommunist identity construction of Romanian women. After 1989, domestic violence increased in Romania, and by 1993, 29 percent of women treated by the Forensic Hospital in Bucharest were victims of domestic violence.[51] According to the average news in the Romanian mass media, conjugal rape, beating, and incest are widespread, especially as the Romanian legislation does not regulate private life. Outside the family, violence against women is mainly manifest in the form of rape. In this case, the burden of proof is a humiliating task for women and it is the reason why many of them do not report it, especially if they are unmarried, divorced, or if the rapist is a colleague or friend.[52]

A new form of violence against women is the trafficking of women for the purpose of sexual exploitation, either explicit or under the cover of promised jobs such as waitressing, working as a domestic, or as a dancer. Prostitution is thus booming and not only within national borders, as Romanian women are increasingly present on the streets of Western Europe. Eastern European women and girls are also sent to the Middle and Far East, and to the United States, in many cases replacing Asian and Latin American women. The evidence shows that they are young and relatively well educated.[53] Romanian girls can be found mainly in Turkey, Greece, and Italy.

Sexual harassment—which is only recently being considered by Romanian legislation—is another prevalent form of violence, especially in employment situations, when the woman is expected to perform sexual favors, and sometimes even in the context of passing an exam in the academy.[54] Finally, there is no legislation against public verbal aggression against women as women. This is part of a suburban culture's promiscuous jargon whereby women are commonly addressed, for example, as their sexual organ, a disrespectful form of communication frequently encountered in postcommunism and its newly gained feeling of verbal "freedom" coupled with machismo.

The present agenda of most of the Romanian political parties relegates women's problematic together with disabled, children, and elderly people's issues[55]—regarding them as socially incapable, second-class citizens. As politicians, men draw on an utterly sexist rhetoric, while the mass media's approach to violence against women is tragicomic, with women being regarded exclusively as sex objects. It would not be wrong to say that the sexist narratives stemming out from the intellectual house of contemporary Romania makes it easily recognizable as a phallocratic establishment, one that crosses ethnic boundaries, and which is not unique in the Eastern European context.

With the fall of communist quotas for women's participation in political positions—quotas which, I would argue, were highly hypocritical in the national-communist patriarchy, since women were still expected to be obedient and submissive, continuing to exert power only through men—we are faced today with a very low participation of women in political or decision-making bodies. After the 1996 presidential, parliamentary and local elections, there was only one woman presidential counselor, Zoe Petre, no Romanian women in ministerial positions (compared with 15 percent in Slovakia, 8.3 percent in Poland, and 5.6 percent in Hungary), and only 4.1 percent at the sub-ministerial level (compared with 16.2 percent in Bulgaria and 14 percent in Albania).[56] Only 6 percent of Romanian women were successful in parliamentary elections and 7 percent in local councils. There were no women prefects and only 2.7 percent were mayors, although women represent the main office holders in local authorities—70 percent—since in local elections individuals rather than parties are voted.[57]

On the other hand, in 1997, there were 28 percent women in legislative, senior official, and managerial posts, behind other Eastern European countries, but in a better position than some Western European countries (Germany, 27 percent; Denmark, 23 percent; and Italy, 18 percent).[58] This Romanian contrast is worthy of further comment, since, on the one hand, after 1989, Eastern European women experienced a worsening of their socioeconomic and political conditions, while, on the other hand, they continue to be more influential than their Western European counterparts at some particular levels of decision making. Again, the explanations in this case may vary from contiguity of work structure with the communist institutional framework, to women's—at least those who have accepted the rules of the new market economy—post-double/triple burden positive attitude toward initiative and decision making. After the November 2000 parliamentary elections, there are thirty-seven women in *Camera Deputaților* (the Deputies Chamber, which is the Lower House)— that is, 10.7 percent—and eight women in the Senate—that is, 5.7 percent.[59]

Another sign of political marginalization is that, for the decade 1990-2000 there were no women in decision-making positions at the Legislative Council, The Constitutional Court, the Court of Accounts, the Council of Concurrence, the Service of External Information, the Romanian Service of Information, or the Service of Special Telecommunications.[60]

From a different point view, as is the case with the rest of Eastern Europe, the approach of some of the most vocal intellectuals and the position of the mass media regarding gender issues unveils the bleak background against which feminism must develop in postcommunism.[61]

The common discourse presents women only within the gender politics of patriarchy. Thus, educated women are generally referred to as "our ladies," "the beautiful sex," "the eternal feminine," "the woman as myth."[62] These stereotypes are linked to romantic love, a form of conservatism, whereby the woman is an unreachable icon, not an active person. Others, the nationalist conservatives, generally conceive woman as the Mother Nation, hence her traditional role is breeding children, the future of the Nation.[63] Paradoxically, individual peasant women are represented as backward and premodern, usually stupid and inferior, although as the backbone of the Nation (for the nationalists) or, in an elitist way, idealized like the Romanian pristine fairy, *Ileana Cosînzeana*[64] (for the romantics). Newspapers deal with women's emancipation by advertising striptease clubs where the clients are women, while, in adjacent news items on the same page, abortion is approached almost cynically, mainly because many journalists are men. Rape is always sensational news and is depicted in detail, designed to stir laughter and not compassion—as is the rule in the pages of the info-scandal newspaper, *Evenimentul Zilei.*

Generally, when newspapers portray women's profiles, it is usually in the context of domesticity, not as directing a business or having political power. Strong women are generally demonized[65]; they are often associated with a transgressive gender symbol, androgyny. No wonder that they all declare not to be feminists, speaking as persons, not women. Indeed, to be a feminist is considered even by such strong women as either shameful and subversive in an immoral way, or as a residue of communist politics. In general, women are expected to speak tentatively, not assertively, otherwise they would be considered too opinionated and impolite; their utterance should be reserved, indirect, less personal, and emotionless, otherwise they would be accused of unfemininity and hysteria. This discursive discrimination is what Feminist Theory has traditionally criticized as the patriarchal imaginary whereby women are considered as the domain of subjectivity, of feelings, and aesthetics, while men are attributed to the realm of objectivity, reason, and science. As Alison M. Jaggar says, women are usually associated with "interdependence, community, connection, sharing, emotion, body trust, absence of hierarchy, nature, immanence, process, joy, peace and life" while men are seen as masters of "independence, autonomy, intellect, will, wariness, hierarchy, domination, culture, transcendence, product, asceticism, war and death."[66] Finally, women criticizing or plainly protesting against the status quo, at a personal or public level, are not only considered mediocre by not focusing on *the real issues*, but they are also individualized outside their gender, an *it*-enemy who—as Norma Alarcón has expressed it in the literature on gender and nationalism with regards to the symbolic construction of women as reproducers of both people and culture—have now betrayed the community, the nation, and the country.[67] Woman's intention of "self-invention" as a new, empowered subject in her own right, speaking independently of her community, tactics expressed through singular, or more or less organized protests and new women-oriented strategies, is seen by such communities as an "inappropriate" gesture to the woman's culture, while change itself is seen as a danger to an alleged community "authenticity."[68]

For many *true* Romanian liberals, feminism is "definitive barbarism," "a rage against the great moments of culture, from Plato to Kant," "a new eugenics," "the intellectual castration of men," and "blind revisionism."[69]

Locating the Postcommunist Romanian Feminist Movement

In spite of this context that brings evidence to the fact that "the political unconscious is gendered,"[70] there is an incipient feminist movement unevenly located at different levels: educational, NGOs and interest group politics, electoral, and bureaucratic/statist.

At the academic level, feminist or gender studies programs have mushroomed since 1993 at the Bucharest University, and since 1996 at both the *Cluj* and *Iaşi* universities. Most important, the Faculty of Political Science at the National School for Political and Administrative Studies, in Bucharest, offers a one-year Master's of Arts in Gender Studies. In addition, scholarly volumes on various gender topics have started to appear within the Romanian postcommunist intellectual interstices.[71] However, it is unclear how pervasive academic feminism is today and if, no matter how empowering its intentions, it is not currently reduced to some form of sectarianism.

At the level of NGOs, the situation is complex. Although in reality their organizational and operational engagement can vary, I consider that the present Romanian NGOs connected to a fluid notion of feminism can be classified into three organizational forms, which does not preclude their intersection or the dynamic character of their nature: *feminist organizations, women's organizations,* and *women-friendly organizations. Feminist organizations,* such as the Bucharest-based *AnA: Societatea pentru Analize Feministe* (AnA: Society for Feminist Analyses), and academic feminists in general, base their activism on an assimilated form of feminist consciousness. Usually they are in close contact with Western scholars, conferences, and publications. *Women's organization,* such as some women or youth organizations within political parties or trade unions, generally support the party or the trade union politics—themselves male dominated—being motivated by a low feminist consciousness if any at all, since feminism tends to be rejected as a "communist residue." These organizations tend to be conservative and do not pursue feminist goals, which might arise only incidentally within the party or trade union. This, in fact, represents a discourse and practice remnant of the old Marxizant *proletarian equality* formula, which has notoriously made gender subjectivity secondary to the working class's position as *the essential* subject in history, while regarding feminism per se as *bour-*

geois. In the West, feminism has long ago expressed its dissatisfaction with the gender blindness pervasive throughout Marxist thought, whereby women's oppression or discrimination is considered substantially less important than or even nonexistent compared with class exploitation. This gender blindness has led feminists such as Heidi Hartmann to the conclusion that: "[Marxist] categories give no clues about why *women* are subordinate to *men* inside and outside the family and why it is not the other way around. *Marxist categories, like capital itself, are sex-blind*."[72]

Finally, there are *women-friendly organizations*, which, although not rejecting feminism, pursue other interests and approach women's issues only secondarily. This is typical of human rights organizations and Western private philanthropic associations in Romania. Nevertheless, new NGOs continue to appear in grassroots movements, and Romanian women's interests are now included in some fifty NGOs. Such NGOs concentrate on issues such as "women's equality, health care, education, professional groups," Christian moral education, and social assistance; comparatively, Romania is better than Georgia with 43, but behind Russia with 600, Estonia with 160, and Ukraine with 70.[73] The two leading feminist NGOs in Romanian civil society, both openly assuming their feminist stance, are, as mentioned above, *AnA: Societatea pentru Analize Feministe*, which cooperates with such international programs as the European Communities' 1989 "*Pologne/Hongrie: Assistance à la Restructuration Economique*" (PHARE)—today addressing other ten Eastern European countries, including Romania—and the United Nations Development Programme (UNDP), and *Gender: Centrul de studii ale identității feminine* (Gender: Center for the Study of Feminine Identity). They all act in conjunction with other women's organizations such as *Asociația Fetelor Ghizi* (The Association of Women Touristic Guides), *Ariadna: Asociația Jurnalistelor* (Ariadna: The Association of Women Journalists), or various NGOs focused on human rights.[74] However, there are few if any such associations in the rural area, which brings one to the conclusion that feminism in Romania tends to be more of an urban phenomenon.

Electoral feminism has not proven to be an efficient strategy yet. In 1995 and in light of the 1996 parliamentary elections, a number of feminist NGOs organized a platform for equal democracy, also assembling *women's organizations* from various political parties. Nonetheless, the 1996 election results were quite opposite to the original feminist initiative, with women being generally marginalized. Analyzing this failure, it became obvious that there was a lack of a common feminist agenda, of associational experience, of solidarity and feminist consciousness, and of a common language that should empower women's politics, along the ideas that feminism as a label must be avoided as compromising and that gender policies should be redirected toward social assistance, not toward consciousness raising and emancipation.[75]

As a matter of bureaucratic/statist feminist strategy, like other Eastern European countries, Romania has a governmental section for equal opportunities, "The Department for the Advancement of Women and Family Policies" (DAWFP), created in 1995 within the Ministry of Labor and Social Protection.[76] There is also "the Department for Child, Woman and Family Protection" within the institution of the Ombudsman, and "the Sub-Commission for Equal Opportunities" within the Parliamentary Commission for European Integration—both founded in 1997. In 1998, DAWFP drafted "the Women and Men Equal Opportunities Bill" and "the Law on Parental Leave" (adopted in 1998). In 1997, DAWFP also created a "Pilot Center for the Assistance and Protection of Women-Victims of Domestic Violence," generally favoring cooperation with human rights NGOs rather than with feminist organizations.[77] As prostitution has become a chronic social phenomenon with international ramifications, lobbying for the human rights protection of sex workers, "the Sub-Commission for Equal Opportunities" drafted a bill of law on "the Statutory Recognition of Prostitution" in 1998 (since then still subject to parliamentary debates).[78] Finally, in August 2000, the government also adopted the law no. 137 against any forms of discrimination, including sex and sexual orientation, thus instituting the liberal feminist principle of equality.[79]

Gender, Women, and Difference

In present Romania, gender issues and feminism have a negative popular and political perception. This situation is correlated with the overwhelming use of conspiratorial scenarios, the prevalence of personal opinion over information, of political journalism, and of more recently mythified voices over scholarly studies, and which, as a substitute for professional, scientific, and critical arguments in political debates, dominate the discursive stage. In this sense, faced with unexpected or too sophisticated situations that involve critical thinking and protest, many political actors use conspiracy theories (e.g., the terrorists in the Romanian revolution, the Jewish international plot, the West against Romania, even an attack on Romanian culture) as a pseudo-reasoning method. Accordingly, feminism is largely perceived as a Western importation designed to destabilize the traditional Romanian social *cosmic* order and national ethos, a conspiracy directed to *abolish men* and their socioeconomic and political power, and to make homosexuality and lesbianism mandatory. Thus, as a criterion of identification, gender remains entrapped in a wider problematic of denied difference that in the West has been analytically linked with various politics of pan-subjectivities. In the Eastern European case, the most analyzed one until now has been the intersection between two subjectivities: gender and ethnicity (under the rubric gender and nation/nationalism).[80] But, as I am suggesting, there are many other grids of identification, many other subjectivities and differences that are weaving into the identity construction of an individual recognized as subject, as citizen. Hence, in present-day Romania some aspects of difference—ethnic, religious, gender, sexual—are bitterly rejected within wider processes of *authentic* identification expressing contempt toward those perceived as inferior or alien. Due to their dissimilitude in the Romanian postcommunist context, Roma, Hungarians, Jews, women, queer, the poor, disabled, the aged, recent immigrants or refugees from Asian and African countries (such as Somalia and Bangladesh), and the preoccupation with an environment, where problems range from air pollution to cyanide spills into transnational rivers, are generally regarded as inferior, alien, or, in a word, as "the other."[81]

There are many Western constructions and deconstructions of contemporary progressive public policies directed against multiple discrimination. Some theories, recognizing that there are intersecting cognitive orders, where common values cut across traditionally organized identities, include: Chantal Mouffe's "coalition politics" as "the partial fixation of identities through the creation of nodal points" within a "radical and plural democracy"[82]; Nancy Fraser's "multiple intersecting differences," as "cross-cutting axes of difference and subordination"[83]; Nira Yuval-Davies's "transversal politics" as a dialogical alliance politics both "'rooting' and 'shifting'" identities;[84] or Rosi Braidotti's "nomadic subjects," as "the simultaneous occurrence of . . . axes of differentiation such as class, race, ethnicity, gender, age, and others."[85] These radical democratic forms of empowerment may deconstruct previously antiracist, democratizing, but elitist, identity politics of "multiculturalism," which—as Yuval-Davies justly points out—tends to dialogue only with community leaders (usually male), "ignoring questions of power relations" and representation within communities, themselves inner universes of epistemological diversity.[86]

Like feminism, the politics of pan-subjectivities is also considered either alien or unsuitable for Romania, a "Western importation." Also, from a tactical viewpoint, the idea of coalition politics, or the politics of pan-subjectivities, is absent within the general machismo and highly personalized politics governing both state politics and community leadership. I would argue that Romanian society and politics still perceive the activism of minority subjectivities (such as national minorities, women, queer, and environmentalists) as subversive and incompatible with paramount national, ethno-religious concerns.

Related to this plural subordination, two interesting notes complete the intersection of gender with the alterity of other subjectivities in Romania. No matter how marginal a national (e.g., Hungarian, Roma, or Jewish) or cultural (e.g., sexual preference) minority, women's claims as relations of power still remain peripheral within that very minority, mainly because the leadership is generally male and it customarily develops a traditional or multicultural politics devoid of a relational gender problematic. This has already been argued in relation to the experience of African-American feminism that came in conflict not only with racism but also with the heterosexism embedded in the activism of the civil rights movement, among others creating the pro-coalition politics paradigm, which Patricia Hill Collins calls "matrix of domination"[87] and bell hooks names "yearning," "cutting across boundaries of race, class, gender, and sexual practice."[88] Also relevant here is another case integral in the Second Wave Western feminism, and it refers to the struggles of lesbians in the gay movement. According to Cheshire Calhoun, lesbian feminism has different claims from gay men, as they oppose not only patriarchy's heterosexuality but the gay movement's patriarchy as well.[89]

In the case of Romania, on the one hand, the discourse of national minorities regarding the preservation and assertion of their culture precludes feminist activism within them. Overall, national minorities tend to be more conservative as they focus mainly on ethnic politics, not on gender or ethno-gender ideas. The most dramatic situation in Romania is that of Roma women, especially young girls, who live under overlapping levels of discrimination: by Roma men (gender subordination), by Romanians (ethnic and gender subordination), and by the "minimalist citizen" postcommunist condition (civic and political subordination). On the other hand, the rights of queers (homosexuals, lesbians, bisexuals, hermaphrodites, transsexual, and transgender) encounter perplexing reactions of conservatism and denial in contemporary Romania.[90] Their situation is among the most difficult in the category of otherness. If, in the case of gender, there existed a previously formal, although hypocritical and ultimately antifeminist egalitarian policy under communism, in the case of queer, their claims challenge an intersection of discrimination never addressed before: the heterosexual norm within the patriarchal order of the precommunist, national-communist, and postcommunist systems. As the next chapter shows it, in order to claim political recognition, queers in Romania have to confront an increased alterity from the traditional heterosexual law, based on their performative, multiple, and mediated identifications in the paradigm: sex, gender, and sexuality.[91]

Overall, the formative experiences on the side of a majority seemingly unaware of issues of otherness during centuries of building the nation-state are forcefully obstructing the imaginary blueprint on which the process of constructing a postcommunist, gendered, and inclusively democratic world can be engraved.

East-West Feminist Dialogues

In what analytical terms can one discuss feminism in Eastern Europe? As a discursive political space for conceptual dialogue, the knowledge exchange that takes place between Western and Eastern European scholars represents the crux of a wider debate regarding *what fits* and *what does not fit* the socioeconomic, cultural, political, and historical particularities of each Eastern European country. Criticism from both Easterners and Westerners, and particularly by postcolonial feminists, has been addressed to Western feminists who take for granted "the Eastern woman,"[92] essentializing and ethnocentrically universalizing her features through an act of appropriation and misrepresentation. As I have mentioned before, while the Croatian writer Slavenka Drakulić "survived communism" and "even laughed," she nevertheless felt unable to answer Western feminists' questions regarding Yugoslav women's experiences of empowerment.[93] In line with postcolonial thought, Frances Elisabeth Olsen mentions Western feminism's assumptions that all women have the same definitions and experiences of gender, sexuality, and patriarchy cross-culturally (East-to-East and East-to-West) and that gender is a paramount issue in transitional/transformation societies, unlike poverty, privatization, weak civil society and political parties for example. This criticism also considers that Western feminists are trying to influence local political agendas and, through a policy of patronage, influence the distribution of power in various ways. Thus, I should add that, as previously revealed by Michel Foucault with regards to the discourse of sex, the clinic, or archeology of knowledge[94]—and considering the contemporaneous globalizing condition of the world—such a feminist geopolitics may easily exercise transtemporal and transgeographic "epistemological validation" or "epistemological discrimination" (Vrinda Dalmiya and Linda Alcoff),[95] East and West, North and South. Nevertheless, Olsen also recognizes that each side can influence the other in terms of new ideas and tactics (e.g., by assessing the values of a market strategy or the use of language in women's politics).[96]

From a theoretical standpoint, I would like to point out that the debate on both sides seems to be dwelling between the levels of analysis of any East-West coherent scholarly dialogue: descriptive and analytical on the one hand (the *Weltanschauung* or *Verstehen* dimension), and prescriptive/normative on the other. However, the conflation between these levels of analysis (analytical-normative) is present many times even in the Eastern European case: Eastern European feminists usually tend to conflate these dimensions and often reject Western feminism altogether as another "-ism," in spite of the fact that gender, for example, is an analytical dimension, itself an instrument, a lens of investigation in the intimacies of *any* society. Due to this conflation, many Eastern European feminists (as well as antifeminists) remain prisoners of the "Hegelian-Marxist dilemma" regarding the necessary dialectical historical stages. According to this logic and to predominant feminist and antifeminist rhetoric, until Romania for example becomes as modern as the West—in other words, until it enters a fictitious notion of stable, Western-like modernity—it cannot have a feminist movement, and, according to these opinions, debating about feminism in the meantime is thus superfluous. Moreover, according to this logic, it follows then that until Romania should become "postmodern," "postindustrial," and "postmaterialist" it cannot have Third Wave/difference feminism(s).[97] Yet, the very Western definition of gender as "socially," "historically,"[98] and thus locally and contextually constructed, is useful as an analytical-theoretical tool for surveying gender relations any*where* and any*time*, as is the case here with Romania—even if the dynamic of patriarchy or women's history and politics are revealed to be specifically different, thus claiming particular prescriptive ideas.

Also, we cannot deny the fruitful ideational exchange that has helped Eastern Europeans shape a conceptual space for gender and a political stage for feminism, both apprehended as integrated problematics. Such issues would otherwise remain volatile and split into detached categories (e.g., abortion, sexual preference, equal opportunities, domestic violence, etc.) within a chaos of subjectivities struggling for political recognition as political identities against a religious-based morality and on the background of national-communist sexual and gender arrangements. As a consequence, feminism in Eastern Europe and Romania resides in a different set of presuppositions about empowerment than in the West: both as theory and practice it is prefeminist and still unarticulated within a comprehensive gender problematic. As a consequence, feminism tends to be conflated with heterosexual women's politics, usually *white*—since the ethno-racial opposition to Roma women, for example, is only rarely brought up in feminist debates—which does not mean that certain measures have not been already taken.[99] And, for all its democratic stance, feminism is middle-class, usually academic, and transnational, being linked to human rights NGOs or Western private philanthropy—as I have argued above. This is co-terminus with the fact that Eastern European feminists seem not to be aware of the notion of *positionality*, or *voice*, or *standpoint* in feminism (and social sciences more generally), which otherwise expresses epistemological and empirical unbound diversity, intersecting cognitive orders, as well as the uniqueness of the individual's experiential subject-positioning within various axes of identification such as sex, gender, sexual preference, ethnicity, race, religion, age, ableness, and location in the urban or rural and national or Diasporic milieus. Finally, like other non-Western feminists, some Eastern European feminists occasionally tend to have the features of what Kwame Anthony Appiah has described in postcolonial theory—and was subsequently employed by postcolonial feminism—as *"comprador* intelligentsia" who "mediate[s] trade in cultural commodities of world capitalism at the periphery,"[100] in this case often, yet indiscriminately importing Western feminism at all costs, even as "the vagina monologues."[101] Once more, like other symbols highly appreciated by the West such as civil society or human rights, feminism sometimes proves to be a catch-all symbol, chic nonetheless, and an objective to be appropriated by certain groups and individuals who may seek legitimacy and status—personal, professional, and, many times, financial—from the West.[102]

From a linguistic point of view, there are no Romanian words for the conceptual heritage of Western women's and gender studies (such as womanhood, femaleness). Interestingly, the noun *gender* was translated in Romanian as *gen social* (social genus) only in the mid-1990s, although it is not part of the common language, being used only by academic feminists. Moreover, the use of masculine nouns for professional categories represents the rule, although a Romance language, Romanian generally uses nouns with a different suffix for the feminine (e.g., *profesor* and *profesoară* for man professor and woman professor). As I have argued, there are contradictory ideals about feminism and emancipation, varying from engagement in the public sphere (ideas supported by feminist academics) to the willful return of a great number of women to the private sphere, yet also to their energetic engagement in various public work and decision-making bodies, even if not under the banner of feminism.

From a feminist point of view, this brings me to the conclusion that a *feminist-relevant language*, a new, empowering women's *"sayable"* is now required in Romania, as is the case in other Eastern European contexts. Yet, this feminist language should not be conflated with the notion of "women's writing" (*écriture feminine*) conveyed, among others, by Hélène Cixous[103] and other literary feminists of French essentialist persuasions. From a feminist theoretical perspective, the feminist language I am talking about recognizes the existence of intersecting subject-positionings and nonessentialist differences along gender, sexuality, ethnicity, religion, ableness, or age lines. Finally, it seems that it is precisely this feminist language that needs to be first created in Romania as a background to a novel and comprehensive feminist awareness, and in order to carve discursive feminist spaces and a gender politics beyond traditional patriarchal and heterosexist orders.

Listening to its rhetoric and claims to political recognition, some Western feminists have integrated Eastern European feminism in a progression time warp, considering it to be similar to the activism of Second Wave Western feminism,[104] a feminism that traditionally sought *equality* not *difference*, or, when more radical feminists like Mary Daly[105] sought difference, they proclaimed an essentialist female distinction. I would like to agree with this view, yet also point out that the way feminism evolves in Romania has its own contextual specificities that transcend such an ideological progression, otherwise criticized, as explained, by postcolonial feminist authors as essentializing, or ethnocentrically universalizing, or valorizing a Western-based standpoint epistemology of modernity. In this sense and according to the laws passed, policies enacted, and the general academic and political discourse about gender politics as "gender justice" and "equity," Romania seems to be promoting—when it does so—a form of top-down, institutional, mainstream *liberal* feminism. Yet, as explained, few NGOs and private academic institutions do promote various affirmative actions with regards to women and minorities, especially Roma women. In general, pan-identity politics such as "coalition politics" between various social movements do not have a tradition in Romania. What feminism or "coalition politics" lacks there is the foundation that would otherwise enable their existence: feminist political consciousness and a vocal politics of democratic social movements on a background of a more articulated civil society. Finally, until the country's elites realize the modern and democratic aspect of a feminist-empowering perspective in society and politics, the crude reality is that, without Western funding and transnational feminist politics, the Romanian feminist movement, although unevenly starting to exist and trying to respond to the Romanian reality, is still uncertain.

In the end, as expressed in the introduction to this book, through my research I have discovered a present Romanian society that proves to be inhabited more by *subjectivities, practices,* and *experiences* of oppression and resistance, and less by developed, democratic *political identities.* Furthermore, I have explained that, as they are understood in Western politics, *political identities* are built up on notions of cohesive solidarity, social movements, and vocal identity politics of inclusion/exclusion, which, from my perspective, do not have a parallel in the Romanian case. Instead, *practices, subjectivities,* and *experiences of identity construction as women* are more pervasive than a *feminist identity politics* of a corresponding, integrated *social movement.* Finally, as was the case under communism, this absence of a Western-like grassroots politics does not invalidate an everyday life-based *biopolitics* of resistance grounded in the *microreality* of the quotidian, as women continue to construct, struggle with, and transcend their subjectivities from one patriarchy, communism, to another patriarchy, postcommunism.

Notes

1. This title is inspired from Betty Friedan's *Feminine Mystique* (New York: W. W. Norton, 1963) and, by comparison, it refers to the reinstitution of patriarchal gender roles in postcommunism.

2. Slavenka Drakulić, *How We Survived Communism and Even Laughed* (New York: HarperPerennial, 1993), 22.

3. Vladimir Pasti, Mihaela Miroiu, and Cornel Codiță, *România—Starea de fapt: Societatea* vol. I [Romania—As a Matter of Fact: Society] (Bucharest: Nemira, 1997), 30.

4. Jane Jaquette and Sharon L. Wolchik, "Women and Democratization in Latin America and Central and Eastern Europe," in *Women and Democracy: Latin America and Central and Eastern Europe,* ed. Jane Jaquette and Sharon L. Wolchik (Baltimore: The Johns Hopkins University Press, 1998), 4.

5. World Bank, *2000 World Development Indicators,* <http://www.worldbank.org> (24 June 2002).

6. My general use of the notion "woman" or "women" here refers to adult women. I will specify the notion of young girls when this category will be analyzed. Also, my use of these concepts engenders nonessentialist understandings of women, recognizing that gender intersects with various axes of identification, such as sexuality, ethnicity, religion, or age. This should help deconstruct the corporate notion of a fictitious "Romanian woman," which, occluding civic-based, cross-subjectivity definitions, seems to permeate as a discursive paradigm and a legacy of national-communism in postcommunism.

7. *Recensământ 2002* [Census 2002], <http://www.recensamant.ro/> (17 July 2002).

8. Pasti, Miroiu, and Codiță, *Romania,* 182.

9. Pasti, Miroiu, and Codiță, *Romania*, 181-2.

10. See also Doina Pasca Harsányi, "Women in Romania," in *Gender Politics and Post-Communism: Reflections from Eastern Europe and the Former Soviet Union*, ed. Nanette Funk and Magda Muller (New York: Routledge, 1993), 39-52; and Mariana Hausleitner, "Women in Romania: Before and after the Collapse," in *Gender Politics and Postcommunism: Reflections from Eastern Europe and the Former Soviet Union*, ed. Nanette Funk and Magda Muller (New York: Routledge, 1993), 53-61.

11. Susan Gal and Gail Kligman, *The Politics of Gender after Socialism: A Comparative-Historical Essay* (Princeton: Princeton University Press, 2000), 13, 41. See also chapter 2.

12. Throughout this chapter, my use of the term "Romanian feminists" refers solely to academic feminists.

13. See also Mary Ellen Fisher and Doina Pasca Harsányi, "From Tradition and Ideology to Elections and Competition: The Changing Status of Women in Romanian Politics," in *Women in the Politics of Postcommunist Eastern Europe*, ed. Marilyn Rueschemeyer (Armonk: M. E. Sharpe, 1994), 201-23.

14. As is the case with the notions "woman" or "Romanian woman," my use here of "Romanian peasant woman" is only analytical.

15. For a discussion on self-sacrifice in Eastern European societies, see Barbara Einhorn, *Cinderella Goes to Market: Citizenship, Gender and Women's Movements in East Central Europe* (London: Verso, 1993).

16. Harsányi, "Women in Romania," 40.

17. Andrei Simić, "Machismo and Cryptomatriarchy: The Traditional Yugoslav Family," in *Gender Politics in the Western Balkans: Women and Society in Yugoslavia and the Yugoslav Successor States*, ed. Sabrina P. Ramet (University Park: The Pennsylvania State University Press, 1999), 11-29.

18. Simić, "Machismo and Cryptomatriarchy," 25.

19. Simić, "Machismo and Cryptomatriarchy," 25.

20. It is not clear if this reference to Pauker, as it is used in the Romanian common parlance (both in communism and postcommunism), does not hide nuances of anti-Semitism. On Ana Pauker, see Robert Levy, *Ana Pauker: The Rise and Fall of A Jewish Communist* (Berkeley: University of California Press, 2001).

21. See also Mihaela Miroiu, "Ana's Land. The Right to Be Sacrificed" in *Ana's Land: Sisterhood in Eastern Europe*, ed. Tanya Renee (Boulder: Westview Press, 1997), 137-138. On "supererogation," see David Heyd, *Supererogation: Its Status in Ethical Theory* (Cambridge: Cambridge University Press, 1982).

22. Catriona Kelly, Hilary Pilkington, David Shepherd, and Vadim Volkov, "Introduction: Why Cultural Studies?," in *Russian Cultural Studies: An Introduction*, ed. Catriona Kelly and David Shepherd (Oxford: Oxford University Press, 1998), 1-17.

23. Simić, "Machismo and Cryptomatriarchy," 15-6.

24. Drakulić, *How We Survived Communism*.

25. R. G. Waldeck, *Athene Palace* (New York: Robert M. McBride & Company, 1942).

26. Gheorghe Crutzescu, "The Mogoșoaia Bridge," in *Bucharest: A Sentimental Guide*, ed. Aurora Fabritius, Erwin Kessler, and Adrian Solomon, trans. Florin Bican, Alina

116   *Chapter Six*

Cârâc, Michi Constantinescu Fărcaş, Daniela Neacşu, Adrian Solomon, Monica Voiculescu, and Ioana Zirra (Bucharest: The Romanian Cultural Foundation, 2001), 56-67.

27. Constantin Bacalbaşa, "The Bucharest of Former Times," in *Bucharest: A Sentimental Guide*, ed. Aurora Fabritius, Erwin Kessler, and Adrian Solomon, trans. Florin Bican, Alina Cârâc, Michi Constantinescu Fărcaş, Daniela Neacşu, Adrian Solomon, Monica Voiculescu, and Ioana Zirra (Bucharest: The Romanian Cultural Foundation, 2001), 74-6.

28. Dan C. Mihăilescu, "The Rules of Bucharest Chic," in *Bucharest: A Sentimental Guide*, ed. Aurora Fabritius, Erwin Kessler, and Adrian Solomon, trans. Florin Bican, Alina Cârâc, Michi Constantinescu Fărcaş, Daniela Neacşu, Adrian Solomon, Monica Voiculescu, and Ioana Zirra (Bucharest: The Romanian Cultural Foundation, 2001), 87-8. See also chapter 3.

29. See Mihail Sebastian. *Journal 1935-1944: The Fascist Years*, trans. Patrick Camiller, Introduction and notes, Radu Ioanid (Chicago: Ivan R. Dee, 2000. Published in association with the United States Holocaust Memorial Museum).

30. Mihăilescu, "The Rules of Bucharest Chic," 88.

31. These women conveyed to me that they generally did not report this condition to a doctor.

32. Christine Valmy, a native of Romania who owns a U.S.-based cosmetic empire today, was a one-time employee of such Romanian skin, hair, and body care centers under communism.

33. For a similar case in post-Soviet Russia, see Nancy Condee, "Body Graphics: Tattooing the Fall of Communism," in *Consuming Russia: Popular Culture, Sex, and Society Since Gorbachev*, ed. Adele M. Barker (Durham: Duke University Press, 1999), 339-61.

34. It is unclear whether, like their Western counterparts, Romanian urban youth practice more profound piercing such as genital piercing, or if they experience body mutilation or implants. Cosmetic surgery—mainly reconstructive—existed under communist Romania and is now developing through private cosmetic surgery clinics.

35. For an analysis of the body as a "message board" in American society, see Joan Jacobs Brumberg, *The Body Project: An Intimate History of American Girls* (New York: Vintage Books, 1998).

36. See Walter M. Bacon Jr. and Louis G. Pol, "The Economic Status of Women in Romania," in *Women in the Age of Economic Transformation: Gender Impact of Reforms in Post-Socialist and Developing Countries*, ed. Nahid Aslanbeigui, Steven Pressman, and Gale Summerfield (New York: Routledge, 1994), 43-58; and Doina Pasca Harsányi, "Participation of Women in the Workforce: The Case of Romania," in *Family, Women, and Employment in Central-Eastern Europe*, ed. Barbara Lobodzinska (Westport: Greenwood Press, 1995), 213-17.

37. UNICEF, *Women in Transition: The MONEE Project. Regional Monitoring CEE/CIS/Baltics* 6 (Florence: UNICEF, 1999), 31.

38. UNICEF, *Women in Transition*, 32.

39. Einhorn, *Cinderella Goes to Market*, 220.

40. In 1997, women's share among entrepreneurs was 26 percent, among the highest in the region. UNICEF, *Women in Transition*, 103.

41. Unlike postcommunism and the diversification of lifestyles and career options, an academia degree under communism (which was roughly the equivalent of a Bachelor degree) was generally considered one of the most important personal and professional status factors. This is a reason why youth from both urban and rural milieus would put all their efforts into being accepted by one of the few state universities that existed at that time, an acceptance that relied upon getting the highest scores in a certain number of written and oral exams. In many cases, parents would invest enormous sums of money in their children's private tutoring, a preparation specially designed to ensure their entrance into the academia. Failure to be accepted in the academia was considered failure in life.

42. Data for 1997. UNICEF, *Women in Transition*, 32.

43. Particularly with regards to work practices, this "fractal" situation can be employed as a comparative paradigm useful to understand contemporary private/public divisions that are noticeable today not only in Eastern Europe, but in a world of globalization, "restructuring" (in the "North") and "structural adjustment" (in the "South" or East"). For example, such a public/private interconnected "fractality" can also be observed in the case of "structural adjustment policies" (SAP), flexibilization of work, and the feminization of poverty, as these are analyzed by Development Studies and "Women/Gender in/and Development" research. According to this literature, SAP have created new household survival strategies in the "South" and "East," whereby "public" work is in effect executed in or supplemented by work done in the "privacy" of the household, thus creating "fractal" time/identities/activities. See, for example, the notion of the "informal sector" in the South, which best exemplifies the "private/public fractality" mentioned by Gal and Kligman. M. Patricia Connelly notes that, in Latin America, "women are increasingly involved in some combination of formal and informal labor as well as housework. Informal sector work provides the intermediate link between paid formal sector work and unpaid household work, having some characteristics of both"; occasionally "women receive wages for domestic services." Women constitute the greatest majority in the informal sector, which basically refers to "small-scale manufacturing, retail trade, small-scale transport, self-production (e.g., gardens, cooperative child care, labor exchange for house construction), as well as illegal or quasi-legal activities (e.g., beer brewing, smuggling, begging, drug cultivation)." See M. Patricia Connelly, "Gender Matters: Global Restructuring and Adjustment," *Social Politics*, (Spring 1996): 17-8.

44. UNICEF, *Women in Transition*, 33. For data on Romania, see also AnA: Society for Feminist Analyses, *Romanian National Report on Institutional Mechanisms for the Advancement of Women (Since the Beijing Conference)* (Bucharest, 1999), 18-9.

45. UNICEF, *Women in Transition*, 66.

46. See also Gail Kligman, *The Politics of Duplicity: Controlling Reproduction in Ceausescu's Romania* (Berkeley: University of California Press, 1998).

47. The situation of Romania in communism can serve as a lesson today, when the right to abortion is, in the name of religion and "life," under question not only in Eastern European but also in Western countries. See, for example, the "Save Roe Now" open letter sent in 2002 by Kim A. Gandy, president of the National Organization for Women (NOW), aimed at gathering support to preserve the 1973 *Jane Roe v. Henry Wade* Supreme Court decision that legalized abortion in the United States. National Organization for Women, "NOW President Kim Gandy Calls for a Filibuster Strategy to Save *Roe*," 22 January 2002, <http://www.now.org/press/01-02/01-22.html> (1 August 2002).

48. UNICEF, *Women in Transition*, 63. See also Joseph Ascroft, "Către o strategie de afirmare-educație-planificare familială" [Toward a Strategy of Family Affirmation-Education-Planification] 22, no. 6, 1998, <http://www.dntb.ro/22/1998/6/suplim/5.html> (10 March 2000); and Adriana Băban and David P. Henry, "Aspecte ale sexualității în epoca Ceaușescu" [Sexuality Aspects in Ceaușescu's Times] 22, no. 6, 1998, <http://www.dntb.ro/22/1998/6/suplim/1.html> (10 March 2000).

49. UNICEF, *Women in Transition*, 60.

50. Pasti, Miroiu, and Codiță, *Romania*, 184.

51. UNICEF, *Women in Transition*, 84.

52. See also Pasti, Miroiu, and Codiță, *Romania*, 186-87.

53. UNICEF, *Women in Transition*, 87. See also Hunt Swanee, "Women's Vital Voices," *Foreign Affaires* no. 76 (July 1997): 2-7.

54. Sexual harassment was prevalent during communism as an unquestioned part of gender labor relations. Sexual harassment in education has taught entire generations of young women how to survive (sexual) harassment through the dissimulation of their innate feminine characteristics. Secrecy and denial concerning sexual harassment continues to seal the lips of so many young Romanian women, while the legal system is only now starting to deal with this issue—a chilling proof of the prevalent promiscuity and of women's political impotence, and a legacy of the patriarchy embedded in the communist system and now in postcommunism.

55. In postcommunism, the only parties that do take seriously some of women's problematic are the left-wing *"Partidul Democrației Sociale din România"* (the Party of Social Democracy in Romania), PDSR—today renamed *"Partidul Social-Democrat"* (the Social-Democratic Party)—and *"Partidul Democrat"* (the Democratic Party), PD.

56. UNICEF, *Women in Transition*, 97. For data on Romania, see AnA, *Romanian National Report*, 1999. During a constitutional crisis in December 1999, in the form of an unpredicted cabinet reorganization under a new premier, Mugur Isărescu (acting chairman of the Romanian National Bank) introduced for the first time a woman deputy-minister for Labor and Social Protection, Smaranda Dobrescu. Then, in July 2000, the thirty-two-year-old Daniela Boagiu became deputy-minister for Transportation, replacing Traian Băsescu, the newly elected mayor of Bucharest.

57. UNICEF, *Women in Transition*, 101; AnA, *Romanian National Report*, 20.

58. UNICEF, *Women in Transition*, 99; For data on Romania, see AnA, *Romanian National Report*, 21.

59. Inter-Parliamentary Union, *Women in National Parliaments*, 1 July 2002, <http://www.ipu.org/wmn-e/classif.htm> (25 July 2002).

60. AnA, *Romanian National Report*, 20.

61. See also Einhorn, *Cinderella Goes to Market*.

62. Liliana Popescu, "Șoapte fierbinți și fantezii romantice" [Hot Whispers and Romantic Fantasies], in *Gen și educație* [Gender and Education], ed. Laura Grünberg and Mihaela Miroiu (Bucharest: AnA and PHARE, 1997), 34.

63. See also Spike Peterson, "The Politics of Identification in the Context of Globalization," *Women's Studies International Forum* 19, nos. 1, 2 (1996): 5-15; and Nira Yuval-Davies, "Women and the Biological Reproduction of the 'Nation,'" *Women's Studies International Forum* 19, nos. 1, 2 (1996): 17-24.

64. *Ileana Cosînzeana* belongs to the common Romanian folktale heritage. She is the epitome of beauty and innocence, femininity and youth. Usually kidnapped by a dragon (*balaur* or *căpcăun*) she is rescued by and marries the young, handsome, and smart *Făt-Frumos*—sometimes a prince, other times a peasant.

65. Popescu, "Şoapte fierbinţi."

66. Alison M. Jaggar "Feminist Ethics," in *Encyclopedia of Ethics*, ed. Lawrence Becker with Charlotte Becker (New York: Garland, 1992), 364.

67. Norma Alarcón, "*Traddutora, Traditora*: A Paradigmatic Figure of Chicana Feminism," in *Dangerous Liaisons: Gender, Nation, & Postcolonial Perspectives*, ed. Anne McClintock, Aamir Mufti, and Ella Shohat (Minneapolis: University of Minnesota Press, 1997), 281.

68. Alarcón, "*Traddutora*," 286.

69. Miroiu has made an inventory of such statements expressed by various prominent Romanian intellectuals. See Mihaela Miroiu, "Feminismul ca politică a modernizării" [Feminism as A Politics of Modernization], in *Doctrine politice: Concepte universale şi realităţi româneşti* [Political Doctrines: Universal Concepts and Romanian Realities], ed. Alina Mungiu-Pippidi (Iaşi: Polirom, 1998), 265.

70. Zakia Pathak, "A Pedagogy for Postcolonial Feminists," in *Feminists Theorize the Political*, ed. Judith Butler and Joan W. Scott (New York: Routledge, 1992), 426-41.

71. See Mihaela Miroiu's feminist philosophy in her *Convenio: Despre natură, femei şi morală* [Convening: On Nature, Women, and Morals] (Bucharest: Editura Alternative, 1996) and gender interdisciplinary studies such as Laura Grünberg and Mihaela Miroiu, eds., *Gen şi educaţie* [Gender and Education] (Bucharest: AnA and PHARE, 1997) and Liliana Popescu, ed., *Gen şi politică: Femeile din România în viaţa publică* [Gender and Politics: Romanian Women in Public Life] (Bucharest: UNDP, 1999). Other gender surveys can be found in political science volumes, such as those edited by Pasti, Miroiu, and Codiţă, *Romania*, and by Alina Mungiu-Pippidi, *Doctrine politice*, as well as in bilingual human rights volumes, such as Irina Moroianu-Zlătescu, *Şanse egale. Şanse reale: Studii şi cercetări privind drepturile femeii—Equal Opportunities. Real Opportunities: Studies and Research on Women's Rights* (Bucharest: Institutul Român pentru Drepturile Omului, 1996).

72. Heidi I. Hartmann, "The Unhappy Marriage of Marxism and Feminism: Towards a More Progressive Union," in *Women and Revolution: A Discussion of the Unhappy Marriage of Marxism and Feminism*, ed. Lydia Sargent (Boston: South End Press, 1981), 1-41, quoted in Rosemarie Putnam Tong, *Feminist Thought: A More Comprehensive Introduction*, 2nd ed. (Boulder: Westview Press, 1998), 119. Emphasis in the original.

73. UNICEF, *Women in Transition*, 102; For data on Romanian, see AnA, *Romanian National Report*, 16-7. On gender-related NGOs in postcommunist Romania, see also Laura Grünberg, "Women's NGOs in Romania," in *Reproducing Gender: Politics, Publics, and Everyday Life after Socialism*, ed. Susan Gal and Gail Kligman (Princeton: Princeton University Press, 2000), 307-36.

74. Miroiu, "Feminismul," 269-70.

75. Miroiu, "Feminismul," 270.

76. AnA, *Romanian National Report*, 12.

77. AnA, *Romanian National Report*, 12-5.

78. AnA, *Romanian National Report*, 12-5.

79. The Governmental Ordinance no. 137 (*Ordonanța guvernului*) from 31 August 2000, regarding the prevention and sanctioning of all forms of discrimination, published in *Monitorul Oficial* no. 431, 2 September 2000. On this regulation, see also chapter 7 on queer.

80. On postcommunist gender and nationalism, see Maja Korać, "Understanding Ethno-National Identity and Its Meaning: Questions from Women's Experience," *Women's Studies International Forum* 19, nos. 1, 2 (1996): 133-43; Wendy Bracewell, "Women, Motherhood, and Contemporary Serbian Nationalism," *Women's Studies International Forum* 19, nos. 1, 2 (1996): 125-32; and the contributions of Vlasta Jalušić, Tatjana Pavlović, Žarana Papić, Julie Mertus, Obrad Kesić, and Dorothy Q. Thomas and Regan E. Ralph in *Gender Politics in the Western Balkans: Women and Society in Yugoslavia and the Yugoslav Successor States*, ed. Sabrina P. Ramet (University Park: The Pennsylvania State University Press, 1999).

81. For a similar perspective on Romania, see Pasti, Miroiu, and Codiță, *Romania*, 190-95; and the discussion about "multiculturalism" in chapter 5. I must also stress here that I am referring to the general social perception of these distinctive groups, not to the effective legislation (such as the Constitution, or the antidiscrimination Governmental Ordinance no. 137 mentioned throughout this book), which does protect citizens through *equality* and *affirmative action* dispositions, and, in keeping with the international system of treatises and conventions, grants certain rights to refugees.

82. Chantal Mouffe, "Feminism, Citizenship, and Radical Democratic Politics," in her *The Return of the Political* (London: Verso, 1997), 75, 78.

83. Nancy Fraser, "Equality, Difference and Radical Democracy. The United States Feminist Debates Revisited," in *Radical Democracy: Identity, Citizenship, and the State*, ed. David Trend (New York: Routledge, 1995), 202.

84. Nira Yuval-Davies, *Gender and Nation* (London: Sage Publications, 1997), 125-33.

85. Rosi Braidotti, *Nomadic Subjects: Embodiment and Sexual Difference in Contemporary Feminist Theory* (New York: Columbia University Press, 1994), 1, 4.

86. Yuval-Davies, *Gender and Nation*, 57.

87. Patricia Hill Collins, *Black Feminist Thought: Knowledge, Consciousness, and the Politics of Empowerment*, 2nd ed. (New York: Routledge, 2000), 227.

88. bell hooks, *Yearning: Race, Gender, and Cultural Politics* (London: Turnaround, 1991), 27.

89. See Cheshire Calhoun, "Separating Lesbian Theory from Feminist Theory," in *Feminist Social Thought: A Reader*, ed. Diana T. Meyers (New York: Routledge, 1997), 200-18.

90. See chapter 7 on queer.

91. See Judith Butler, *Gender Trouble: Feminism and the Subversion of Identity* (New York: Routledge, 1990).

92. Chandra Talpade Mohanty, "Under Western Eyes: Feminist Scholarship and Colonial Discourse," in *Dangerous Liaisons: Gender, Nation, & Postcolonial Perspectives*, ed. Anne McClintock, Aamir Mufti, and Ella Shohat (Minneapolis: University of Minnesota Press, 1997), 255-77; Trinh T. Minh-ha, "Not You/Like You: Postcolonial Women and the Interlocking Question of Identity and Difference," in *Dangerous Liaisons: Gender, Nation, & Postcolonial Perspectives*, ed. Anne McClintock, Aamir Mufti, and Ella Shohat (Minneapolis: University of Minnesota Press, 1997), 415-19; and Gayatri C. Spivak, "Can

the Subaltern Speak?" in *The Post-Colonial Studies Reader*, ed. Bill Ashcroft, Gareth Griffiths, and Helen Tiffin (New York: Routledge), 24-8.

93. Slavenka Drakulić, "A Letter from The United States—The Critical Theory Approach," in her *How We Survived Communism*, 123-32.

94. Michel Foucault, *The History of Sexuality: An Introduction* vol.1., trans. Robert Hurley (New York: Vintage Books, 1990); *The Birth of the Clinic: An Archeology of Medical Perception*, trans. A. M. Sheridan Smith (New York: Vintage Books, 1994); and *The Archeology of Knowledge and the Discourse on Language*, trans. A. M. Sheridan Smith (New York: Pantheon Books, 1982).

95. Vrinda Dalmiya and Linda Alcoff, "Are 'Old Wives' Tales' Justified?," in *Feminist Epistemologies*, ed. Linda Alcoff and Elizabeth Potter (New York: Routledge, 1993), 217.

96. Frances Elisabeth Olsen, "Feminism in Central and Eastern Europe: Risks and Possibilities of American Engagement," *Yale Law Journal* 106, no. 7 (1997): 2215-57.

97. On the notion of "feminism" as a "postmaterialist doctrine," see, for example, the volume edited by Mungiu-Pippidi, *Doctrine Politice*. Although commendable for inserting for the first time a chapter on feminism, this volume is problematic on account of its incorporation of "feminism" and "ecology" under the heading of "postmaterialist doctrines." Not only is this theoretically inaccurate but, according to the editor's materialist/postmaterialist framework, it is against her very empowering intentions, and paradoxically invalidates such movements in the Romanian context. Feminist as well as ecological issues do not occur only in Western, postmaterialist, postindustrial societies, but in *all* societies, as analyzed for some decades now by postcolonial feminism, ecofeminism, and Development Studies, as well as by their correlative literature on "women/gender in/and development" ("WAD"/"WID"/"GAD").

98. Joan W. Scott, "Gender: A Useful Category in Historical Analysis," *American Historical Review* 91, no. 5 (1986): 1053-75.

99. See, for example, the affirmative actions focusing on Roma candidates seeking acceptance in the National School for Political and Administrative Studies, in Bucharest.

100. Kwame Anthony Appiah, "The Postcolonial and the Postmodern," in *The Post-Colonial Studies Reader*, ed. Bill Ashcroft, Gareth Griffiths, and Helen Tiffin (New York: Routledge, 1995), 119; and Pathak, "A Pedagogy for Postcolonial Feminists," 438. Emphasis in the original.

101. As elsewhere in the world, Eve Ensler's *The Vagina Monologues*, a book and play of great notoriety in North America, is quite popular with Romanian feminists and, according to a Romanian feminist *Newsletter*, was also staged as an empowering feminist discourse in Bucharest. Eve Ensler, *The Vagina Monologues* (New York: Villard Books, 2000).

102. On the argument about the occasional yet inescapable farce and highly personalized "parlor politics" (111) that, regarding some Eastern European "favored cliques" (83)—from Russia to Poland, and from government executives, NGOs, and local banks, to intellectuals and international philanthropists—has accompanied the honorable, yet often naïve, intentions of some Western-funding of the postcommunist transformation, see Janine R. Wedel's award-winning book *Collision and Collusion: The Strange Case of Western Aid to Eastern Europe 1989-1998* (New York: St. Martin's Press, 1998).

103. Hélène Cixous, "The Laugh of the Medusa," trans. Keith Cohen and Paula Cohen, in *New French Feminisms: An Anthology*, ed. Elaine Marks and Isabelle de Courtivron (Hemel Hempstead: Harvester Wheatsheaf, 1981), 245-64.

104. On such an idea about Eastern European feminism, see also Nanette Funk, "Feminism East and West," in *Gender Politics and Post-Communism: Reflections from Eastern Europe and the Former Soviet Union*, ed. Nanette Funk and Magda Muller (New York: Routledge, 1993), 318-330.

105. See Mary Daly, *Gyn/Ecology: The Metaethics of Radical Feminism* (Boston: Beacon Press, 1978).

Chapter Seven

Between Ars Erotica *and* Scientia Sexualis: *Queer Subjectivity and the Discourse of Sex*

That sexuality is not, in relation to power,
an exterior domain to which power is applied,
that on the contrary it is a result and an instrument of power's designs.

— Michel Foucault, *History of Sexuality*[1]

Activism for the rights of queers (homosexuals, lesbians, bisexuals, hermaphrodites, transvestites, and transsexuals) encounters widespread reactions of conservatism and denial in contemporary postcommunist Romania. Sinners from an ethico-religious viewpoint, and outcasts in the juridico-political discourse of the state apparatuses, queers are either considered pariah in present Romanian society, or they are victims through omission. Emerging from the niches of marginality, the queer body is displaced through meaning instability—castrated male/asexual women. Queer personalities become a matter of hybridity, presence/absence liminal, amoebic space, usually imagined as a lack. Their bodies and subjectivities are textually inscribed by the hegemonic discourses of the Romanian state and social mechanisms, agencies where profound conservatism, as explained in the previous chapter, has survived, although weakened today, from precommunist times into the postcommunist socioeconomic, cultural, and political transformation. As proved by other political struggles for identity recognition and democratization, the Romanian conceptual blueprint continues to accommodate only with great difficulty any otherness from the accepted traditional norm: ethnic Romanian, Christian-Orthodox, white, male, and heterosexual.

From an identity construction positionality, this study investigates the present state of Romanian queer experience. First, the chapter presents Romanian postcommunism as a background for the construction of a queer identity. Then, the research tries to locate Eastern European queer experience between what Michel Foucault calls *"scientia sexualis"* and *"ars erotica,"* searching for Romanian queer subjectivity and its specificities compared with the construction of Western queer identity. The chapter also makes a brief excursus through cases of queer discrimination and follows the battle with a law (the Penal Code) that continued to incriminate same-sex relations until 2001. Finally, the chapter seeks spaces of marginality, liminality, and the subversive, where queer subjectivities emerge as border identities, operating in the dim light of semiopen, social margins.

Retrospectively, it looks as if the year 1989 and its subsequent changes were prefaced in Eastern Europe under the heading of national identity versus ethnic politics. However, present marketization, globalization, pan-European integration, and revival of precommunist traditional-conservative gender orders seem to concur toward profound renegotiations of the way identities and subjectivities are produced. Gender roles are being realigned and contradictory ideas of femininity and masculinity clash.

As the previous chapter has explained, in postcommunist Romania this globalization and marketization has brought unemployment, part-time jobs, and the feminization of poverty, especially in agriculture and low productivity sectors. Discourses on sexuality and sexual health, and awareness of sexual practices, diseases, and protection are more markedly to be found within urban limits, varying according to the social status and age of populations. Meanwhile, the predominantly rural milieu still dwells in archaic understandings of sexuality under the norms of heterosexuality and motherhood. On the other hand, Ceauşescu's pro-natalist policies, which brought so many deaths and mutilations due to illegal, unsafe abortion techniques, have made the adult population of women particularly cautious about sexuality, which is many times perceived as a duty to the male partner. Deviations from these norms occur mainly in the urban environment, where the younger, culturally pro-Western generations prove to have a level of sexual awareness and sophistication comparable to their Western counterparts, although sometimes their activities border on prostitution.[2] However, such urban overt sexual-related discourses and behavior function as border subjectivities between public and private, official and unofficial, and, until recently, legal and illegal realms. As explained throughout this book, Susan

Gal and Gail Kligman call these dichotomous situations—activities, spheres, and identities—"fractals."[3] Such "fractal," border subjectivities function, as expressed above, at the margins of underground and public cultures and discourses, in spite of the general sociopolitical climate denunciating homosexuality—which is perceived by older generations, average women, and rural systems of value as Western-type *libertinage*. This fractality in the construction of the queer subject is also co-terminus with what the poet and literary critic Eva Kosofsky Sedgwick calls the "epistemology of the closet," a form of oblique interaction of the gay person with their social environment, one based on the notion of the "open secret."[4] Functioning between "private/public," "inside/outside," and "subject/object," this form of queer subjectification expressed through veiled openness or leaky secrecy:

> erects new closets whose fraught and characteristic laws of optics and physics exact from at least gay people new surveys, new calculations, new draughts and requisitions of secrecy or disclosure. . . . The gay closet is not a feature only of the lives of gay people. But for many gay people it is still the fundamental feature of social life.[5]

At the level of everyday life, such queer "fractal" subjectivities were also practiced against article 200 from the Penal Code, which indicted until 21 June 2001, as will be discussed below, same-sex relations (if committed in public or causing public scandal).[6] This means that, in the last decade of struggle to make queer subjectivity accepted, there existed various levels of dislocation in the way power operated between political discourses that denied homosexual identity and queer as border, "fractal" subjectivity. Since strictures were not rigorously enforced, the letter and spirit of law (the Penal Code) and anti-queer politico-religious discourses in general were laxly enforced in current social practices, leaving quite a bit of room for queer expression in everyday life. This laxity, then, opened up sites of subversive subjectivities, among which are queer. Such queer subjectivities functioned and, after 21 June 2001, continue to function within "fractal" enclaves permissive of certain levels of agency flexibility. Within this liminal space of daily life, queer subjectivity dwells in an uncertain, yet undeterred shifting positionality.

Thus, although until 2001, legal, political, and religious anti-queer discourses fully operated at the public sphere and public culture levels, I can nevertheless say that, in light of the flexible and liminal position held by queers in postcommunist Romania, after 1989 the pathologization of homosexuality has weakened compared with the muscular, ideological criminalization of queer sexuality under communism. Extrapolating this disrupted nature between state discourses (as expressed in the Penal Code) and the reality of a civil society and everyday life that function on "fractal" public/private levels embedding negotiated and subversive queer subjectivities, one can conclude that state and civil society in postcommunist Romania functioned until the recent abolition of article 200 as two, parallel, if not utterly conflicting discourses. After 21 June 2001, when the incrimination of same-sex relations was entirely repelled, the disjuncture shifted entirely within civil society since, although the state does not indict gay/lesbian sexual relations anymore, nevertheless general social, moral, and religious acceptance of these practices continues to do so.

Before going into the analysis of Romanian queer subjectivity there are three influential facts worthy of attention as they contribute to the building of a negotiated identity and queer politics in present Romania.

First, in terms of the legislative steps that have brought about the disincrimination of same-sex relations in Romania, as I have previously mentioned, until 21 June 2001 the Romanian Penal Code indicted homosexuality "if committed in public or causing public scandal," a clause of publicity introduced by the Law no. 140 from 1996. Before the 1996 law, article 200 from the Romanian Penal Code universally indicted same-sex relations irrespective of whether they were public or private. This can be said to constitute the main difference between communist and postcommunist criminalization of queer sexuality until its entire abolition in 2001. However, the Antidiscrimination Governmental Ordinance no. 137 from 31 August 2000, represented an alternative venue to claim queer difference, since it had specifically instituted the liberal principle of equality among citizens, punishing any forms of discrimination based on "difference, exclusion, restriction or preference, race, nationality, ethnicity, language, religion, social category, convictions, sex or *sexual orientation*, belonging to a disadvantaged category or any other criteria infringing . . . basic human rights."[7] On the other hand, this legislation had also instituted for the first time "affirmative actions" or "special measures" with regard to national minorities and some "disadvantaged categories,"[8] defined as "persons who are in a position of inequality compared with the majority of citizens due to their social origins, or a handicap, or if they face attitudes of rejection and marginalization due to specific causes such as a chronicle noncontagious disease, or HIV infection, or the status of refugee or asylum-seeker."[9] As a consequence, this ordinance protected queer identity both through normative, liberal dispositions implementing equality and nondiscrimination, and normative politics of difference expressed in special affirmative actions. As this book is being written, the use in practice of this Governmental Ordinance for claiming or protecting a position of queer identity is unclear. Finally, in order to avoid lack of clarity, subjectivism, and dispositions conflicting with other situations qualified as indictable by the Romanian Penal Code, the abolition of article 200 in June 2001 has triggered the realignment of the entire section "crimes regarding sexual life." Article 200 did not have a life of its own outside criminal law and a holistic approach could not neglect other articles from this section as well as other penal provisions indirectly linked to this problematic.[10] Since the Governmental Emergency Ordinance no. 89 from 2001, particularly in article 197, "rape" now includes the rape of same-sex persons; similarly, article 198, which condemns "sexual relations with a minor," now addresses pedophilia of either sex; and article 201, "sexual perversions," now goes beyond its traditional treatment by the Romanian communist medical ideology in connection with "sexual deviations," then including homosexuality.[11]

Second, before 21 June 2001, since paragraph 5 from article 200 indicted any forms of queer proselytism, propaganda, or association, there were and indeed still are few if any scholarly published materials on the issue of Romanian queer at this date, let alone organizations and apparent queer subcultures. However, benefiting from the vague application of the Romanian law and in light of the "fractal" nature of public/private embeddings and of queer subjectivity itself—and, not to forget, with the help of international organizations and foreign governments—a queer-dedicated NGO, *Bucharest Acceptance Group* (ACCEPT), has boldly assumed in the 1990s an active role in democratizing at least the juridical, if not the socioethical acceptance of queer in postcommunist Romania. As explained in the previous chapter, many identity politics NGOs in Romania are funded mainly by international organizations. In the case of Romanian queer politics, financial sponsorship comes from the Netherlands, Canada, Finland, and the United States.[12]

Third, as the new century of cyber-technology unravels its televisual and information consciousness toward the East, the Internet—a major tool available for queer activism—was able to supplant the lack of a queer local activism by providing more means for strategically fighting back intolerance in Romania. It is within this transnational political cyber-subculture, cyber-postcommunism, where both ACCEPT and other foreign gay and lesbian as well as human rights organizations voiced their concerns, battles, narratives of discrimination, hopes, and negotiations for power. In terms of transnational operations of power, due to such cyber-communities, the issue of queer transcended and de-territorialized Romanian politics, coming back with a vengeance gained through international recognition and pressure. It was a struggle for identity recognition and democratization fought from both an insider-without and an outsider-within positionality, a feature of hybridity specific to the cyberspace and contemporary global politics. Such a transnational operation of power successfully managed to fight against dogmatic state discourses and legislation as well as civil society's intolerant elements, such as the Church and other anti-queer (usually nationalist) organizations. This transnational politics also empowered those voices from within the same civil society who sought to democratize the acceptance of otherness. But what remains fundamental here is the international character of pressure that was exercised over state apparatuses and civil society, without which, realistically speaking, little could have been accomplished in the renegotiation of queer identity and empowerment of queer politics. Finally, such a form of Internet-based activism may also be discussed in the context of Donna Haraway's "cyborg,"[13] a political figuration of global feminism/activism, which subverts and transforms systems of domination—"compulsory heterosexuality" (Adrienne Rich)[14] in this case—through an intervention in communication networks.

"Romanian LesBiGays," as they call themselves on Internet, remain one of the main focal points of intolerance in contemporary Romania. The issue of queer represents a problem largely perceived by the Romanian state and society as one of the most ghastly—as criminality in the extreme and the epitome of the so-called "antinatural."

Mapping Postcommunist Sexuality:
Between "Scientia Sexualis" and "Ars Erotica"?

When trying to locate Romanian queer experience it is desirable to map such an Eastern European experience—itself an intermediary between East and West—within various other sexual discourses.[15] Michel Foucault gives us a perceptive picture of the way the "repressive hypothesis" was institutionalized in the seventeenth century Western society, as sex became regulated in discourses of power.[16] From its ethical construction as sin, the discourse of sex, like madness, becomes a pathologized, scientific one.[17] Yet Foucault also makes a spatial and temporal division between this Western *scientia sexualis* and the early, Eastern *ars erotica* of the ancient Greeks and the Orient. Within this Foucauldian understanding of a politics of sexuality, I argue here that the Romanian mapping of sexual desire is neither Western nor Eastern. From the standpoint of a politics of sexual preference, Romania is a hybrid where many traditions of identity construction and gender and sexuality regimes meet. Thus, a politics of sexuality in Romania must, therefore, be understood with its eclectic heritages of Thraco-Roman, Slavic, Ottoman, Austro-Hungarian, precommunist "bourgeois" and French high culture, Russian/Soviet, and postcommunist gender and sexuality norms and production of gendered and sexual subjectivities; with its division between enlightened/Westernized, or nationalist-conservative elites and overwhelming peasant values; with a traditional role that subdues women to patriarchy and relegates them to motherhood; with the dominance of the Christian-Orthodox Church as an epistemic center of both religious and ethical family and identity values; and with precommunist gender politics and legacies as well as postcommunist international, more progressive influences—all with consequences over the dynamic of morals codes and sexual subjectification. According to the current main discourses, with their strong lineages in previous centuries of traditional-conservative identity politics, gender and sexuality are socially perceived as apolitical ethico-religious subjectivities, since neither the political class nor society at large recognizes gender and sexuality as subjectivities with political claims per se. In other words, gender and sexuality are not yet accepted as political identities, and are relegated to the domain of religious morality. In this sense, the Foucauldian binary mapping of sexuality as *scientia sexualis* versus *ars erotica* is displaced in the following way in Romanian postcommunist political and social discourses: obeying the gender/sexuality regime set out by the Christian-Orthodox religion, by traditionally conservative and overwhelmingly peasant values functioning under the myth of motherhood, occasionally combined with urban, precommunist "bourgeois" yet patriarchal gender subjectification, and by communist antiabortion legacies of body alienation, Romania reserves neither *scientia* nor *ars* for the discursive domain over sexuality. Accordingly, sexuality discourses refer to sexuality either as heterosexual reproduction, or as homosexual sin (the ethico-religious and peasantist-rural discourse), or as homosexual criminal and pathological behavior (the medico-legal-political discourse until 2001). There are no Victorian puritanical *scientia sexualis* discourses, although the communist state did manage to elaborate its version of a puritan science, distributing homosexuality and lesbianism in the medical domain of the pathological, while the law recognized the queer only through the profile of the outcast and the criminal.[18]

As for *ars erotica*, it is a realm generally unknown for the Romanian dominant discursive practices—although some form of tolerated queer subjectivities existed within the artistic environment of communist Romania.[19] The representation of sexuality in Romania is not freed from any "absolute law of the permitted and the forbidden"; it does not stand, as Foucault says about *ars erotica*, "first and foremost in relation to itself . . . experienced as pleasure, evaluated in terms of its intensity, its specific quality, its duration, its reverberations in the body and the soul."[20] There are no Oriental psalmist poems about the art of making love, such as the Ottoman book of eroticism, *Bahnâme*.[21]

On the contrary, according to the dominant social and political discourses, sexuality obeys the heterosexual norm under the cult of motherhood, peasant values, and the ethico-religious hegemony of the Christian-Orthodox faith and Church.[22] Neither *ars* nor *scientia*, neither *sexualis* nor *erotica*, sexuality in Romania has only one recognized purpose: procreation. This implies the triad of the official patriarchal normalcy: "compulsory heterosexuality," motherhood, and traditional values (peasant and religious). In other words, sexuality remains fundamentally linked to the politics of reproduction.[23] As sexuality was until recently publicly exposed through regulation, the state managed to appropriate the citizen body as a Kafkaesque infernal machine of the *Penitentiary Colony* type, and textually inscribe it with its heterosexual normalcy and reproductive politics. However, this was not a recent statist attempt to violate body boundaries. Ceauşescu's pro-natalist policies already made the uterus a vulgar state property, with all the frightening consequences induced by this forced appropriation: illegal abortions, surveillance, repressed sexuality, maternal and infant mortality, imprisonment, hemorrhage, death, child abandonment, AIDS, international trafficking in children, and urban street children.[24] On an average basis, the body was not recognized as a personal value neither under Ceauşescu's puritanical reproductive policies—although, as explained in the previous chapter with regards to alternative femininities and lifestyles, in some urban differentiated private and public spaces an attention for the body was indeed observed—nor before communism, as traditional values of patriarchal heterosexism and the supremacy of peasantist communitarianism always held the upper hand. In postcommunism, as a consequence of a peasantist culture that does not traditionally discuss the body and of Ceaușescu's antiabortion politics, the body continues to be an unspoken subject matter, although, as expressed in the previous chapters, urban teenagers do engage in novel forms of a body-based popular culture and personal politics. Thus, although women from the rural environment and the suburbia seem to be estranged from their bodies, apparently being afraid of sexuality per se,[25] alternative lifestyles and body-based sexual practices do exist at least in the urban, artistic, and youth milieus—as this chapter wishes to present.

Deconstructing the Postcommunist Queer Subject

In order to locate the queer experience in Eastern Europe, three theorists are useful here: Joan W. Scott's definition of gender,[26] Michel Foucault's approach to "sex" as a discursively unifying moment between state apparatuses and the body,[27] and Judith Butler's poststructuralist/psychoanalytic, discursive configurations of sex, gender, and desire.[28] Scott defines gender as a cultural and political construct, a social category of analysis referring to either women or men.[29] For Scott, history and power are gendered terrains, while gender becomes a relationship of power and culture. In this sense, as a historical and cultural construct, gender relations and identities are deconstructed as local, particular, contextual, and discursively placed subjectivities and practices. This idea serves as a background for understanding the special construction of queer in postcommunist Eastern Europe—Romania being the case here. Second, in a Foucauldian sense, "sex" is the moment of interface between the body and the gendered identity, which is grafted onto the material of the body by the ideological discourses of state apparatuses. Whether through democracy or intolerance, the body is textually reshaped and rewritten within hetero- or nonhetero-gender regimes. Finally, on this background, Butler refines the idea of a textually inscribable body. She splits identity into sex, gender, and sexuality as subjectivities, hence cultural, discursive, and ultimately political, constructs. Butler makes sex, gender, and sexuality fluid signifiers within a poststructuralist continuous shifting and deferring of meaning and identity. Searching for queer subjectivity in this light, "sex" is conceived as culturally constructed from the viewpoint of gender. Ultimately, it is gender that sexes the body as "'prediscursive,' prior to culture, a politically neutral surface *on which* culture acts."[30] In this sense, "[g]ender is the repeated stylization of the body, a set of repeated acts within a highly rigid regulatory frame that congeal over time to produce the appearance of substance, of a natural sort of being."[31] Once gender is revealed as performative subjectivity and in the context of the criticism of phallogocentrism, there are no "women" and "men" as firm identities, but only subjectivities and continuous gender performances that allocate and dislocate desires within one body and from one body to another.[32]

This line of thought is most helpful for locating and analyzing queer subjectivity in postcommunist Romania. As a consequence, is it possible to speak in the context of postcommunist Eastern Europe about queer as a clearly defined identity of the Western type, one constructed through visible and loud struggles for political recognition? The approach to the construction of the Eastern European/postcommunist queer subject is more nuanced. Today, due to the "fractal" organizing principle ordering the postcommunist everyday life and in light of its social unacceptability opposed to its subversive, flexible, and liminal production, queer seems to be more of a matter of subjectivity. This means that, according to Joan Scott's definition of experience as one being located in practices and in deconstructed, discursively placed subjectivities,[33] and following Laurie Essig's empirical analysis of queer in postcommunist Russia, queer subjectivity emerges defined as *experience*, a series of repeated acts, "a verb"; it has no clear-cut identification, subcultures, or even self-representations "as queer" ("as subject").[34] In other words, the postcommunist queer subject can be defined as a fluid, free-floating subjectivity, and as lacking an identity. The latter is generally produced, as it happens in the West, through a Foucauldian "insurrection of subjugated knowledges"[35] and incitement to discourse, overt public exposure, subcultures and styles, loud claims and struggles for political and social recognition—none of which currently exists in postcommunist Romania.

As expressed before, Essig makes the same assertion with regard to the post-Soviet queer subject, noting that in present Russia there exists a "queer style" but not a "queer subculture."[36] In other words, this means that, from a discursive point of view and due to particular Eastern European cultural, social, and historical formative experiences, those engaging in same-sex relations have never become a "homosexual species," a homosexual/lesbian subject, although the sexual acts themselves were punishable as crimes, occasionally seen as "curable": "queerness [is] seen as a set of acts, not an unchangeable core of self-identity."[37] As in postcommunist Russia, Romania does not have a queer subculture, as queerness here does not correspond to an existing and firmly (self-) defined identity. Queerness is an unstable notion, a discursive reality, "a set of signs" and acts that are "readable as queer," and a performative subjectivity.[38] In other words, there are queer-performative subjectivities functioning in the absence of queer identities.

Also, in terms of constructing the very queer subjectivity, what makes the situation dramatically different from Western conceptions of the queer subject is that such an Eastern European queer subjectivity is based on "gender performance," not "sexual practices."[39] As Essig explains, this means that a woman performing femininity in a same-sex relation can think of herself as "straight" if not breaking the gender performative code corresponding to "heterosexuality"—and this irrespective of the fact that her sexual practice is, according to Western discourses, lesbian. In the same line of thought, a bisexual woman who has both heterosexual and lesbian relations can continue to perceive herself as "heterosexual," not queer, again if not breaking the masculine/feminine gender performance corresponding to "heterosexuality" in either relationships. Finally, a similar thing can be said about gay/bisexual men, who can think of themselves as "heterosexual," again if not breaking "norms of gender performance."[40] In these situations it is gender (gender performance) that is the element that distinguishes "straightness" from "queerness," not sex (sexual practice). Located in "the flexible and fleeting space of subjectivities":

> Queer subjectivities, unlike queer "subculture" or "identity," are not limited to a well-defined group of persons. Queer subjectivities build an amorphous structure that does not attach itself to individual bodies. Instead, individual bodies participate in creating and consuming queer subjectivities, speaking at times for themselves, at times for others.[41]

There are more complex situations when, as explained when mapping Eastern European queer experience as that *between* Foucauldian Western *scientia sexualis* and Eastern, ancient *ars erotica*, such gender performers would not classify themselves at all, leaving forms of homo-/lesbo-eroticism outside any identification, let alone the taxonomy of otherness. Even the notions of "homosexuality," "lesbianism," and "bisexuality" can be thought of as historical imports fraught with negative political signifiers. They are the cultural constructs of a Christian morality, which, according to a Nietzschean Foucault, subverted the noble *ars erotica* of the pre-Christian world. Similarly, in his examination of sexuality and gay/lesbian movements under the postulate of "same-sex erotic universality," Peter Drucker says that "in the tropics there is no sin," implying that Western ideas of sexual normalcy become ineffectual in non-Western worlds.[42] Under such circumstances, Western definitions of "queer," "straight," or "identity" become superfluous. So does the notion of "transsexuality," which merely slips into "transgenderism," and thus shifts its meaning toward desire for opposite gender not necessarily sex/body.

It can thus be concluded that sexual practices that challenge Western traditional definitions of sexual normalcy or deviance, basing queer subjectivity on gender not sexual difference can be encountered everywhere outside the Western world. Even the ancient Greek world and the Ottoman empire considered same-sex relations as a matter of normalcy; and in Mexico those sexual practices that are defined by the Western discourse as homosexual are not apprehended by the locals as deviant, or "homosexual." According to Ana Maria Alonso and Maria Teresa Koreck, the passive, "effeminate males"—the *"jotos"* or *"putos"*— are contrasted to the "masculine males"—the *"machos."*[43] The latter can engage in active sexual practices with both *jotos* and women without being disgraced as homosexuals or aberrant. On the contrary, *machos'* sexual versatility with both women and *jotos* is seen as a sign of magnified virility, not weakness, which, as passivity, would otherwise be associated with the *jotos*. Another example refers to Chicano men who:

> embrace a "gay" identity (based on the European-American sexual system) [and] must reconcile this sexual identity with their primary socialization into a Latino culture that does not recognize such a construction: there is no cultural equivalent to the modern "gay man" in the Mexican/Latin-American sexual system.[44]

Finally, the *hijra* in India is considered both "eunuch" and "hermaphrodite."[45] Neither woman nor man, "an alternative gender," *hijra* "attracts people with many different kinds of cross-gender identities, attributes, and behaviors— people whom we in the West would differentiate as eunuchs, homosexuals, transsexuals, hermaphrodites, and transvestites," and is harmonized by Hinduism beyond Western sexual anxieties.[46]

As explained, the Romanian heterosexual norm coupled with patriarchy has always functioned unchallenged until the moment when, with the help of the international community, the democratization efforts that preceded the fall of communism engaged in a protest against the heterosexual norm inscribed both in social and political discourses and legal documents. Thus, it is necessary here to follow up on a narrative of queer discrimination coupled with a transnational, de-territorialized queer politics that has influenced and pressured the democratization of the Romanian juridical practices and hegemonic discourses embedded both in state apparatuses and civil society.

The Face of Discrimination

"Human-rights advocate found murdered; authorities blame 'homosexual killing.'"[47] This headline from the 1998 Romanian media demonstrates the treatment of homosexuality as the domain of the sinner/pathological/criminal. The article describes the killing of a human rights activist for the League for the Defense of Human Rights (LADO), a lawyer and journalist, Ştefan Itoafă. Although Itoafă was investigating some high officials in the city, the police explained the murder in terms of a "sex crime," making public the victim's asserted homosexuality. Echoing the deaths of two famous Romanian pop stars, Ioan Luchian Mihalea, tortured and killed in 1993, and Mihaela Runceanu, killed and set on fire in her apartment in 1989 just before the Revolution, this more recent "sex crime" stirred new conservative passions while presenting the queer both with a pathological and a malefactor versatility, an object of public disdain and a factor of increased imperilment. If, in 1993, the police gave the details of Luchian Mihalea's homosexual life almost with no reserves, in the case of Runceanu, a bisexual killed during communist times, the crime remained surrounded with the air of a mysterious burglary and sexual intrigue. When the police intervene in such cases, their treatment of victims is brutal and abusive. Abuses of this type are documented usually with the help of international organizations, such as the International Gay and Lesbian Human Rights Commission (IGLHRC), Human Rights Watch (HRW), Amnesty International, or the Helsinki Committee for Human Rights, organizations that bring these situations before of the UN and the European Union (particularly as Romania seeks European Union membership). In this context, human rights activist Scott Long from IGLHRC revealed other police abuses in cases of homosexuality investigations in Iaşi, Cluj, Baia Mare, and Maramureş for the period 1995-1997. According to the victims' declarations, the procedure was intimidating and brutal, and in some cases without any legal mandate; it was also disrespectful of any forms of privacy and intimate life, and filled with expletives.[48] The identification with the Roma minority in some cases created a situation of double discrimination.

At other times, homosexuality made exciting newspaper headlines, when stories from police files leaked into the hands of cynical and sarcastic journalists looking for bombastic exposures. Such is the one from the newspaper *Ziua*, from 3 September 1997: "Policemen interrupt a torrid homosexual round . . . in the Cişmigiu Park."[49] Particularly before amending article 200 with the clause of publicity in 1996, police and penitentiary brutality were assertively powerful. In 1992, Marian Mutaşcu and Ciprian Cucu from Timişoara were forcibly dragged by policemen and, on account of their homosexuality, incarcerated without official charge. Then they were both sentenced to two and one years in jail respectively, a period of time when they were repeatedly beaten, sexually assaulted and raped by other inmates, since their homosexuality had apparently been disclosed by the police itself. After Amnesty International intervened, the two had their sentences suspended. However, as Cucu was not allowed to return to high school due to the public perception of him as a menace, he finally sought political asylum in the United States (where he received this status in 1996), while Mutaşcu committed suicide.[50]

A similar situation happened to forty-year-old Mariana Cetiner, indicted for "luring another woman into sexual intercourse." Arrested in 1995, she was found guilty in 1997 and, although released following a successful appeal in early 1997, she was rearrested and put to serve the remainder of her sentence, during which she was abused and beaten. Finally, in 1998 President Emil Constantinescu pardoned Cetiner who, despite her release, remains an outcast in her overwhelmingly conservative society.[51] There are many other cases and each has its own specificity.

It was clear that the Penal Code needed to be democratically reexamined and realigned to modern European standards, which is what happened in June 2001 regarding the famous article 200. This became a necessity particularly as article 200 from the Penal Code indicted actions that could overlap with cases of pedophilia or sexual molestation. In 1997, *Ziua* presented the case of a British Protestant priest who was waiting to be judged in Bucharest for homosexuality and pedophilia. It was discovered that he was engaging in sexual relations with various minor boys of around fourteen years old usually living in the railway station *"Gara de Nord"* surroundings,[52] a neighborhood notorious as headquarters of street children.

But then again, how could the criminal code distinguish between crime and legality, between licit and illicit actions? The battle to abolish article 200 from Romanian law, a battle fought both from within and without with the help of international organizations and pressure groups, becomes here an illustrative moment of democratic politics in postcommunist Romania.

The Battle with the Law

After 1989 and the fall of the communist atheist and ideologically revolutionary ethic, the epistemic source for ethical values in Romania was situated in a temporal leap backwards into premodern charismatic forms; that source was religion, rather than the more rational, civic or political, cultures most associated with democracy. Usually, changing moral values comes prior to changing a legal system; it is a cause-effect relationship. Nevertheless, under international pressure and de-territorialized politics, opposite power operations can happen: laws can change while society remains intolerant at large, as happens today in Romania regarding the acceptance of queer subjectivity. As previously mentioned, the Orthodox Church had a lot to say about this change, but its conservatism and political power hampered further democratizations. In this sense, the head of the Romanian Orthodox Church, Patriarch Teoctist, made public his disavowal of homosexuality in a protest to the Romanian Parliament, when, in 1994, the legislative assembly embarked on a road to ease the provisions against homosexuality through the clause of publicity. Radio Free Europe reported that Teoctist said in a public statement that "it was not necessary for Romania to abandon its values in order to integrate with West European standards and institutions" and that "the country should maintain the old formulation of the Penal Code, which made any homosexual act a crime punishable by imprisonment." Around one hundred students in Theology, the report continued, protested in front of the Parliament, asking for a total ban on homosexuality and its "proselytism."[53] Father Dumitru Radu, Professor at the Faculty of Theology and a representative of the Orthodox Church, expressed a similar point of view at the 1995 symposium organized in Bucharest by ACCEPT under the auspices of the United Nations Educational, Scientific, and Cultural Organization and the European Center for Higher Education (UNESCO -CEPES). He considered that queer rights are not "human rights" but a "plague," a "sexual deviance," and a "violation of nature." Homosexuals are sinners since, by considering the body "one's own business" and preaching their sexual practice, they create a "sick youth." Father Dumitru Radu concluded: "[t]olerance is not unlimited."[54]

The battle to abolish article 200 was hard and was orchestrated at several national and international, political and civil society levels. Pressures came from Amnesty International, the Helsinki Committee for Human Rights, HRW, IGLHRC, and the International Gay and Lesbian Association (ILGA) among others, with reports to the Council of Europe and the European Parliament. Also, ACCEPT, the Romanian NGO active since 1996, engaged in reforming Romanian legislation with respect to gay and lesbian human rights as well as re-educating Romanian society on accepting homosexual relations. For its effort, ACCEPT was nominated in 1999 for the Andrei Sakharov Prize by the Green Group in the European Parliament, also winning the "Égalité" ("Equality for Gays and Lesbians in the European Institutions") Prize, awarded in Brussels, at the European Commission headquarters.[55] In 1994, in yet another instance of discrimination and protest, the newspaper *Tineretul liber* presented the case of five Finnish homosexual artists (dancers and musicians) who had been banned from participating in an international gay and lesbian art festival in Bucharest, initially booked at the *Ion Creangă* Theater, then at a *Casa de cultură*. Nonetheless, the newspaper *Tineretul liber* concluded that, under such circumstances, Elton John's or Karl Lagerfeld's products should also be banned in Romania.[56] As a sign of "fractal" behaviors and lax application of Romanian law, it is noteworthy that such an artistic event could be organized in Romania in the first place, under circumstances of a general interdiction of any homosexual activity, association, and proselytism. Eventually, gay members from the European, Canadian, Dutch, British, and Danish Parliaments visited Romania in order to challenge the antigay laws and address individual protests, while Amnesty International urged its members to engage in a letter campaign of protest targeting the Romanian authorities. "Arci Gay Milano"—the Milan queers—protested in front of the Italian-Romanian Chamber of Commerce, and, in 1996, the New York group "Penniless Anarchist Queer Nuisance" (PAQ'N) took over the Romanian consulate, while the Londonese "OutRage!" and the "Lesbian Avengers" boycotted the government-sponsored Romanian National Opera's performance of Aida at London's Royal Albert Hall. Finally, in 1997, "OutRage!" and ILGA issued a call for international boycott of Romania's wine exports.[57]

The Subversive?

In the interstices of both civil and political societies' intolerance regarding queer, one can still find some interestingly subversive, anticultures of democratization. An incipient queer subculture of resistance in the Romanian "fractal" public/private spaces can be perceived through various mosaics of queer representation.

In the fall of 1997, Babes-Boylai University in Cluj-Napoca organized a conference entitled "Expressing Sexuality: Biology, Culture, Theory and Psychology of Homosexuality," an occasion gathering leading Romanian and American scholars as well as human rights organizations. Although the foreign guests openly expressed their sexual orientation, there was a general feeling that among the Romanian audience there was extreme reluctance toward openness.[58] However, the very fact that—benefiting from a substantial participation of Romanian professors in psychology, psychiatry, philology, philosophy, and anthropology—such an event took place is indicative that the queer experience managed to find an expression and, I can say, acceptance at least at some progressive levels of the Romanian academy.

Other "fractal" spaces of the subversive exist by virtue of a romantic integration of queer practices into wider artistic configurations such as literature, maybe because literature is both artistic and political, and its subtexts can easily cover or expose challenging subjectivities and narratives. Some foreign and Romanian novels dealing with the subject of homosexuality trace lineages either into romantic periods or to famous personalities open about their queer sexual lives.[59] Among them are *Îngerul Destinului* (Destiny's Angel) by Dominique Fernandez (1995), a novel describing the life of the Italian cinematographer Pier Paolo Pasolini in an ultra-Catholic Italy,[60] *Mihail* by Panait Istrati, a gay novel that was initially published in 1939 then republished in 1996 with the new title *Adolescența lui Mihail Zografi* (The Adolescence of Mihail Zografi),[61] and the no less famous *Viața lui Oscar Wilde* (The Life of Oscar Wilde).[62] Alina Mungiu-Pippidi, a publisher of political analysis and a playwright, presented her new play *Moartea lui Ariel* (Death of Ariel) in the newspaper *Adevărul* in 1998. According to the author, although not reflecting the case of the pop star Ioan Luchian Mihalea, the text was nevertheless inspired by Mihalea's death. It is a script about "the life of a woman married to a homosexual" and "intolerance in Romania," says the writer.[63]

Finally, Romanian gays and lesbians do have their places of company, connecting in bars, clubs, discos, and restaurants, beaches, and cruising areas, escort facilities, and health and AIDS services, usually located in cities and important towns, such as Bucharest, Cluj, Brașov, Sibiu, and Iași. This is a sign that, in the end, each subjectivity manages to find its niche of being and becoming, a form of visibility in more or less marginal boundaries, throughout the web of what Foucault describes as power circulating through individuals, understood as nodal points,[64] in spite of conservative or blatantly discriminating socially embedded gender regimes. What remains to be seen in the years to come is if this new form of quick, yet uncertain, visibility favored by Western-based transnational politics, and functioning, as Sedgwick says, through a vexed "epistemology of the closet," will go beyond queer bar subculture and cyber-activism, thus avoiding a mere mimicry of Western progressive identity politics.

There are some notes that must accompany the overall presentation of Romanian queer subjectivity. On one hand, I must consider the present postcommunist context framed by patriarchy and heterosexuality. In this sense, lesbian subjectivity collides into homosexuality, the general Romanian discourse on queer conflating all forms of nonhetero-eroticism to "homosexuality of both sexes." In her call for a separate lesbian theory, Cheshire Calhoun alerts us to the predicament of finding a voice for lesbian feminism in the gay men's liberation movement.[65] Unlike gay men, lesbian women face both patriarchal and heterosexual discrimination. In the Romanian case, as expressed before, lesbian and bisexual women's sexuality is furthermore appropriated, commodified, objectified as a form of private eroticism for the straight man, while denying the very subjectivity of the lesbian woman. On the other hand, the statutory recognition of gay and lesbian sex has a connotation of panic for both civil and political society: the sort of eschatological fear that queer will become the rule, a mandatory sexual practice subverting the binary hetero-/nonhetero-opposition and devaluing heterosexuality altogether. Finally, gay and lesbian activism is intrinsically connected to the gendered reality of postcommunist Romania. Very few women dare engage in feminist activities and even fewer have the courage to openly declare their feminist stance, a situation explained by the pervasive perception that to be a feminist means to be a lesbian, the latter comprehended within a pejorative signification. Men working on gender issues (which, it should not be forgotten, also include masculinities), fall under the suspicion of being gay. And, as we know by now, to be gay or lesbian is a socially perceived ethico-religious sin, a pathology and shame. Thus, beyond the negatively perceived feminist movement, there is a still deeper level of marginalization: gay and lesbian rights-related activities, with the further implication that activists, or anyone debating on this subject, must necessarily be queer and not a democratic, progressist person. In this hierarchization of power negotiation and discrimination, to be a gay/lesbian/bisexual is socially perceived as better only to being a serial killer.

Finally, this chapter has tried to present a comprehensive yet nuanced account of queer subjectivity in postcommunist Romania. First, the background on which queer subjectivities are produced was exposed as a "fractal" organization of time, space, activities, and identities. On the basis of a troubled epistemology of the "open secret," Romanian postcommunist queer subjectivity managed to find a liminal, dim niche of representation, in spite of legal and social intolerant discourses, themselves prone to "fractal," lax applications in everyday life. Second, queer subjectivity was mapped as an eclectic, hybrid sexual discourse, one functioning at the border of Foucault's Western and Eastern erotic maps. Third, and based on this nuanced mapping of sexual practices, queer identity was deconstructed and located as performative subjectivity, one operating in the absence of clear-cut political identities. Moreover, unlike many Western theorizations of queer identity construction, such a subjectivity was apprehended as situated in gender performances, not sexual practice, in gender roles, not sexual difference or body. Finally and more important, from a political science point of view regarding operations of power, the chapter hopefully revealed one of the most powerful forms of politics de-territorialization. Such a transnational politics was inflicted by international queer and human rights activism on Romanian intolerant politico-legal state apparatuses and ethico-religious elements within civil society. Moreover, this de-territorialized, transnational politics brought together, like never before, international and Romanian civil societies in their effort against traditional and still hegemonic repressive patriarchal heterosexism.

In the end, after following so many local and global operations of power in the construction of the Romanian queer subject and politics, we can return here to Michel Foucault and his insight that fundamentally marks this entire chapter on queer, identity, and politics: "That sexuality is not, in relation to power, an exterior domain to which power is applied, that on the contrary it is a result and an instrument of power's designs."[66]

Notes

1. Michel Foucault, *History of Sexuality: An Introduction* vol.1., trans. Robert Hurley (New York: Vintage Books, 1990), 152.

2. For example, in the daily newspaper *România liberă*, from 30 June 2000, are advertisements in a section called "Întâlniri pe fir" (Dates on Wire) for couples seeking a bisexual—generally female—third partner or vice-versa (3 ads); for "complete" and erotic Thai massage (9 ads); for offers of oral sex (1 ad), sex with "erotic toys" (1 ad), and "S&M" (1 ad); and for *ménage à trois*, and sex with Russian and Ukrainian young girls and women. There were no ads regarding offers or requests of homosexual sex. "Întâlniri pe fir," *România liberă*, 30 June 2000, 22. From this trend, one could conclude that lesbians and bisexual women face a double objectification based on their gender (usually conflated to their biological sex) and sexuality. While gay men's sexuality is overtly seen as a menace, bisexual or lesbian women's sexuality is considered an additional excitement for the straight man, a new object of private eroticism that precludes awareness of lesbian subjectivity and claims of identity legitimacy. I wish to thank Adrian Coman from ACCEPT-Romania for this clarification.

3. Susan Gal and Gail Kligman, *The Politics of Gender after Socialism: A Comparative-Historical Essay* (Princeton: Princeton University Press, 2000), 13, 41.

4. D. A. Miller, "Secret Subjects, Open Secrets," in D. A. Miller, *The Novel and the Police* (Berkeley: University of California Press, 1988), p. 207, quoted in Eva Kosofsky Sedgwick, "Epistemology of the Closet," in *The Lesbian and Gay Studies Reader*, ed. Henry Abelove, Michèle Aina Barale, and David M. Halperin (New York: Routledge, 1993), 45-6.

5. Sedgwick, "Epistemology of the Closet," 45-6.

6. On 21 June 2001, the Romanian Government passed the Emergency Ordinance no. 89 repealing article 200 from the Romanian Penal Code, while also modifying other

articles from the section "Crimes Related to Sexual Life." Then, on 30 January 2002, as published in *Monitorul Oficial*, the Law no. 61 for the adoption of the Government Ordinance no. 89/2001 came into force (Bucharest Acceptance Group, *Accept Fact Sheet: Status of article 200 of the Romanian Penal Code on same-sex relations*. 1 February 2002). Until 21 June 2001, the most politically relevant incriminatory dispositions from article 200 from the Penal Code were paragraphs 1. and 5.: "[Par. 1.] Sexual relations between persons of the same-sex, committed in public or causing public scandal, are punishable by one to five years imprisonment. . . . [Par. 5.] Urging or seducing a person into committing sexual acts between persons of the same-sex as well as the propaganda of association or any other encouraging acts committed with this view are punishable by one to five years imprisonment."

7. Governmental Ordinance no. 137, 31 August 2000, article 2, par. 1, *Monitorul Oficial* no. 431, 2 September 2000. My emphasis.

8. Governmental Ordinance no. 137, article 2, par. 5.

9. Governmental Ordinance no. 137, article 4.

10. See also Romanian LesBiGays on Internet, "ACCEPT's Proposed New Legislation," 7 May 1998, <http://www.geocities.com/WestHollywood/1811/despre200. htm> (30 March 2000).

11. Some of these "sexual perversions" listed as "sexual deviances" are "autoeroticism," "homosexuality" and "lesbianism," and "hypersexuality and hypereroticism" including "sadism," "masochism," "exhibitionism," "voyeurism," "pedophilia," "fetishism," "narcissism," "zoophilia," "gerontophilia," "necrophilia," "azoophilia/pygmalionism," "transsexualism," and "transvestism." Constantin Ursoniu, *Igiena Sexuală* [Sexual Hygiene] (Timişoara: Editura Facla, 1980), 176-86.

12. ACCEPT, <http://www.accept-romania.ro/englishabout.html> (7 June 2002).

13. Donna Haraway, "A Manifesto for Cyborgs: Science, Technology, and Socialist Feminism in the 1980s," in *Feminist Social Thought: A Reader*, ed. Diana T. Meyers (New York: Routledge, 1997), 501-31.

14. Adrienne Rich, "Compulsory Heterosexuality and Lesbian Existence," in *Feminism in Our Time: The Essential Writings, World War II to the Present*, ed. Miriam Schneir (New York: Vintage Books, 1994), 312.

15. This chapter uses paradigms of queer identity construction insofar as they are relevant to a gender/queer approach that maps the Eastern European queer experiences in comparison with Western constructions of queer identity. Accordingly, this article does not make use of Queer Theory in general, which, through its specific Western problematic and prescriptive character, may look superfluous for the Eastern European postcommunist context. For a debate on the value of Western feminist theories for the Eastern European postcommunist empirical reality, see the previous chapter.

16. Foucault, *History of Sexuality*.

17. Michel Foucault, *Birth of the Clinic: An Archeology of Medical Perception*, trans. A. M. Sheridan (New York: Vintage Books, 1994).

18. See Ursoniu, *Igiena Sexuală*, 176-86.

19. Under communism, some Romanian artists whose homosexual, lesbian, or bisexual behavior was notorious (mainly within artistic boundaries) were constantly questioned by the police. The cases of Mihaela Runceanu and Ioan Luchian Mihalea—killed due to their sexuality—are discussed in this chapter. In the postcommunist artistic

environment, one of the more notable cases was the 1993 release on channel one of the National Television of a controversial video-clip representing some scenes of lesbian eroticism, with music interpreted by a famous Romanian pop star.

20. Foucault, *The History of Sexuality*, 57.
21. Sema Nilgün Erdoğan, *Sexual Life in Ottoman Society*. (Istanbul: Dönençe, 1998).
22. On the Romanian Orthodox Church and homosexuality, see Lavinia Stan and Lucian Turcescu, "The Romanian Orthodox Church and Post-Communist Democratisation," *Europe-Asia Studies* 52, no. 8 (December 2000): 1467-88.
23. Gail Kligman defines the "politics of reproduction" as "the intersection between politics and the life cycle, whether in terms of abortion, new reproductive technologies, international family planning programs, eugenics, or welfare." Gail Kligman, *The Politics of Duplicity: Controlling Reproduction in Ceausescu's Romania* (Berkeley: University of California Press, 1998), 5.
24. See also Kligman, *The Politics of Duplicity*, 17-8, 240-51.
25. Adriana Băban, "Women's Sexuality and Reproductive Behavior in Post-Ceauşescu Romania: A Psychological Approach," in *Reproducing Gender: Politics, Publics, and Everyday Life after Socialism*, ed. Susan Gal and Gail Kligman (Princeton: Princeton University Press, 2000), 239-48.
26. Joan W. Scott, "Gender: A Useful Category in Historical Analysis," in *American Historical Review* 91, no. 5 (1986): 1053-1075.
27. Foucault, *The History of Sexuality*.
28. Judith Butler, *Gender Trouble: Feminism and the Subversion of Identity*. (New York: Routledge, 1990).
29. See Scott, "Gender."
30. Butler, *Gender Trouble*, 7. Emphasis in the original.
31. Butler, *Gender Trouble*, 33.
32. On this performativity of identity and sexual desire, see also Cheshire Calhoun, "Separating Lesbian Theory from Feminist Theory," in *Feminist Social Thought: A Reader*, ed. Diana T. Meyers (New York and London: Routledge, 1997), 208.
33. Joan W. Scott, "Experience," in *Feminists Theorize the Political*, ed. Judith Butler and Joan W. Scott (New York: Routledge, 1992), 23, 26, 37. See also chapter 2.
34. Laurie Essig, "Publicly Queer: Representations of Queer Subjects and Subjectivities in the Absence of Identity," in *Consuming Russia: Popular Culture, Sex, and Society Since Gorbachev*, ed. Adele M. Barker (Durham: Duke University Press, 1999), 282.
35. Michel Foucault, "Two Lectures," in *Power/Knowledge: Selected Interviews and Other Writings, 1972-1977*, ed. Colin Gordon (New York: Pantheon Books, 1981), 81.
36. Essig, "Publicly Queer," 283.
37. Essig, "Publicly Queer," 298 en. 2. See also Laurie Essig, *Queer in Russia: A Story of Sex, Self, and the Other* (Durham: Duke University Press, 1999). Similarly, the now defunct article 200 from the Romanian Penal Code indicted "same-sex relations committed between persons of the same-sex," that is, it indicted the *acts*, not the "homosexuals" or "lesbians," who, as *subjects*, were considered "the authors" of these crimes.
38. Essig, "Publicly Queer," 283.
39. Essig, "Publicly Queer," 282.
40. Essig, "Publicly Queer," 282. On late nineteenth and early twentieth centuries Russian homosexual subculture as a self-perceived matter of "normalcy," straightness, or

heterosexuality, see Dan Healey, "Masculine Purity and 'Gentlemen's Mischief': Sexual Exchange and Prostitution between Russian Men, 1861-1941," *Slavic Review* 60, no. 2 (2001): 233-65.

41. Essig, "Publicly Queer," 283.

42. Peter Drucker, "'In the Tropics There Is No Sin,' Sexuality and Gay-Lesbian Movements in the Third World," *New Left Review* no. 218 (1996): 75-101.

43. Ana Maria Alonso and Maria Teresa Koreck, "Silences: 'Hispanics,' AIDS, and Sexual Practices," in *The Lesbian and Gay Studies Reader*, ed. Henry Abelove, Michèle Aina Barale, and David M. Halperin (New York: Routledge, 1993), 115.

44. Tomás Almaguer, "Chicano Men: A Cartography of Homosexual Identity and Behavior," in *The Lesbian and Gay Studies Reader*, ed. Henry Abelove, Michèle Aina Barale, and David M. Halperin (New York: Routledge, 1993), 255.

45. Serena Nanda, *"Hijras* as Neither Man Nor Women," in *The Lesbian and Gay Studies Reader*, ed. Henry Abelove, Michèle Aina Barale, and David M. Halperin (New York: Routledge, 1993), 542.

46. Nanda, *"Hijras,"* 542, 544, 547.

47. Romanian LesBiGays on Internet. *Latest News*, 17 November 1998, <http://www.geocities.com/WestHollywood/1811> (30 March 2000).

48. *Ziua* and Romanian LesBiGays on Internet. "Scott Long, consilier al organizaţiei 'Human Rights Watch' din SUA, va informa Comunitatea Europeană şi ONU despre abuzurile din România" [Scott Long, counselor to the organization "Human Rights Watch" from the United States, will inform the European Community and the UN about the abuses from Romania], 6 July 1997, <http://www.geocities.com/Hollywood/ 1811/baiamare.html> (30 March 2000); Long Scott and Bogdan Voicu, "Police Abuses Against Suspected Homosexuals in Baia Mare and Iaşi, Romania," in *Romanian LesBiGays on Internet*," 23-28 September 1996, <http://www.geocities.com/ West Hollywood/1811/scott.htm> (30 March 2000); Cornel Sabou, *Ziua* and Romanian LesBiGays on Internet, "Scandalul homosexualilor anchetaţi ilegal de Poliţia Maramureş" [The scandal of the homosexuals illegally investigated by the Maramureş Police], 23 July 1997, <http://www.geocities.com/WestHollywood/1811/baiamare2.htm> (30 March 2000); and Romanian Action for Gay Men, Lesbians and Bisexuals, "U.S. Activists Denounce Romania," 15 January 1998, <http://www.raglb.org.uk/news30.htm> (30 March 2000).

49. Romanian LesBiGays on Internet. "Poliţiştii întrerup o toridă partidă de homosex . . . în parcul Cişmigiu," *Ziua,* 3 September 1997, ed. Adrian Newell Păun, 1998, <http://www.geocities.com/WestHollywood/1811/amantii.htm> (30 March 2000).

50. Romanian LesBiGays on Internet, "Romanian Gay Man Wins Asylum in U.S.," <http://www.geocities.com/WestHollywood/1811/news.html> (30 March 2000).

51. Romanian Action for Gay Men, Lesbians and Bisexuals, "Mariana Cetiner Thanks Supporters," 6 April 1998, <http://www.raglb.org.uk/news33.htm> (30 March 2000).

52. Romanian LesBiGays on Internet, "Britanicul John Michael Taylor este arestat pentru relaţii sexuale cu un minor" [The British John Michael Taylor Is Arrested for Engaging in Sexual Relations with a Minor], October 1997, <http://www.geocities.com/ WestHollywood/1811/taylor.htm> (30 March 2000).

53. Michael Shafir, "Romanian Patriarch on Homosexuality," *RFE/RL Daily Report* 213, 9 November 1994, quoted in Romanian LesBiGays on Internet, <http://www.geocities.com/WestHollywood/1811/9nov94.html> (17 July 2002).

54. Bucharest Acceptance Group, "Report on the Symposium Homosexuality: A Human Right? Rapporteur Jennifer K. Tanaka, Bucharest: UNESCO-CEPES," 31 May 1995, <http://geocities.com/WestHollywood/1811/acc1995.html> (30 March 2000).

55. Romanian Action for Gay Men, Lesbians and Bisexuals, "Greens Nominate Romanian Gay and Lesbian Rights Group for the Sakharov Prize," 17 September 1999, Strasbourg, <http://www.geocities.com/WestHollywood/1811/> (30 March 2000) and <www.accept-romania.ro> (20 June 2002).

56. Romanian LesBiGays on Internet, "Kom Ut International Press Release: Nordic Artists Prohibited from Performing in Romania," 20 July 1994, <http://www.geocities.com/WestHollywood/1811/20jul94.html> (30 March 2000).

57. Romanian Action for Gay Men, Lesbians and Bisexuals, "International Boycott of Romania Launched to Protest Article 200," 22 January 1997, <http://www.raglb.org.uk/ news19.htm> (30 March 2000).

58. Romanian LesBiGays on Internet, "The Conference Expressing Sexuality: Biology, Culture Theory, and Psychology of Homosexuality," 13 September 1997, <http://www.geocities.com/WestHollywood/1811/cluj97.html> (30 March 2000).

59. Romanian LesBiGays on Internet, "Books with Gay Themes Published in Romania," <http://www.geocities.com/WestHollywood/1811/book.html> (30 March 2000).

60. Dominique Fernandez, *Îngerul destinului* (Bucharest: Editura RAO International, 1995), quoted in Romanian LesBiGays on Internet, "Books with Gay Themes."

61. Panait Istrati, *Mihail*, trans. Alexandru Thalex (Bucharest: Editura Cartea Românească, 1939), republished with a new title, *Adolescenţa lui Mihail Zografi* (Bucharest: Editura Albatros, 1996), quoted in Romanian LesBiGays on Internet, "Books with Gay Themes."

62. Robert H. Shepherd, *Viaţa lui Oscar Wilde*, trans. N. H. Negrin (Bucharest: Editura Librăriei Alexandru Stănculescu, 1920-1921), quoted in Romanian LesBiGays on Internet, "Books with Gay Themes."

63. *Adevărul* in Romanian LesBiGays on Internet, "Despre teatru cu Alina Mungiu-Pippidi," April 1998, <http://www.geocities.com/WestHollywood/1811/trebuie.htm> (30 March 2000).

64. Foucault, "Two Lectures," 98-9.

65. Calhoun, "Separating Lesbian Theory," 200-18.

66. Foucault, *A History of Sexuality*, 152.

Conclusion

The initial question of this book was: What will the *flâneur* encounter while strolling through Bucharest and through the politics of its everyday life? Indeed, what constitutes identity and politics in postcommunist Romania? In this sense, the purpose of this book was to construct a cultural-political cartography of the intimacies of Romanian postcommunist society and politics, while asking from a standpoint of the quotidian and of identity construction and identity politics: What can one see and understand when looking into the present state of affairs of Romanian discourses, culture, society, and politics?

Thus, the *flâneur* was presented with the communist aesthetical experience of subjectification, which "socialist realism," or the "popular/proletarian aesthetics" was, while also looking for various forms of counter-hegemonic subcultures located in a *biopolitical* popular culture, in *biostructures*, and in precommunist "bourgeois" and Western-influenced synchronic/diachronic discourses. That chapter also followed the way in which "popular aesthetics" is recirculated and resignified in postcommunism. Here, the focus was on the aesthetics produced and consumed by the new aesthetic actors in postcommunism, the *nouveaux riches*, while the cultural logic of postcommunism was revealed as one dominated by syncretism, carnivalesque, kitsch, and consumption.

The discussion of youth and popular culture located everyday life and politics at a Foucauldian, sub-civil society level of surfaces and nodal points. In particular, the politics of youth was discovered in the private sphere of the family, a biostructure extended to the close network of relatives and friends, which successfully proved to secrete a popular culture-based rebellious rock politics, a body and *jouissance*-experienced pop culture, and a form of subjectification as

145

resistance-identity during communism. Intersecting politics, pop culture, and musical genres—from classical music and jazz, to pop, rock, rap, and hip-hop—and introducing two generations of youth, "Blue Jeans" and "Generation PRO," the discussion also unveiled the de-territorialized character of Western popular culture, one that continuously pervaded Eastern European/Romanian forms of public and private culture since early, even precommunist times.

Another noticeable feature of present popular culture introduced here is its hate speech dimension, as exemplified by the discourse of anti-Semitism as "the mythical Jew." As the relevant chapter introduced it, through its expression in various discourses, in the printed press and, more recently, in cyberspace, "the mythical Jew" brings popular culture at one of its most significant intersections with politics. Finally, as explained, in postcommunism this discourse functions as a symbolic, subject-reflected experience embedded in past representations, yet recirculated as a legacy with new complexities brought by transnational politics in the absence of its synchronic ethnic minority.

The research on women, identities, and politics presented the construction of women as discursive subjects as well as one of the more visible connections between identity construction and identity politics in the form of women's politics. The chapter introduced the reader to the formative experiences of women as subjects within competing femininity discourses—peasant, Balkan "cryptomatriar-chal," Bolshevik-proletarian, yet also precommunist "bourgeois" (diachronic) and Western popular culture (synchronic). It also presented women's integration into a feminized postcommunist transformation as "second-class citizens"—from work practices, health and issues of family planning, and violence, to political participation, and their representation in the mass media. While women's politics was located at educational, NGOs and interest group politics, electoral, and bureaucratic/statist levels, the relevant chapter also problematized larger notions of difference and pan-subjectivities, within which gender and feminism are integral. Discussing the possibilities of an East-West feminist and scholarly dialogue, the research also expressed the need for a "women's *sayable*" or "feminist language," finding present Romanian feminism to be more of a matter of transnational feminist politics and liberal feminism intersecting with some private cross-subjectivities affirmative actions.

An extension of previous gender considerations, the chapter on queer identity insisted on the liminal position that the queer subject holds in Romania. On a background of a "fractal" organization of time, space, practices, and identities, queer subjectivity in postcommunist Romania was revealed not only as a matter of a space of presence/absence, or a discourse of the "open secret," but as an experience that has managed to find a border, a dim niche of representation, in spite of socially intolerant discourses (and legal indictment until September 2001). While deconstructing the practices that create subjectivities, practices that stand beyond Foucauldian definitions of *scientia sexualis* or *ars erotica*, from a transnational politics point of view regarding operations of power, the research sought to reveal one of the most powerful forms of politics de-territorialization, which has brought together international and Romanian civil societies in their fight against conservatism and discrimination.

Finally, the syncretic "final vocabulary" and "limits of the *sayable*" in post-communism were revealed as being framed—from a popular culture point of view —by precommunist-"bourgeois," "socialist realist," and "carnivalesque" aesthetics; by youth subversive politics and various other intellectual and popular culture spaces of counter-hegemonic discourses interweaved in the quotidian fabric of communism; and by recycled, select intolerant discourses. This eclectic discursive order was also unveiled as being conditioned by traditional gender codes, peasant culture, and religious ethic, by a patriarchy fused with nationalism and conservatism, by the feminization of a postcommunist transformation that is developing at a fast, yet uneven pace, and by Western influences, and de-territorialized, transnational politics. Accordingly, postcommunism itself was uncovered as an eclectic discursive universe that easily manages to transcend an immediate totalitarian/communist past, to invoke a larger concept of *yesterday* in its historicity, and to recirculate and recombine various synchronic and diachronic symbolic systems—pre-/post-/communist, East and West.

From a different perspective focused on identity construction and identity politics, entering Romania this way has presented a highly uneven, undulating picture where the *flâneur* could encounter, for example, a weakly developed feminist movement (usually centered on academic feminists and Western funding) while society remains highly sexist and women have to face daily practices of patriarchy and discrimination in the face of which they develop enduring practices of resistance. At another level, the *flâneur* has encountered anti-Semitic discourses that pervade both popular and, to some degree, high culture but with no corresponding Jewish minority, which would otherwise presuppose further reflections on ethnic politics; queer practices of resistance and homophobic practices of discrimination but with no clearly defined queer subcultures, movements, or identity; finally, youth popular culture but with no visible youth politics. Ultimately, the discussion about *what constitutes identity politics in present postcommunist Romania* was revealed to be more about *subjectification practices of oppression and resistance, de-territorialized, transnational politics,* and *discursive syncretism* rather than coherent identity politics and local, democratic social movements—which, as the empirical material reveals, are made relatively inadequate as paradigms capable of explaining at least the last decade as well as present postcommunist Romanian identity and politics.

Thus, the empirical exploration seems to lead us toward the conclusion that *practices* and *experiences* of *identity construction* represent the ultimate foundation of *political identities.* But the absence of clear-cut political identities and local, democratic, cohesive social movements cannot nullify the existence of more subtle forms of politics located in Foucauldian surfaces and networks of power within sub-civil society *biostructures*—such as the family, the community, or the city—in discursively created subjectivities, and in practices of identification through oppression and resistance, or *resistance-duplicity*. When social movements exist—as is the case with Western democracies—the political voice of their represented groups is stronger. But should this political voice be absent or muted—as in the Romanian case—this situation cannot be interpreted as *an absence of politics*, of practices of identification. In other words, the absence or weakness of social movements politics and of a reactive civil society cannot disqualify the existence of more subtle micropolitics of oppression-resistance located in the materiality of everyday life and its *biostructures*. It is my hope that this book has rendered visible such a micropolitics—a micropolitics of the quotidian, or a *biopolitics* of popular culture, that would remain obfuscated if examined through a framework that values less the situatedness of knowledges and epistemological praxes, and places more emphasis on general, abstract concepts such as identity politics and social movements. This is also, as explained, the reason why this book has chosen as its methodologies Cultural Studies and Feminist Theory, as these bodies of knowledge have successfully managed to mesh in the theoretical arena new dimensions of life and politics that express the daily lived life and interaction of individuals with their discursive construction as pluralistic subjects. Such new dimensions of micropolitics are: everyday life, and epistemologies of the quotidian; gender, sex, the body, nature, queer theory, and difference (post)feminism; the public sphere, the media, cyberspace, and global popular culture; subjectivity, identity, fragmentation, difference, and diversity; class, ethnicity, religion, age, and ableness; and literature, TV, the media, the university, popular culture, and folklore.

In the end, I would like to stress that neither each nor all of the subjectivities, practices, and discourses discussed here reflect a holistic picture of contemporary Romanian society, culture, and politics. Such a lived life is irreducible solely to popular culture, gender, women, queer, aesthetics, consumption, *nouveaux riches*, youth, rock and rap subcultures, discursive anti-Semitism, or the feminization of the postcommunist transformation. Everyday life in postcommunist Romania is more complex and, beyond a *cinévérité* realism that can strike the *flâneur*, it will continue to reveal erstwhile hidden and often charming subtleties to those who take an interest.

In regards to Bucharest and the Bucharestians—the originating point of this book—I would like to return here and poetically rejoin Alex Leo Șerban, who, in his "'Everything Must Go,' Or Five Reasons Why I Stayed in Bucharest Instead of Moving to Paris, Florence, or New York," has inspiringly laid down an affectionate satire of the city's quintessential ethos: "Filth" as "self-reproducing" "sub-junk," old "cobbled streets," romantic and shaded "ivy-clad houses," and cats and stray dogs.[1] As for the city's denizens, Șerban concludes with this fluid sentiment: the Bucharestian is "a native juggler" who has "a natural disposition to elaborate on grief rather than on gaiety," who has a short-lived élan, who is "perpetual[ly] naïve, fallible because misinformed," and who is "eternally trustworthy because at this very moment what s/he says is true."[2]

Notes

1. Alex Leo Şerban, "'Everything Must Go,' Or Five Reasons Why I Stayed in Bucharest Instead of Moving to Paris, Florence, or New York," in *Bucharest: A Sentimental Guide*, ed. Aurora Fabritius, Erwin Kessler, and Adrian Solomon, trans. Florin Bican, Alina Cârâc, Michi Constantinescu Fărcaş, Daniela Neacşu, Adrian Solomon, Monica Voiculescu, and Ioana Zirra (Bucharest: The Romanian Cultural Foundation, 2001), 243-4.

2. Şerban, "'Everything Must Go,'" 245.

Selected Bibliography

This selected bibliography contains both Western and Romanian material. With regards to the notion of "academic material," in the Romanian case I must add that, unlike the Western material of this kind, to this date Romanian books and journals with academic relevance—at least those relevant for the topic and genre of this book—are generally not (blind) peer reviewed. Few exceptions do exist, yet their importance on the Romanian academic market is unclear at the time this book is being written. As such, I relied on the empirically rich or erudite character of narrative, on the important testimonial value of some journals or memoirs, and on the national and international prestige of some authors or publications. By contrast, those Romanian nonacademic sources used in this book include articles published in newspapers and journals, reports, surveys, legislation, fact sheets, and songs. In the end, taking advantage of cyberspace and its global connecting powers, I must acknowledge the use of important Internet material, ranging in nature from academic to journalistic, and from reports to sites of political activism.

ACCEPT. <http://www.accept-romania.ro/englishabout.html> (7 June 2002).

Alarcón, Norma. "*Traddutora, Traditora*: A Paradigmatic Figure of Chicana Feminism." Pp. 278-97 in *Dangerous Liaisons: Gender, Nation, & Postcolonial Perspectives*, edited by Anne McClintock, Aamir Mufti, and Ella Shohat. Minneapolis: University of Minnesota Press, 1997.

Almaguer, Tomás. "Chicano Men: A Cartography of Homosexual Identity and Behavior." Pp. 255-73 in *The Lesbian and Gay Studies Reader*, edited by Henry Abelove, Michèle Aina Barale, and David M. Halperin. New York: Routledge, 1993.

Alonso, Ana Maria, and Maria Teresa Koreck. "Silences: 'Hispanics,' AIDS, and Sexual Practices." Pp. 110-26 in *The Lesbian and Gay Studies Reader*, edited by Henry Abelove, Michèle Aina Barale, and David M. Halperin. New York: Routledge, 1993.

Altera. <http://www1.proeuropa.ro/ALTERA/altera.htm> (30 July 2002).

AnA, Society for Feminist Analyses. *Romanian National Report on Institutional Mechanisms for the Advancement of Women (Since the Beijing Conference)*. Bucharest, 1999.

Appadurai, Arjun. "Disjuncture and Difference in the Global Cultural Economy." Pp. 220-30 in *The Cultural Studies Reader*, edited by Simon During, 2nd ed. New York: Routledge, 1999.

Appiah, Kwame Anthony. "The Postcolonial and the Postmodern." Pp. 119-24 in *The Post-Colonial Studies Reader*, edited by Bill Ashcroft, Gareth Griffiths, and Helen Tiffin. New York: Routledge, 1995.

Arendt, Hannah. *Antisemitism: Part One of the Origins of Totalitarianism*. New York: Harcourt Brace & Company, 1958.

Arpad, Joseph J. "The Question of Hungarian Popular Culture." *Journal of Popular Culture* 29, no. 2 (Fall 1995): 9-28.

Ascroft, Joseph. "Către o strategie de afirmare-educaţie-planificare familială," 22, no. 6. 1998. <http://www.dntb.ro/22/1998/6/suplim/5.html> (10 March 2000).

Bacalbaşa, Constantin. "The Bucharest of Former Times." Pp. 73-6 in *Bucharest. A Sentimental Guide*, edited by Aurora Fabritius, Erwin Kessler, and Adrian Solomon, translated by Florin Bican, Alina Cârâc, Michi Constantinescu Fărcaş, Daniela Neacşu, Adrian Solomon, Monica Voiculescu, and Ioana Zirra. Bucharest: The Romanian Cultural Foundation, 2001.

Bacon, Walter M. Jr., and Louis G. Pol. "The Economic Status of Women in Romania." Pp. 43-58 in *Women in the Age of Economic Transformation: Gender Impact of Reforms in Post-Socialist and Developing Countries*, edited by Nahid Aslanbeigui, Steven Pressman, and Gale Summerfield. New York: Routledge, 1994.

Bakhtin, Mikhail. *Rabelais and His World*. Translated by Helene Iswolsky. Bloomington: Indiana University Press, 1988.

Banc, C., and Alan Dundes, eds. *You Call This Living? A Collection of East European Political Jokes*. Athens: The University of Georgia Press, 1990.

Barker, Adele Marie. "Rereading Russia." Pp. 3-11 in *Consuming Russia: Popular Culture, Sex, and Society Since Gorbachev*, edited by Adele M. Barker. Durham: Duke University Press, 1999.

———. "The Culture Factory: Theorizing the Popular in the Old and New Russia." Pp. 12-45 in *Consuming Russia: Popular Culture, Sex, and Society Since Gorbachev*, edited by Adele M. Barker. Durham: Duke University Press, 1999.

———. "Going to the Dogs: Pet Life in the New Russia." Pp. 266-77 in *Consuming Russia: Popular Culture, Sex, and Society Since Gorbachev*, edited by Adele M. Barker. Durham: Duke University Press, 1999.

Barthes, Roland. *The Pleasure of the Text*. Translated by Richard Miller. New York: The Noonday Press, 1980.

Baudrillard, Jean. *Simulacra and Simulation (The Body, in Theory: Histories of Cultural Materialism)*. Translated by Sheila Faria Glaser. Ann Arbor: University of Michigan Press, 1995.

Băban, Adriana. "Women's Sexuality and Reproductive Behavior in Post-Ceauşescu Romania: A Psychological Approach." Pp. 225-53 in *Reproducing Gender: Politics, Publics, and Everyday Life after Socialism*, edited by Susan Gal and Gail Kligman. Princeton: Princeton University Press, 2000.

Băban, Adriana, and David P. Henry. "Aspecte ale sexualităţii în epoca Ceauşescu." *22*, no. 6. 1998. <http://www.dntb.ro/22/1998/6/suplim/1.html> (30 March 2000).

Benjamin, Walter. *Illuminations*. Edited and with an Introduction by Hannah Arendt, translated by Harry Zohn. New York: Shocken Books, 1968.

Boia, Lucian. "Iluzia 'Salvatorului.'" *Curentul*, 12 March 1999. <http://www.curentul. ro/curentul.php> (12 March 1999).

———. *Istorie şi mit în conştiinţa românească*. Bucharest: Humanitas, 1997.

Bourdieu, Pierre. *Distinction: A Social Critique of the Judgement of Taste*. Translated by Richard Nice. Cambridge: Harvard University Press, 1984.

Boym, Svetlana. "From the Toilet to the Museum: Memory and Metamorphosis of Soviet Trash." Pp. 383-96 in *Consuming Russia: Popular Culture, Sex, and Society Since Gorbachev*, edited by Adele M. Barker. Durham: Duke University Press, 1999.

Bracewell, Wendy. "Women, Motherhood, and Contemporary Serbian Nationalism." *Women's Studies International Forum* 19, nos. 1, 2 (1996): 125-32.

Braham, Randolph L. *Romanian Nationalists and the Holocaust: The Political Exploitation of Unfounded Rescue Accounts.* New York: The Rosenthal Institute for Holocaust Studies—The City University of New York, 1998.

Braidotti, Rosi. *Nomadic Subjects: Embodiment and Sexual Difference in Contemporary Feminist Theory.* New York: Columbia University Press, 1994.

Braun, Aurel. "The Incomplete Revolutions: The Rise of Extremism in East-Central Europe and the Former Soviet Union." Pp. 138-60 in *The Extreme Right: Freedom and Security at Risk,* edited by Aurel Braun and Stephen Scheinberg. Boulder: Westview Press, 1997.

Brumberg, Joan Jacobs. *The Body Project: An Intimate History of American Girls.* New York: Vintage Books, 1998.

Bucharest Acceptance Group, *Accept Fact Sheet: Status of Article 200 of the Romanian Penal Code on same-sex relations.* 1 February 2002.

————. "Report on the Symposium Homosexuality: A Human Right?" 31 May 1995. Bucharest: UNESCO-CEPES. <http://geocities.com/WestHollywood/1811/acc1995. html> (30 March 2000).

Butler, Judith. *Gender Trouble: Feminism and the Subversion of Identity.* New York: Routledge, 1990.

Calhoun, Cheshire. "Separating Lesbian Theory from Feminist Theory." Pp. 199-218 in *Feminist Social Thought: A Reader,* edited by Diana T. Meyers. New York: Routledge, 1997.

Campbell, Neil, and Alasdair Kean. *American Cultural Studies: An Introduction to American Culture.* New York: Routledge, 1997.

Cantacuzino, Şerban, "Inns, Churches, Parks and Avenues." Pp. 22-55 in *Bucharest: A Sentimental Guide,* edited by Aurora Fabritius, Erwin Kessler, and Adrian Solomon, translated by Florin Bican, Alina Cârâc, Michi Constantinescu Fărcaş, Daniela Neacşu, Adrian Solomon, Monica Voiculescu, and Ioana Zirra. Bucharest: The Romanian Cultural Foundation, 2001.

Călinescu, Matei. *Five Faces of Modernity: Modernism, Avant-Garde, Decadence, Kitsch, and Postmodernism.* Durham: Duke University Press, 1987.

Cărtărescu, Mircea. "Nuova guardia. Ura şi galeriile de fotbal," *Dilema* no. 357 (Dec. 1999). <http://www.algoritma.ro/dilema/357/MirceaCA.htm> (10 January 2000).

Certeau, Michel de. *The Practice of Everyday Life.* Translated by Steven F. Rendall. Berkeley: University of California Press, 1984.

Cixous, Hélène. "The Laugh of the Medusa." Pp. 245-64 in *New French Feminisms: An Anthology*, edited by Elaine Marks and Isabelle de Courtivron, translated by Keith Cohen and Paula Cohen. Hemel Hempstead: Harvester Wheatsheaf, 1981.

Collins, Patricia Hill. *Black Feminist Thought: Knowledge, Consciousness, and the Politics of Empowerment*. 2nd ed. New York: Routledge, 2000.

Condee, Nancy. "Body Graphics: Tattooing the Fall of Communism." Pp. 339-61 in *Consuming Russia: Popular Culture, Sex, and Society Since Gorbachev*, edited by Adele M. Barker. Durham: Duke University Press, 1999.

Connelly, M. Patricia. "Gender Matters: Global Restructuring and Adjustment." *Social Politics* (Spring 1996): 14-31.

Coupland, Douglas. *Generation X: Tales for an Accelerated Culture*. New York: St. Martin's Press, 1992.

Crutzescu, Gheorghe, "The Mogoşoaia Bridge." Pp. 56-67 in *Bucharest: A Sentimental Guide*, edited by Aurora Fabritius, Erwin Kessler, and Adrian Solomon, translated by Florin Bican, Alina Cârâc, Michi Constantinescu Fărcaş, Daniela Neacşu, Adrian Solomon, Monica Voiculescu, and Ioana Zirra. Bucharest: The Romanian Cultural Foundation, 2001.

Dalmiya, Vrinda, and Linda Alcoff. "Are 'Old Wives' Tales' Justified?" Pp. 217-44 in *Feminist Epistemologies*, edited by Linda Alcoff and Elizabeth Potter. New York: Routledge, 1993.

Daly, Mary. *Gyn/Ecology: The Metaethics of Radical Feminism*. Boston: Beacon Press, 1978.

db Jurnal. Revista Online a Mişcării Legionare din România. <http://dbjurnal.hypermart.net> (8 July 2002).

Derrida, Jacques. *Positions*. Translated and annotated by Alan Bass. Chicago: The University of Chicago Press, 1981.

Drakulić, Slavenka. *How We Survived Communism and Even Laughed*. New York: HarperPerennial, 1993.

Drucker, Peter. "'In the Tropics There Is No Sin,' Sexuality and Gay-Lesbian Movements in the Third World." *New Left Review* no. 218 (1996): 75-101.

Durandin, Catherine. "Cred că a fost supraevaluată capacitatea de ideal a Estului." Pp. 32-42 in *Fin de siècle: Un nou început*, edited by Petre Răileanu. Bucharest: Atlas, 1999.

During, Simon. "Introduction." Pp.1-28 in *The Cultural Studies Reader*, edited by Simon During, 2nd ed. New York: Routledge, 1999.

Dyer, Rychard. "Entertainment and Utopia." Pp. 371-81 in *The Cultural Studies Reader*, edited by Simon During. 2nd ed. New York: Routledge, 1999.

Eco, Umberto. *Travels in Hyperreality*. London: Picador, 1986.

————. *A Theory of Semiotics*. Bloomington: Indiana University Press, 1976.

Einhorn, Barbara. *Cinderella Goes to Market: Citizenship, Gender and Women's Movements in East Central Europe*. London: Verso, 1993.

Eliade, Mircea. *The Sacred & The Profane: The Nature of Religion*. New York: A Harvest Book, 1987.

Elteren, Mel van. "Conceptualizing the Impact of U.S. Popular Culture Globally." *Journal of Popular Culture* 30, no. 1 (Summer 1996): 47-89.

Ensler, Eve. *The Vagina Monologues*. New York: Villard Books, 2000.

Erdoğan, Sema Nilgün. *Sexual Life in Ottoman Society*. Istanbul: Dönençe, 1998.

Eskenasy, Victor. "Anti-Semitic Rhetoric and Propaganda on the Web." *Der Fall Antonescu—Cazul Antonescu*. 9 January 2001. <http://home.t-online.de/home/totok/ion2f.htm> (27 January 2001).

Essig, Laurie. "Publicly Queer: Representations of Queer Subjects and Subjectivities in the Absence of Identity." Pp. 281-302 in *Consuming Russia: Popular Culture, Sex, and Society Since Gorbachev*, edited by Adele M. Barker. Durham: Duke University Press, 1999.

————. *Queer in Russia: A Story of Sex, Self, and the Other*. Durham: Duke University Press, 1999.

Felsenstein, Frank. *Anti-Semitic Stereotypes: A Paradigm of Otherness in English Popular Culture, 1660-1830*. Baltimore: Johns Hopkins University Press, 1995.

Finkelstein, Norman G. *The Holocaust Industry: Reflections on the Exploitation of Jewish Suffering*. New York: Verso, 2000.

Fisher, Mary Ellen, and Doina Pasca Harsányi. "From Tradition and Ideology to Elections and Competition: The Changing Status of Women in Romanian Politics." Pp. 201-23 in *Women in the Politics of Post-Communist Eastern Europe*, edited by Marilyn Rueschemeyer. Armonk: M. E. Sharpe, 1994.

Fiske, John. *Understanding Popular Culture*. New York: Routledge, 1991.

Florian, Alexandru. "The Holocaust in Romanian textbooks." Pp. 237-85 in *The Tragedy of Romanian Jewry*, edited by Randolph L. Braham. New York: The Rosenthal Institute for Holocaust Studies—The City University of New York, 1994.

Florian, Radu. *Criza unei lumi in schimbare*. Bucharest: Editura Noua Alternativă, 1994.

Forgacs, David, and Robert Lumley, eds. *Italian Cultural Studies: An Introduction*. New York: Oxford University Press, 1996.

Fotea, Daniela Caraman. *Meridianele Cîntecului*. Bucharest: Editura Muzicală, 1989.

Foucault, Michel. "The Birth of Biopolitics." Pp. 73-9 in *Ethics: Subjectivity and Truth: Essential Works of Foucault 1954-1984* vol. I, edited by Paul Rabinow, translated by Robert Hurley and others. New York: The New Press, 1998.

————. "Technologies of the Self." Pp. 223-51 in *Ethics: Subjectivity and Truth: Essential Works of Foucault 1954-1984* vol. I, edited by Paul Rabinow, translated by Robert Hurley and others. New York: The New Press, 1998.

————. *Discipline and Punish: The Birth of the Prison*. Translated by Alan Sheridan. New York: Vintage Books, 1995.

————. *The Birth of the Clinic: An Archeology of Medical Perception*. Translated by A. M. Sheridan. New York: Vintage Books, 1994.

————."Politics and the Study of Discourse." Pp. 53-72 in *The Foucault Effect: Studies in Governmentality*, edited by Graham Burchell, Colin Gordon, and Peter Miller. Chicago: The University of Chicago Press, 1991.

————. *The History of Sexuality: An Introduction*. Vol. I. Translated by Robert Hurley. New York: Vintage Books, 1990.

————. *The Archeology of Knowledge and the Discourse on Language*. Translated by A. M. Sheridan Smith. New York: Pantheon Books, 1982.

————. "Two Lectures." Pp. 78-108 in *Power/Knowledge: Selected Interviews and Other Writings, 1972-1977*, edited by Colin Gordon. New York: Pantheon Books, 1981.

Fraser, Nancy. "Equality, Difference and Radical Democracy. The United States Feminist Debates Revisited." Pp. 197-208 in *Radical Democracy: Identity, Citizenship, and the State*, edited by David Trend. New York: Routledge, 1995.

Friedan, Betty. *The Feminine Mystique*. New York: W. W. Norton, 1963.

Funk, Nanette. "Feminism East and West." Pp. 318-330 in *Gender Politics and Post-Communism: Reflections from Eastern Europe and the Former Soviet Union*, edited by Nanette Funk and Magda Muller. New York: Routledge, 1993.

Gal, Susan, and Gail Kligman. *The Politics of Gender after Socialism: A Comparative-Historical Essay*. Princeton: Princeton University Press, 2000.

Garaudy, Roger. *Miturile fondatoare ale politicii israeliene*. Bucharest: Alma Tip, 1998.

Gilberg, Trond. *Nationalism and Communism in Romania: The Rise and Fall of Ceausescu's Personal Dictatorship*. Boulder: Westview Press, 1990.

Giurescu, Dinu C., *Distrugerea Trecutului României*. Bucharest: Editura Museion, 1994.

Glassman, Bernard. *Anti-Semitic Stereotypes without Jews: Images of the Jews in England, 1290-1700*. Detroit: Wayne State University Press, 1975.

Gordy, Eric. "'Turbasi' and 'Rockeri' as Windows into Serbia's Social Divide." *Balkanologie* IV, no. 1 (2000): 55-81.

Government of Canada. *Canadian Multiculturalism Act*. <http://lois.justice.gc.ca/en/C-18.7/29236.html> (25 July 2002).

Grossberg, Lawrence. *We Gotta Get out of This Place: Popular Conservatism and Post-modern Culture*. New York: Routledge, 1992.

Grosz, Elizabeth. "Bodies and Knowledges: Feminism and the Crisis of Reason." Pp. 187-215 in *Feminist Epistemologies*, edited by Linda Alcoff and Elizabeth Potter. New York: Routledge, 1993.

———. "A Note on Essentialism and Difference." Pp. 332-44 in *Feminist Knowledge: Critique and Construct*, edited by Sneja Gunew. New York: Routledge 1992.

Grünberg, Laura, and Mihaela Miroiu, eds. *Gen şi educatie*. Bucharest: AnA & PHARE, 1997.

Grünberg, Laura. "Women's NGOs in Romania." Pp. 307-36 in *Reproducing Gender: Politics, Publics, and Everyday Life after Socialism*, edited by Susan Gal and Gail Kligman. Princeton: Princeton University Press, 2000.

Gutmann, Amy, ed. *Multiculturalism*. Princeton: Princeton University Press, 1994.

Haraway, Donna. "A Manifesto for Cyborgs: Science, Technology, and Socialist Feminism in the 1980s." Pp. 501-31 in *Feminist Social Thought: A Reader*, edited by Diana T. Meyers. New York: Routledge, 1997.

———. *Simians, Cyborgs, and Women*. London: Free Association Books, 1990.

Harding, Sandra. "Rethinking Standpoint Epistemology: What Is 'Strong Objectivity'?" Pp. 49-82 in *Feminist Epistemologies*, edited by Linda Alcoff and Elizabeth Potter. New York: Routledge, 1993.

————. "Feminism, Science, and the Anti-Enlightenment Critiques." Pp. 83-106 in *Feminism/Postmodernism*, edited by Linda J. Nicholson. New York: Routledge, 1990.

Harsányi, Doina Pasca. "Participation of Women in the Workforce: The Case of Romania." Pp. 213-17 in *Family, Women, and Employment in Central-Eastern Europe*, edited by Barbara Lobodzinska. Westport: Greenwood Press, 1995.

————. "Women in Romania." Pp. 39-52 in *Gender Politics and Post-Communism: Reflections from Eastern Europe and the Former Soviet Union*, edited by Nanette Funk and Magda Muller. New York: Routledge, 1993.

Hartsock, Nancy C. M. "The Feminist Standpoint: Developing the Ground for a Specifically Feminist Historical Materialism." Pp. 461-83 in *Feminist Social Thought: A Reader*, edited by Diana T. Meyers. New York: Routledge, 1997.

Hausleitner, Mariana. "Women in Romania: Before and after the Collapse." Pp. 53-61 in *Gender Politics and Post-Communism: Reflections from Eastern Europe and the Former Soviet Union*, edited by Nanette Funk and Magda Muller. New York: Routledge, 1993.

Healey, Dan. "Masculine Purity and 'Gentlemen's Mischief': Sexual Exchange and Prostitution between Russian Men, 1861-1941." *Slavic Review* 60, no. 2 (2001): 233-65.

Heyd, David. *Supererogation: Its Status in Ethical Theory*. Cambridge: Cambridge University Press, 1982.

Hîncu, Dumitru. "Traveling to Bucharest between the Wars." Pp. 138-8 in *Bucharest: A Sentimental Guide*, edited by Aurora Fabritius, Erwin Kessler, and Adrian Solomon, translated by Florin Bican, Alina Cârâc, Michi Constantinescu Fărcaş, Daniela Neacşu, Adrian Solomon, Monica Voiculescu, and Ioana Zirra. Bucharest: The Romanian Cultural Foundation, 2001.

Holograf, "Sunt un Balcanic." *Holografica*. Bucharest: Media Pro Music, 2000.

hooks, bell. *Yearning: Race, Gender, and Cultural Politics*. London: Turnaround, 1991.

Horkheimer, Max, and Theodor Adorno. "The Culture Industry: Enlightenment as Mass Deception." Pp. 32-41 in *The Cultural Studies Reader*, edited by Simon During, 2nd ed. New York: Routledge, 1999.

Iancu, Mişu, ed. *Cântece, cântece, cântece ale unor compozitori evrei din România*. Bucharest: Hasefer, 1996.

Institute for Jewish Policy Research Online Report. "Antisemitism and Xenophobia Today: Romania." <http://www.axt.org.uk/antisem/countries/romania/index.html> (8 July 2002).

Inter-Parliamentary Union, *Women in National Parliaments*. 1 July 2002. <http://www.ipu.org/wmn-e/classif.htm> (25 July 2002).

International Third Position. <http://dspace.dial.pipex.com/third-position/index.html> (8 July 2002).

Ioan, Augustin, "Bucharest—Memory Walled-In." Pp. 159-76 in *Bucharest: A Sentimental Guide*, edited by Aurora Fabritius, Erwin Kessler, and Adrian Solomon, translated by Florin Bican, Alina Cârâc, Michi Constantinescu Fărcaş, Daniela Neacşu, Adrian Solomon, Monica Voiculescu, and Ioana Zirra. Bucharest: The Romanian Cultural Foundation, 2001.

Ioanid, Radu. *The Holocaust in Romania: The Destruction of Jews and Gypsies under the Antonescu Regime, 1940-1944*. Chicago: Ivan R. Dee, 2000.

———. "Introduction." Pp. vii-xx in Mihail Sebastian. *Journal 1935-1944: The Fascist Years*. Translated by Patrick Camiller, Introduction and notes by Radu Ioanid. Chicago: Ivan R. Dee, 2000. Published in association with the United States Holocaust Memorial Museum.

"Intâlniri pe fir." *România liberă*, 30 June 2000.

Jaggar, Alison M. "Feminist Ethics." P. 364 in *Encyclopedia of Ethics*, edited by Lawrence Becker with Charlotte Becker. New York: Garland, 1992.

Jameson, Fredric. *Postmodernism, Or, The Cultural Logic of Late Capitalism*. Durham: Duke University Press, 1991.

Jaquette, Jane, and Sharon L. Wolchik, "Women and Democratization in Latin America and Central and Eastern Europe." Pp. 1-28 in *Women and Democracy: Latin America and Central and Eastern Europe*, edited by Jane Jaquette and Sharon L. Wolchik. Baltimore: The Johns Hopkins University Press, 1998.

Kapur, Jeeta. "Globalization and Culture: Navigating the Void." Pp. 191-217 in *The Cultures of Globalization*, edited by Fredric Jameson and Masao Miyoshi. Durham: Duke University Press, 1998.

Kelly, Catriona, and David Shepherd, eds. *Russian Cultural Studies: An Introduction*. Oxford: Oxford University Press, 1998.

Kelly, Catriona, Hilary Pilkington, David Shepherd, and Vadim Volkov. "Introduction: Why Cultural Studies?" Pp. 1-17 in *Russian Cultural Studies: An Introduction*, edited by Catriona Kelly and David Shepherd. Oxford: Oxford University Press, 1998.

Kidd, William, and Siân Reynolds, eds. *Contemporary French Cultural Studies*. London: Arnold/New York: Oxford University Press, 2000.

King, Deborah K. "Multiple Jeopardy, Multiple Consciousness: The Context of a Black Feminist Ideology." Pp. 220-42 in *Feminist Social Thought: A Reader*, edited by Diana T. Meyers. New York: Routledge, 1997.

King, Robert R. *A History of the Romanian Communist Party*. Stanford: Hoover Institution Press—Stanford University, 1980.

Kligman, Gail. *The Politics of Duplicity: Controlling Reproduction in Ceausescu's Romania*. Berkeley: University of California Press, 1998.

————. *The Wedding of the Dead: Ritual, Poetics, and Popular Culture in Transylvania*. Berkeley: University of California Press, 1988.

Korać, Maja. "Understanding Ethno-National Identity and Its Meaning. Questions from Women's Experience." *Women's Studies International Forum* 19, nos. 1, 2 (1996): 133-43.

Kuller, Harry. *Presa evreiască bucureşteană 1857-1994*. Bucharest: Hasefer, 1996.

Kymlicka, Will. *Multicultural Citizenship*. Oxford: Clarendon Press, 1995.

Laignel-Lavastine, Alexandra. "Fascisme et communisme en Roumanie: enjeux et usage d'une comparaison." Pp. 201-54 in *Stalinisme et nazisme: Histoire et mémoire comparées*, edited by Henry Rousso. Bruxelles: Éditions Complexe, 1999.

Lal, Vinay. *South Asian Cultural Studies*. Manohar: Delhi, 1996.

Levy, Robert. *Ana Pauker: The Rise and Fall of A Jewish Communist*. Berkeley: University of California Press, 2001.

Liiceanu, Gabriel. *The Păltiniş Diary: A Paideic Model in Humanist Culture*. Translated by James Christian Brown. Budapest: Central European University Press, 2000.

Livezeanu, Irina. *Cultural Politics in Greater Romania: Regionalism, Nation Building, and Ethnic Struggle, 1918-1930*. Ithaca: Cornell University Press, 1995.

Lorde, Audre. "Age, Race, Class, and Sex: Women Redefining Difference." Pp. 374-80 in *Dangerous Liaisons: Gender, Nation, & Postcolonial Perspectives*, edited by Anne McClintock, Aamir Mufti, and Ella Shohat. Minneapolis: University of Minnesota Press, 1997.

Manega, Miron. "Cui îi este frică de manele?" *Naţional*, 27 January 2001. <http://www.nationalpress.ro/> (28 January 2001).

Manu, Emil. *Cafeneaua literară*. Bucharest: Editura Saeculum I.O., 1997.

Marcuse, Herbert. *One-Dimensional Man: Studies in Ideology of Advanced Industrial Society*. Boston: Beacon Press, 1992.

Mignolo, Walter D. "Globalization, Civilization Processes, and the Relocation of Languages and Cultures." Pp. 32-53 in *The Cultures of Globalization*, edited by Fredric Jameson and Masao Miyoshi. Durham: Duke University Press, 1998.

Mihăilescu, Dan C. "The Rules of Bucharest Chic." Pp. 87-8 in *Bucharest: A Sentimental Guide*, edited by Aurora Fabritius, Erwin Kessler, and Adrian Solomon, translated by Florin Bican, Alina Cârâc, Michi Constantinescu Fărcaş, Daniela Neacşu, Adrian Solomon, Monica Voiculescu, and Ioana Zirra. Bucharest: The Romanian Cultural Foundation, 2001.

Milea, Ada. "Perspectiva." *Republica Mioritică România*. Bucharest: Intercont Music, 1999.

Milner, Andrew. *Contemporary Cultural Theory: An Introduction*. London: UCL Press, 1994.

Minh-ha, Trinh T. "Not You/Like You: Postcolonial Women and the Interlocking Questions of Identity and Difference." Pp. 415-9 in *Dangerous Liaisons: Gender, Nation, & Postcolonial Perspectives*, edited by Anne McClintock, Aamir Mufti, and Ella Shohat. Minneapolis: University of Minnesota Press, 1997.

Miroiu, Mihaela. "Feminismul ca politică a modernizării." Pp. 252-74 in *Doctrine politice: Concepte universale şi realităţi româneşti*, edited by Alina Mungiu-Pippidi. Iaşi: Polirom, 1998.

———. "Ana's Land. The Right to Be Sacrificed." Pp. 136-40 in *Ana's Land: Sisterhood in Eastern Europe*, edited by Tanya Renne. Boulder: Westview Press, 1997.

———. *Convenio. Despre natură, femei şi morală*. Bucharest: Alternative, 1996.

Mişcarea legionară. <www.miscarea-legionara.com> (8 July 2002).

Mohanty, Chandra Talpade. "Under Western Eyes: Feminist Scholarship and Colonial Discourses." Pp. 255-77 in *Dangerous Liaisons: Gender, Nation, & Postcolonial Perspectives*, edited by Anne McClintock, Aamir Mufti, and Ella Shohat. Minneapolis: University of Minnesota Press, 1997.

Moore, Barrington Jr. *Social Origins of Dictatorship and Democracy: Lord and Peasant in the Making of the Modern World*. Boston: Beacon Press, 1966.

Moreiras, Alberto. "Global Fragments: A Second Latinamericanism." Pp. 81-102 in *The Cultures of Globalization*, edited by Fredric Jameson and Masao Miyoshi. Durham: Duke University Press, 1998.

Moroianu-Zlătescu, Irina. *Şanse egale, Şanse reale: Studii şi cercetări privind drepturile femeii—Equal Opportunities, Real Opportunities: Studies and Research on Women's Rights*. Bucharest: Institutul Român pentru Drepturile Omului, 1996.

Moroianu-Zlătescu, Irina, and Ioan Oancea. *The Legislative and Institutional Framework for National Minorities from Romania.* Bucharest: The Romanian Government—The Council for Ethnic Minorities, 1994.

Mouffe, Chantal. *The Return of the Political.* London: Verso, 1997.

Mungiu-Pippidi, Alina, ed. *Doctrine politice: Concepte universale şi realităţi româneşti.* Iaşi: Polirom, 1998.

Nanda, Serena. *"Hijras* as Neither Man Nor Women." Pp. 542-52 in *The Lesbian and Gay Studies Reader,* edited by Henry Abelove, Michèle Aina Barale, and David M. Halperin. New York: Routledge, 1993.

National Organization for Women. "NOW President Kim Gandy Calls for a Filibuster Strategy to Save *Roe.*" 22 January 2002. <http://www.now.org/press/01-02/01-22.html> (1 August 2002).

Nelson, Lynn Hankinson. "Epistemological Communities." Pp. 121-59 in *Feminist Epistemologies,* edited by Linda Alcoff and Elizabeth Potter. New York: Routledge, 1993.

Niessen, James P. "Romanian Nationalism: An Ideology of Integration and Mobilization." Pp. 273-304 in *Eastern European Nationalism in the Twentieth Century,* edited by Peter F. Sugar. Washington: The American University Press, 1995.

Noua Dreaptă. <http://www.nouadreapta.org/> (8 July 2002).

Oişteanu, Andrei. *Imaginea evreului în cultura română.* Bucharest: Humanitas, 2001.

———. "'Evreul imaginar' versus 'evreul real.'" *Sfera Politicii,* no. 60 (1998): 34-40.

———. "'Imaginary Jew' versus 'Real Jew' in Romanian Folklore and Mythology." Pp. 266-92 in *Identitate/alteritate în spaţiul cultural românesc,* edited by Al. Zub. Iaşi: Editura Universităţii "Alexandru Ioan Cuza," 1996.

Olsen, Frances Elisabeth. "Feminism in Central and Eastern Europe: Risks and Possibilities of American Engagement." *Yale Law Journal* 106, no.7 (1997): 2215-57.

Oushakine, Serguei Alex. "The Quantity of Style: Imaginary Consumption in the New Russia." *Theory, Culture, and Society* 17, no. 5 (2000): 97-120.

———. "In the State of Post-Soviet Aphasia: Symbolic Development in Contemporary Russia." *Europe-Asia Studies* 52, no. 6 (Sept. 2000): 991-1016.

Pagina României Naţionaliste. <http://pages.prodigy.net/nnita/> (8 July 2002).

Pasti, Vladimir, Mihaela Miroiu, and Cornel Codiță. *Romania—Starea de fapt. Volumul I: Societatea.* Bucharest: Nemira, 1997.

Pathak, Zakia. "A Pedagogy for Postcolonial Feminists." Pp. 426-41 in *Feminists Theorize the Political*, edited by Judith Butler and Joan W. Scott. New York: Routledge, 1992.

Peterson, Spike. "The Politics of Identification in the Context of Globalization." *Women's Studies International Forum* 19, nos. 1, 2 (1996): 5-15.

Pilkington, Hilary. "'The Future is Ours': Youth Culture in Russia, 1953 to the Present." Pp. 368-86 in *Russian Cultural Studies: An Introduction*, edited by Catriona Kelly and David Shepherd. Oxford: Oxford University Press, 1998.

Popescu, Liliana, ed. *Gen și politică: Femeile din Romania în viața publică.* Bucharest: UNDP, 1999.

————. "Șoapte fierbinți și fantezii romantice." Pp. 34-9 in *Gen și educație*, edited by Laura Grünberg and Mihaela Miroiu. Bucharest: AnA & PHARE, 1997.

Ramet, Sabrina P., ed. *Gender Politics in the Western Balkans: Women and Society in Yugoslavia and the Yugoslav Successor States.* University Park: The Pennsylvania State University Press, 1999.

————. *Rocking the State: Rock Music and Politics in Eastern Europe and Russia.* Boulder: Westview Press, 1994.

Recensământ 2002. <http://www.recensamant.ro/> (17 July 2002).

Rich, Adrienne. "Compulsory Heterosexuality and Lesbian Existence." Pp. 310-26 in *Feminism in Our Time: The Essential Writings, World War II to the Present*, edited by Miriam Schneir. New York: Vintage Books, 1994.

Roman, Carol. *Laureați ai premiului Nobel răspund la întrebarea: Există un secret al celebrității?* Bucharest: Editura Politică, 1971.

Roman, Denise. "On Survival and Critical Universalism in a Romanian Model in Humanist Culture." In *The European Legacy: Toward New Paradigms* 7, no. 6 (December 2002). Forthcoming.

————. "Gendering Eastern Europe: Pre-Feminism, Prejudice, and East-West Dialogues in Post-Communist Romania." *Women's Studies International Forum* 24, no. 1 (2001): 53-66.

————. "Poststructuralism." Pp. 308-10 in *Encyclopedia of Postmodernism*, edited by Victor E. Taylor and Charles E. Winquist. New York: Routledge, 2001.

Romania.org. "Facts and Figures." <http://www.romania.org> (24 June 2002).

Romanian Action for Gay Men, Lesbians and Bisexuals. "U.S. Activists Denounce Romania." 15 January 1998. <http://www.raglb.org.uk/news30.htm> (30 March 2000).

———. "Mariana Cetiner Thanks Supporters." 6 April 1998. <http://www.raglb.org.uk/news33.htm> (30 March 2000).

———. "Greens Nominate Romanian Gay and Lesbian Rights Group for the Sakharov Prize." 17 September 1998. Strasbourg. <http://www.geocities.com/WestHollywood/1811/> (30 March 2000).

———. "International Boycott of Romania Launched to Protest Article 200." 22 January 1997. <http://www.raglb.org.uk/news19.htm> (30 March 2000).

Romanian Government, "Ordonanţa guvernului no. 137." *Monitorul Oficial* no. 431, 2 September 2000.

———. "Ordonanţa de urgenţă no. 89." *Monitorul Oficial* no. 338, 26 June 2001.

———. "Ordonanţa de urgenţă no. 31." *Monitorul Oficial* no. 214, 28 March 2002.

Romanian LesBiGays on Internet. *Latest News.* 17 November 1998. <http://www.geocities. com/WestHollywood/1811> (30 March 2000).

———. "Poliţiştii întrerup o toridă partidă de homosex . . . în parcul Cişmigiu." *Ziua*, 3 September 1997. Edited by Adrian Newell Păun. 1998. <http://www.geocities.com/WestHollywood/1811/amantii.htm> (30 March 2000).

———. "Despre teatru cu Alina Mungiu-Pippidi." *Adevărul*, April 1998. <http://www. geocities.com/WestHollywood/1811/trebuie.htm> (30 March 2000).

———. "ACCEPT's Proposed New Legislation." 7 May 1998. <http://www.geocities. com/WestHollywood/1811/despre200.htm> (30 March 2000).

———. "The Conference Expressing Sexuality: Biology, Culture Theory, and Psychology of Homosexuality." 13 September 1997. <http://www.geocities.com/WestHollywood/1811/cluj97.html (30 March 2000).

———. "Romanian Gay Man Wins Asylum in U.S." <http://www.geocities.com/ WestHollywood/1811/news.html> (30 March 2000).

———. "Books with Gay Themes Published in Romania." <http://www.geocities.com/WestHollywood/1811/book.html> (30 March 2000).

———. "Britanicul John Michael Taylor este arestat pentru relaţii sexuale cu un minor." October 1997. <http://www.geocities.com/WestHollywood/1811/taylor.htm> (30 March 2000).

————. "Kom Ut International Press Release: Nordic Artists Prohibited from Performing in Romania." 20 July 1994. <http://www.geocities.com/WestHollywood/1811/20jul94.html> (30 March 2000).

————. "Romanian Patriarch on Homosexuality." *RFE/RL Daily Report* 213, 9 November 1994. Edited by Michael Shafir. In Romanian LesBiGays on Internet, <http://www.geocities.com/WestHollywood/1811/9nov94.html> (17 July 2002).

Romanian Parliament. "Lege nr. 61 din 16 ianuarie 2002 privind aprobarea Ordonanţei de urgenţă a Guvernului nr. 89/2001 pentru modificarea şi completarea unor dispoziţii din Codul penal referitoare la infracţiuni privind viaţa sexuală." *Monitorul Oficial* no. 65, 30 January 2002.

Rorty, Richard. *Contingency, Irony, and Solidarity.* Cambridge: Cambridge University Press, 1989.

Rosenthal, Denise [Denise Roman]. "'The Mythical Jew': Antisemitism, Intellectuals, and Democracy in Post-Communist Romania." *Nationalities Papers* 29, no. 3 (2001): 419-39.

Rusu, Victor. *Iţic şi lumea lui.* Bucharest: Hasefer, 2000.

Ryback, Timothy W. *Rock around the Bloc: A History of Rock Music in Eastern Europe and the Soviet Union.* New York: Oxford University Press, 1990.

Sabonis-Chafee, Theresa. "Communism as Kitsch: Soviet Symbols in Post-Soviet Society." Pp. 362-82 in *Consuming Russia: Popular Culture, Sex, and Society Since Gorbachev*, edited by Adele M. Barker. Durham: Duke University Press, 1999.

Sabou, Cornel, ZIUA, and Romanian LesBiGays on Internet. "Scandalul homosexualilor anchetaţi ilegal de Poliţia Maramureş." 23 July 1997. <http://www.geocities.com/WestHollywood/1811/baiamare2.htm> (30 March 2000).

Sarmale Reci (Mihai Iordache and Florin Dumitrescu). "Prostia-i la putere." *Răpirea din Serai.* Bucharest: Media Pro Music, 1998.

Sava, Iosif. *Harpiştii Regelui David.* Bucharest: Hasefer, 1998.

Scott, Joan W. "Experience." Pp. 22-40 in *Feminists Theorize the Political*, edited by Judith Butler and Joan W. Scott. New York: Routledge, 1992.

————. "Gender: A Useful Category in Historical Analysis." *American Historical Review* 91, no. 5 (1986): 1053-75.

Scott, Long, and Bogdan Voicu. "Police Abuses against Suspected Homosexuals in Baia Mare and Iaşi, Romania." *Romanian LesBiGays on Internet.* 23-28 September 1996. <http://www.geocities.com/WestHollywood/1811/scott.htm> (30 March 2000).

Sebastian, Mihail. *Journal 1935-1944: The Fascist Years.* Translated by Patrick Camiller, Introduction and notes by Radu Ioanid. Chicago: Ivan R. Dee, 2000. Published in association with the United States Holocaust Memorial Museum.

————. *De două mii de ani. Cum am devenit huligan.* Bucharest: Hasefer, 2000.

Sedgwick, Eva Kosofsky. "Epistemology of the Closet." Pp. 45-61 in *The Lesbian and Gay Studies Reader*, edited by Henry Abelove, Michèle Aina Barale, and David M. Halperin. New York: Routledge, 1993.

Şerban, Alex. Leo. "'Everything Must Go,' Or Five Reasons Why I Stayed in Bucharest Instead of Moving to Paris, Florence, or New York." Pp. 243-5 in *Bucharest: A Sentimental Guide*, edited by Aurora Fabritius, Erwin Kessler, and Adrian Solomon, translated by Florin Bican, Alina Cârâc, Michi Constantinescu Fărcaş, Daniela Neacşu, Adrian Solomon, Monica Voiculescu, and Ioana Zirra. Bucharest: The Romanian Cultural Foundation, 2001.

Shafir, Michael. "Romanians Vote for the Past and for Extremists." *RFE/RL Newsline*, 27 November 2000. <http://www.rferl.org/newsline/2000/11/271100.asp> (28 Dec. 2000).

————. "The Man They Love to Hate: Norman Manea's 'Snail House' between Holocaust and Gulag." *East European Jewish Affairs* 30, no. 1 (2000): 60-81.

————. "Radical Politics in East-Central Europe. Part III: X-Raying Post-Communist 'Radical Minds.' C) Conspiracy Theories and Anti-Semitism." *East European Perspectives* 2, no. 1 (January 2000). <http://www.rferl.org/eepreport/2000/01/01-120100.html> (24 July 2002).

————. "The Mind of Romania's Radical Right." Pp. 213-32 in *The Radical Right in Central and Eastern Europe Since 1989*, edited by Sabrina P. Ramet. University Park: The Pennsylvania State University, 1999.

————. "Anti-Semitism without Jews in Romania." *Report on Eastern Europe* 2, no. 26 (1991): 20-32.

Simić, Andrei. "Machismo and Cryptomatriarchy: The Traditional Yugoslav Family." Pp. 11-29 in *Gender Politics in the Western Balkans: Women and Society in Yugoslavia and the Yugoslav Successor States*, edited by Sabrina P. Ramet. University Park: The Pennsylvania State University Press, 1999.

Skocpol, Theda. *States and Social Revolutions: A Comparative Analysis of France, Russia, and China.* Cambridge: Cambridge University Press, 1979.

Solomovici, Teşu. *România Iudaica: O istorie neconvenţională a evreilor din România. 2000 ani de existenţă continuă* vols. I and II. Bucharest: Teşu Publishing House, 2001.

Spivak, Gayatri C., "Can the Subaltern Speak?" Pp. 24-8 in *The Post-Colonial Studies Reader*, edited by Bill Ashcroft, Gareth Griffiths, and Helen Tiffin. New York: Routledge, 1995.

Stallybrass, Peter, and Allon White. "Bourgeois Hysteria and The Carnivalesque." Pp. 382-8 in *The Cultural Studies Reader*, edited by Simon During, 2nd ed. New York: Routledge, 1999.

Stan, Lavinia, and Lucian Turcescu. "The Romanian Orthodox Church and Post-Communist Democratisation." *Europe-Asia Studies* 52, no. 8 (December 2000): 1467-88.

Storey, John. *An Introduction to Cultural Theory and Popular Culture.* 2nd ed. London: Prentice Hall/Harvester Wheatsheaf, 1993.

Suru, Şerban. "Scrisoare deschisă." April 2002. <http://www.miscarea-legionara.com/protest.htm> (25 July 2002).

Swanee, Hunt. "Women's Vital Voices." *Foreign Affaires* 76 (July 1997): 2-7.

Tismaneanu, Vladimir. *Fantasies of Salvation: Democracy, Nationalism, and Myth in Post-Communist Europe.* Princeton: Princeton University Press, 1998.

Tismaneanu, Vladimir, and Dan Pavel. "Romania's Mystical Revolutionaries: The Generation of Angst and Adventure Revisited." *East European Politics and Societies* 8 (Fall 1994): 402-38.

Todorova, Maria. *Imagining the Balkans.* New York: Oxford University Press, 1997.

Tomasi, Luigi. "The New Europe and the Value Orientations of Young People: East-West Comparisons." Pp. 47-64 in *Politics and Religion in Central and Eastern Europe. Traditions and Transitions*, edited by William H. Swatos Jr. Westport: Praeger, 1994.

Tomlinson, John. *Cultural Imperialism.* Baltimore: The Johns Hopkins University Press, 1991.

Tong, Rosemarie Putnam. *Feminist Thought: A More Comprehensive Introduction*, 2nd ed. Boulder: Westview Press, 1998.

Totok, William. "Prolog. " In *Der Fall Antonescu—Cazul Antonescu*, edited by William Totok. 21 August 2000. <http://home.t-online.de/home/totok/ion2c.htm#PROLOG> (27 January 2001).

UNICEF. *Women in Transition: The MONEE Project. Regional Monitoring CEE/CIS/Baltics* 6. Florence: UNICEF, 1999.

Ungureanu, Dănuţ. "Adolescent într-o România bătrână." *Curentul*, 15 May 2001. <http://www.curentul.ro/curentul.php> (16 May 2001).

Ursoniu, Constantin. *Igiena Sexuală.* Timişoara: Editura Facla, 1980.

Verdery, Katherine. *The Political Lives of Dead Bodies: Reburial and Postsocialist Change.* New York: Columbia University Press, 1999.

————. *What Was Socialism, and What Comes Next?* Princeton: Princeton University Press, 1996.

————. *National Ideology under Socialism: Identity and Cultural Politics in Ceauşescu's Romania.* Berkeley: University of California Press, 1991.

————. *Transylvanian Villagers: Three Centuries of Political, Economic, and Ethnic Change.* Berkeley: University of California Press, 1983.

Voicu, George. "*Ravelstein*: Text şi Pretext." *22*, no. 42, (2001). <http://home.t-online. de/home/totok/ion2i.htm#Ravelstein> (31 July 2002).

————. "Teme antisemite în discursul public. II" *Sfera Politicii*, no. 81 (2000): 52-8.

————. "Un text din Le Monde şi replici la el. IV: Indecenţa comparativă," *22*, no. 11 (2000). <http://www.dntb.ro/22/2000/11/7voicu.html> (30 March 2000).

————. "Rechizitoriu cu tîlc." *Sfera Politicii*, no. 32 (1995): 15-7.

Volovici, Leon. "Discussion: Notes on 'Latent Antisemitism.'" *Annual Report.* The Vidal Sassoon International Center for the Study of Antisemitism—The Hebrew University of Jerusalem (1997): 16-8.

————. "Mit şi realitate." Translated by Louis Ulrich. *Sfera Politicii*, no. 32 (1995): 4-8.

————. *Antisemitism in Post-Communist Eastern Europe: A Marginal or Central Issue? ACTA no. 5.* Jerusalem: The Vidal Sassoon International Center for the Study of Antisemitism—The Hebrew University of Jerusalem, 1994.

————. *Nationalist Ideology and Antisemitism: The Case of the Romanian Intellectuals in the 1930s.* Translated by Charles Kormos. Oxford: Pergamon Press, 1991.

Wald, Henri. *Înţelesuri Iudaice.* Bucharest: Hasefer, 1995.

Wald, Lucia, ed. *Lingvişti şi filologi evrei din România.* Bucharest: Hasefer, 1996.

Waldeck, R.G. *Athene Palace.* New York: Robert M. McBride & Company, 1942.

Wedel, Janine R. *Collision and Collusion: The Strange Case of Western Aid to Eastern Europe 1989-1998.* New York: St. Martin's Press, 1998.

Williams, Raymond. *Keywords: A Vocabulary of Culture and Society.* London: Fontana, 1983.

Wolff, Larry. *Inventing Eastern Europe: The Map of Civilization on the Mind of the Enlightenment.* Stanford: Stanford University Press, 1994.

World Bank. *2000 World Development Indicators.* <www.worldbank.org> (24 June 2002).

Yuval-Davies, Nira. *Gender and Nation.* London: Sage Publications, 1997.

———. "Women and the Biological Reproduction of the 'Nation.'" *Women's Studies International Forum* 19, nos. 1, 2 (1996): 17-24.

Ziua and Romanian LesBiGays on Internet. "Scott Long, consilier al organizației 'Human Rights Watch' din SUA, va informa Comunitatea Europeană și ONU despre abuzurile din România." 6 July 1997. <http://www.geocities.com/Holly wood/1811/ baiamare.html> (30 March 2000).

Index

About the Author

Denise Roman holds a Ph.D. degree in Political Science from York University, Canada, and a degree in Law from the University of Bucharest, Romania. Ms. Roman taught Feminist Theory and Gender and Society at Northeastern University, in Boston, and she is a Visiting Scholar with the UCLA Center for the Study of Women. An international editorial advisory board member for *Women's Studies International Forum*, she specializes in critical Cultural Studies, issues of democratization in postcommunist Eastern Europe, and transnational feminism. She is a contributor to the Routledge *Encyclopedia of Postmodernism* and has published articles on Eastern European identity construction and identity politics in various North American, French, and Romanian journals, such as *Nationalities Papers, Balkanologie, Women's Studies International Forum, The European Legacy: Toward New Paradigms, Balcanii*, and *Sfera Politicii*. A native of Bucharest, she is now a Canadian citizen.